William Marvy

Dedicat

*This special edition is dedi
memory of Mr. William Marvy (1909-1993)
who never clipped a lock of hair in his entire
life and yet was enshrined into the Barber
Hall of Fame in 1982.*

Stars and Stripes *forever!*

For almost half a century the William Marvy Company has done its darndest to keep the American barbershop symbol alive and well on Main Street, U.S.A. As the last remaining barber pole factory in the country, they deserve a nice brisk neck rub for keeping those stripes ever turning.

Twelve year-old Bill Marvy bid farewell to his paper route in 1921 to get his start in the barber supply business by sweeping floors in a St. Paul barber supply house. If not for this career change, today's tonsorial symbol might have gone the way of the cigar-store Indian.

At the young age of 16, Marvy became a full-fledged salesman of barber supplies. He was soon calling on barber shop owners throughout the Minnesota countryside. In his travels, Bill noticed the generally dilapidated condition of the signs and poles displayed by his customers. It became obvious to him that the most common problems with barber poles were broken glass, faded stripes and rusty frames.

After several years of tinkering in his spare time, Marvy introduced his "Six Ways Better" barber pole. It was the hit of the 1950 Chicago barber supply trade show. Dealers stood in line to sign up for Marvy's revolutionary shatterproof, lucite-cased acetate cylinder with stainless steel and aluminum frames.

Marvy's new pole did not drive all of his competitors out of business, but his boundless enthusiasm eventually won the game. In a 1985 interview he said, "We were all very excited about barber poles at a time when other manufacturers were just coasting along. In our first six years of business we churned out 5,100 poles. By 1967 our men had made over 50,000 units."

Since the late 1960s the barber pole business has declined at about the same rate as crew cuts, hot towels and shaves. Today the company is operated by Bill's son, Robert Marvy, and has expanded its manufacturing to include sanitizing equipment for barber and beauty shops, along with importing and distributing a wide line of barber and beauty supplies and sundries.

Hardly a day passes without the arrival of several orders for spare parts or an antique pole for restoration. Marvy keeps the collector community aware of his services through modest ads in publications such as "The Antique Trader".

And, of course, brand new barber poles are on hand -- in colors ranging from pink to gold -- for everyone from hair stylists to poodle-parlor operators.

Other trade symbols, like the cigar-store Indian, the pawnbroker's gold balls and the drugstore's mortar and pestle have faded away. But thanks to William Marvy, the rotating red, white and blue stripes will remain upon the American landscape forever. Amen!

Ronald S. Barlow

THE VANISHING AMERICAN BARBER SHOP

Printed in the U.S.A.

ISBN #0-965237-30-3

Library of Congress Card Number 94-76415

CONTENTS

ABOUT THE BOOK

Photographs of early American barber shops are hard to come by. In rarity they rank alongside vintage images of cowboys and Indians, policemen, firefighters, saloons, cigar stores and billiard parlors.

The quest for these scarce photographs began by contacting all 400 members of the National Shaving Mug Collector's Association. Several barber shop memorabilia buffs responded to our letter, including the club's newsletter editor, Michael Griffin, of White Plains, New York. You will find Mike's credit line under half the pictures in this book. His help in writing and pricing the chapter on shaving mugs was invaluable.

Richard Harris, owner of a Boone, Iowa barber shop and mini-museum, also provided valuable assistance in the early research. And another barber shop proprietor, Chris Jones of Hamilton Square, New Jersey, loaned a selection of early advertising material from his 1,000-piece museum collection.

Fellow author Phillip Krumholz of Bartonsville, Illinois, offered his well-honed appraisal skills in compiling the price guide section of the book. (Phil has written three books on shaving history and accessories.)

Another writer, Gerard Petrone of El Cajon, California, located dozens of early newspaper articles about barbers, and Maxine Cook the N.S.M.C.A. librarian, provided photocopies of contemporary magazine articles on barber shop collectibles.

Photo researcher, Susan Hormuth of Washington, D.C., combed the caverns of the Smithsonian Institution and the Library of Congress, where she found a treasure-trove of material dating back to the 1840s.

Other photographs and advertising pieces were found at antique postcard shows and through ads placed in collector publications. The original old barber shop supply catalogs were purchased (at prices ranging up to $500 each) from rare book dealers in New England.

After a six-month buying spree, there was enough material to produce a whole series of barber history books! The problem now became what to keep and what to recycle to other collectors.

About this time, a wonderful surprise arrived in the mailbox in the form of a twelve-page manuscript by William Gambino, an 87-year-old tonsorial artist from Flushing, New York. Mr. Gambino's 50 years of experience behind the chair provided one of the book's most interesting chapters.

The Barlow family collaborated to prepare the book for typesetting. A few months later a truckload of completed books arrived from the printer and it wasn't long before the entire first edition of 10,000 copies was gone from the home-based warehouse.

When suppliers began clamoring for a second edition, we turned to the William Marvy Company. The book was a natural acquisition for them since they are the last manufacturer of barber poles in North America.

William Marvy Company has had a relationship with barbers throughout the United States and Canada since Bill Marvy founded his barber supply company in 1936. The company is now in its second generation of family ownership and operation.

Ronald S. Barlow

INTRODUCTION

There was a time when a saddle-weary stranger could ride into any town, dirty, smelly, sunburned, bewhiskered and hungry, with less than a dollar in his pocket and be cheerfully welcomed at the sign of the bloodstained pole.

Within an hour's time he would be bathed, shorn, shaved, perfumed and manicured, have his boots shined, his moustache curled and his pants pressed. Some barber shops even offered customers a mug of beer and a free cigar! During this grooming session the stranger would be dutifully informed of any local employment opportunities, hear a current weather report and peruse a dog-eared copy of the *Police Gazette*.

Quite transformed, our stranger probably emerged from the barbershop looking as slick as a fresh-plucked cucumber and strolled happily down the boardwalk. He had made several contacts in the shop and knew where to look for room and board and perhaps even suitable female companionship.

All of these benefits to body and soul had been bestowed upon our stranger for less than fifty cents. This was truly the Golden Age of the barber shop in America.

The half century between the end of the Civil War and our entrance into World War I was also the prim and proper "Victorian" period, a time when all townsmen were expected to act respectable, smell agreeable and shave at least three times a week.

Shaving with a straight razor was an art that few men ever really mastered and even fewer wished to be bothered with. Especially when the local barber shop was open 12 hours a day and before church on Sundays. For just a few nickels you could get your face lathered and your neck rubbed while relaxing in dreamland.

Live music was sometimes available, along with local gossip and the latest sporting news. Here one could rub elbows with the town's merchants, bankers and politicians. It was a social hour that most men looked forward to attending at least three or four days a week. But times were slower then; over half the nation's population still lived down on the farm.

An easy-to-enter apprentice system provided plenty of young razor-artists, and their ever-increasing numbers kept rates at very affordable levels. At the turn of the century, barber shops even outnumbered saloons in many towns.

In 1880, approximately 45,000 full-time barbers served a nation of 50 million souls. Today the trade is spread more thinly with 100,000 barbers and 62,000 shops shearing a population of 250 million (including the 10 percent who are bald).

Mr. Gillette's refinement of the safety razor, and our rapid industrialization after World War I spelled a new era for the barber shop in America. Today's tonsorial parlor looks more like a hospital ward than a men's club.

The free cigars, the lurid tabloids and colorful shaving mugs are nowhere in sight. The conversation is often stilted, the music piped-in and the *man* behind your chair may, in fact, be a *woman*.

The "Good Old Days" are gone forever, but collectors of barber shop memorabilia are preserving virtually everything associated with this time-honored profession. We have included a comprehensive *Price Guide Section* in the back of the book for those readers who wish to join in the search.

FROM BARBER TO HAIR STYLIST,
A HISTORY OF TONSORIAL ART

An Egyptian Barber shaves a bewigged customer, one of four hundred on a typical working day.

MEN have always tried to please the fairer sex. Archaeologists tell us that even the most primitive cave dwellers of 20,000 years ago tweezed their whiskers with clam shells and shaved their faces with razor-sharp flints.

Young Romans of 300 B.C. were as anxious for the appearance of mustaches as are today's youth. When the silky down on their lips first sprouted they were entitled to be called *barbatulus*—the slightly bearded—and later on came the proud distinction of being known as *barbatus*—the full bearded. Thus all bearded and unshaven *foreigners* were called, solely on account of their beards, *barbarians* by the Greeks and Romans, and then from the Latin word *barba*—the beard—came the word barber.

Public barber shops in ancient Rome were called *tonstrinae*, in which *tonsura*—the shearing of hair—was performed, usually by woman attendants.

In Egypt, many centuries earlier, barbers were already well established in their trade and highly respected by the populace. Egyptians of the period shaved their beards *and their heads*. Their rulers wore false beards, sometimes made of fine gold wire, but more often of plaited human hair. Even Egyptian queens wore these strap-on goatees along with mohair wigs.

Priests took matters a step further and shaved themselves completely, from head to toe, every three days. Some speculate that the hairless fad was a religious custom, but chances are that the masses shaved their heads to keep cool and vermin-free. A proficient Egyptian barber could shave up to 400 customers a day. This works out to 33 heads an hour over a 12-hour period. Sounds a bit mythological to me, but there were no union rules or coffee breaks in those days.

The Bible Verifies this Egyptian preoccupation with facial hair. When Joseph was summoned to appear before Pharaoh, "A barber was sent for to shave him, so that Pharaoh's sight would not be offended by a dirty face."

Among other Biblical references to shaving, the prophet Ezekiel is recorded as saying, "Take thou a barber's razor and cause it to pass upon thy beard," (a mourning rite).

Greece seems to have been the first country in which wandering freelance barbers began to establish themselves in permanent locations. There, as early as 500 B.C., the sidewalk barber shop was a daily gathering place for everyone from poets to politicians. Customers discussed sports, weather, philosophy, the grain market and upcoming elections. At that time the men of Athens rivalled each other in the excellence of their beards, which were artfully trimmed, curled and perfumed. Their women, according to Ovid, "had a thousand styles of curling their hair."

Greek courtesans were the first ladies to discover that "blondes have more fun." Bleached hair became a status symbol among them and everything from yellow pollen to potassium salt was employed to obtain a provocative shade of tresses.

At the famous Greek gymnasiums and health spas, barbers were the appointed dieticians. They also cut hair, gave enemas, set broken bones and practiced bleeding and minor surgery.

The Greek medical tradition started with Hippocrates, born in 460 B.C., who lived to be one hundred and three years old by simply following his own advice. Physicians today still swear by him!

In the third century B.C., the Greeks, under Alexander the Great, began their conquest of Asia. After losing several important battles to unprincipled Persians, who grabbed their beards, Alexander's cavalrymen were commanded to buy razors. Their clean-shaven example was followed by the civilian populace and beards quickly went out of fashion.

Barbers were unknown in Rome prior to 296 B.C., when Ticinius Mena and his crew of scissor-artists arrived from Sicily. The comfort-loving Romans quickly embraced the tonstrinae and also became the first people to utilize warm water in the shaving process. Being a slave-supported society, most Romans had plenty of idle time to wile away in barber shops and bath houses.

By the second century B.C., bathing had turned into a social occasion. The huge public baths (many containing hundreds of individual cubicles) were outfitted with gardens, shops, libraries, gymnasiums, and marble-seated commodes. You could have dinner and attend the theatre or an art exhibit without ever leaving the premises.

The baths of Diocletian were the largest and could accommodate over 3,000 frolicking citizens at one time. Upper class Romans had private bathing facilities inside their palatial dwellings. These marble-lined rooms had piped-in hot water and heated air. Slaves were trained to the art of tonsura within the home. *Ciniflones* were the slaves who specialized in using the *calamistrum*, or curling irons, on Roman ladies.

Most Roman men preferred the congenial atmosphere of the public baths and barber shops. Citizens of all classes (and both sexes) spent several hours each day being steamed, scraped, bathed, trimmed, shaved, oiled, massaged, perfumed and manicured (more or less in that order).

From Rome the barbering profession spread north, east and west; from Byzantium to Arabia and onward to Spain. During the early Christian era the barbers of Europe flourished or faded according to the customs of their day.

Charlemagne had made long hair the fashion between 768 A.D. and 814 A.D., but each new monarch, or conquering chieftain, had his own hair style, and wise men imitated their betters.

To enumerate the profusion and constant evolution of wigs, coiffures, beards and cosmetics would require several additional volumes. For starters, we recommend *Beards, Their Social Standing, Religious Involvements, Decorative Possibilities and Value in Offense and Defense Through the Ages*, a 300-page tome by Reginald Reynolds. Also of interest is *Principles and Practice of Beauty Culture* by Florence E. Wall.

Not to be overlooked by anyone really interested in the age-old battle of hair is *The Long and Short of It, Five Thousand Years of Fun and Fury over Hair*, by Bill Severn. The author sums up the subject saying, "The debate over hair styles and facial hair adornments has been going on since the beginning of history. Even before Delilah snipped Samson's locks, the ancients had issued edicts for and against hair and beards, long and short. What was forbidden or frowned upon by one generation often became the accepted style for the next."

The Barber Surgeon. The most educated people of the first ten centuries after Christ were the cloistered monks and priests. Neither nobility nor the masses could read or write. These were indeed the Dark Ages; all of the accumulated medical knowledge of the ancient Egyptians, Greeks and Romans had been lost or squirreled away in monastaries.

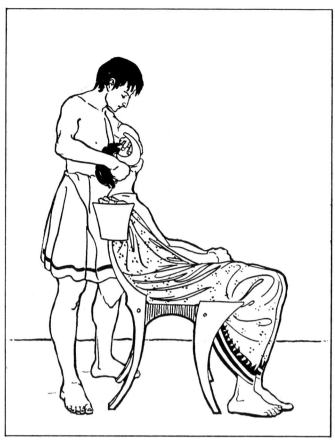

A Greek Barber of the period of Alexander the Great uses a crescent-shaped razor on his snoozing customer.

There were no real physicians or surgeons in this dark period, and most diseases that are commonly curable today were fatal then. Bloodletting and herbal remedies were the accepted methods of "curing" patients. Phlebotomy, or bleeding, was first practiced by the clergy, who also ran pharmacy shops within the walls of their monasteries.

These monks often enlisted young barbers (whom they ostensibly kept on hand for head shaving) as medical apprentices. Bloodletting was a messy, time-consuming chore, and the boy barbers could use the extra cash.

However, at the council of Tours in 1163, the clergy were "Hence forth forbidden to draw blood or act as physicians or surgeons in any manner," on the grounds that such practices were sacrilegious. Thereupon, many barbers moved out of the cloisters into private bloodletting establishments.

Thus began a practical marriage of shaving, haircutting, bleeding, tooth-pulling and minor surgery, which continued uninterrupted for the next 600 years. George Washington was literally bled to death by his personal physician in 1799, after suffering from a prolonged windpipe infection. He died, calmly counting his own pulse, at the age of 67. By 1845, bloodletting instruments had disappeared from most doctor's satchels.

Barber Unions. The first recorded organization of barbers was formed in 1096, in France, when the Archbishop of Rouen prohibited the wearing of beards. From that time onward, the chirurgeons, or barber-surgeons, began to thrive all over Europe.

They served royalty as well as the common people, but were in constant conflict with the more scholarly physi-

Barber-surgeon bleeds a woman.   Woodcut, 1520.

cians who actually read books and studied medicine in an objective manner. The barber-surgeons also stepped on the toes of full-time dentists. When you had a paying customer in your chair, with his mouth half open, why not inspect his teeth and pull out all the loose ones?

Medical, dental and tonsorial factions vied with one another for several centuries, each seeking the favor of reigning kings and councils. Finally, in 1252, an official barbers' association was organized in France. Members sought protection not only from outsiders, but also from each other. Codes of conduct were set up with strict rules to be adhered to. These unions were more powerful than their modern-day counterparts. They were sanctioned by kings and queens, and could enforce regulations with impunity from lawyers and labor arbitrators. One would-be barber was paraded through the streets of London, with trumpets and fifes, bareback on a horse with a urinal hung in front of his face. Even prison terms for violators of Guild rules were not uncommon; however, members often differed in their interpretations of professional boundaries. Some felt that shaving and hairdressing should suffice. Others wished to venture further into the lucrative practice of surgery.

About this time, a group of sophisticated blacksmiths emerged who were also turning their tools and veterinary skills towards human doctoring. Guillotine operators, who were running out of victims, also began to enter the legitimate bloodletting trade. As if this were not enough competition, bathhouse owners in France added shaving and haircutting to their bill of fare and some barbers began to offer food and wine as a sideline.

It was from these interlopers that the earliest barber unions sought relief. One prospectus urged membership as a protective measure against "quacks, smiths and such-like doctors."

Across the channel in England, the "Worshipful Company of Barbers" was established by royal charter in 1308. Richard le Barbour was elected as Master and supervised all of the barber-surgeons in London. He soundly rebuked any among the brotherhood whom he found "acting disgracefully or entering on other trades less reputable."

Reputable indeed? Charles De Zemler in his 1939 book, *Once Over Lightly*, states: "One difficulty encountered by both barbers and surgeons *before the union of their guilds* was their inferior social status. No member of any other of the numerous guilds in London would accept any barber or surgeon on terms of equality, no matter how important he had become. Even the shoemakers, the next lowest to them in rank, would not mingle with the haircutters and doctors." The barber-surgeons were forbidden to take part in any official municipal sessions and were classified with such scoundrels as musicians, executioners, grave-diggers, dog-catchers, singers and actors. All were social pariahs. Even candlestick-makers outranked them. As a later consolation, society offered members of the Guild of Barber-Surgeons a permit to wear a sword in public.

What was the cause of all this disdain? The rotten clergy, those same fellows who had trained the barbers in the art of bleeding just a few years before. Most priests felt that barber shops were the breeding places for sin and sedition. Loose talk and loose morals were associated with barbering and bathing. Between 1500 and 1612 the king of England and emperor of Germany both made public appeals to upgrade the status of barbers, but somehow they could not erase the public's contempt for those who sheared and bled them.

Perhaps it was not unnatural that a class whose business brought its members into such close contact with persons suffering from bodily disease (therefore impure and godless) should be made a target of condemnation.

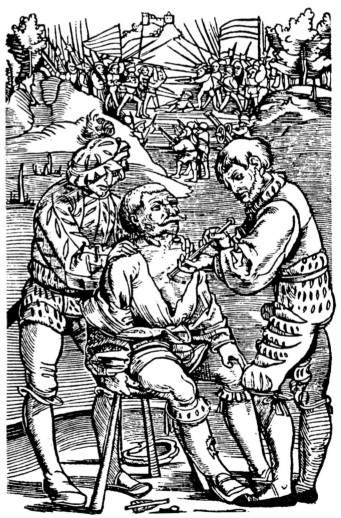

Army barber-surgeon removes an arrow point from a wound. From a woodcut published in 1528.

Monks were not even permitted to visit a steam bath and could indulge in a full tub bath only on great holidays. In stark contrast to the average monk's tonsorial regimen is the following account of the barber/customer relationship adapted from a 14th-century dialogue by John Eliot:

John: What doth the gentle Barber?

Barber: Welcome, Sir.

John: I come to trim my beard and my haire.

Barber: Sit you downe there: you shall be trimd by and by.

John: Will you wash me, for I have great hast.

Barber: Stay a little, I have almost done with this gentleman. (to 'prentice) Come give me some cleane cloathes.

John: What sayth your Almanacke Barber?

Barber: That the moone is just in the eclipse of monie.

John: When is it good to bleed?

Barber: When there are any crownes to be gotten.

John: You are as courteous as the Divell.

Barber: I ask nothing else alwaies; but health and a purseful of monie, for my paramour a pretty conie, and Paradice at the end of my daies. You have your beard tangles and knotty.

John: Undo my lockes with this combe. Rub not so hard. Rub softly.

Barber: (to 'prentice): A Pomander and some soape, ho. Hold up this bason.

John: Wash me gently.

Barber: Shall I cut your haire. Will you have your head shaven? Shall I wash your neck, brest and stomache? Shall I picke your teeth. Boy, where be my Cizars. Give me my Ivorie combe. Sharpen a little the rasor. Shall I cut your mustaches? An earepicker and a tooth-picker, ho. You are almost trimmed. Take this glasse and behold your selfe.

Medical Doctors Emerge. Up until the year 1461, British barbers were not much interfered with in their dental and surgical sidelines. But soon it became obvious to The Council of London that these tonsorial technicians were not the best qualified to practice medicine. People complained how much sicker they felt after treatment than before. In fact, a lot of folks died before they felt well enough to complain. Quackery was rampant.

An ordinance was passed, by the king and council, "forbidding barbers from taking under their care any sick person in danger of death or maiming, without first presenting the patient to a master of the Barber-Surgeon's Guild." (The Guild of Surgeons had been incorporated with the Barbers' Company by an act of Parliament in 1450.) Under the new edict, barbers were restricted by law to bloodletting, toothdrawing, cauterization and regular tonsorial chores. From then on every new surgeon was required to have his diploma signed by a committee of two barbers and two surgeons.

In 1512, the third year in the reign of Henry VIII, it was further enacted "That no person within the city of London, or within seven miles of same, should take upon him to exercise or occupy as a physician or surgeon, except he first be examined, approved and admitted by the Bishop of London or the Dean of St. Paul's, calling to him four doctors of physic, and for surgery other experts in the faculty," This was the real beginning of the College of Surgeons of England.

Barber-surgeon amputates the leg of a wounded soldier. Strassbourg, 1528.

Under a clause in the Act of Henry VIII, barber-surgeons were given the bodies of four executed criminals every year for dissection in the Guild Hall. It is easy to understand how battlefield barber-surgeons quickly outstripped civilian doctors in practical medical knowledge. They had no such limitations imposed upon their delvings into the human anatomy, warm or cold; but their main duty was to keep officers clean-shaven.

The final split between barbers and surgeons in Great Britain did not occur until 1745 when the union of the two guilds was dissolved by an act of George II, which made the surgeons a separate company governed by a 21-member council and a court of examiners from the Royal College of Surgery. This act marked the eventual decline of the barber profession to the status of wigmakers. Similar action was taken in France under the reign of Louis XIV.

By the end of the 18th century, nearly all of Europe's barbers had ceased to practice surgery or dentistry except for those located in small towns and villages in remote areas.

Barbers become Wig Makers. "After British barbers separated from the surgeons' guild in 1745, they digressed into mere mechanics and servants, subject to whims of fashion. When wigs became the rage in the 18th century, barbers became wig makers. Their once proud profession had lost its ancient dignity;" so states A. B. Moler in *The Barber's Manual* of 1898.

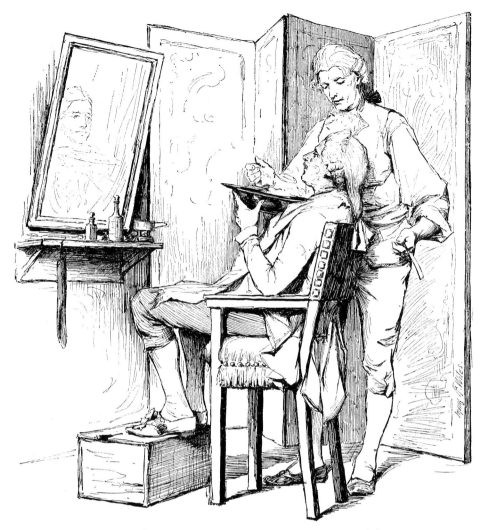

A Colonial barber shop patron holds the traditional notched basin under his chin while being shaved.

Imported European fashions dictated that gentle men folk in Colonial America wear false hair, too. City boys were bewigged by the age of seven and college students wore flat-topped bag-wigs with their queues enclosed in silk or tied with a ribbon. On many occasions, even Negro house servants were required to wear powdered wigs.

Barber shops kept these fragile hairpieces groomed and repaired. Only farmers, merchants, tradesmen and country folk wore their own hair.

The young rebel, Thomas Jefferson, wore his natural bright red hair as a student in college, but later gave in to the wig makers when he became a politician. During the American Revolution, town dwellers were so unnerved by the sight of long-haired hillbilly recruits marching with the continental army, that they refused to look upon them.

Edward Hazen's book, *Panorama*

of Professions and Trades, published in 1837, recorded the eventual decline of wigs for men: "The fashion, except in cases of baldness, is now nearly banished from Europe and America. However, the manufacture of wigs and false curls is still an important branch of the business of the barber."

An interesting footnote to even a casual perusal of Hazen's 1837 book is that none of the dozens of tradesmen illustrated therein are anything other than short-haired and clean-shaven. Even the blacksmith and his swarthy crew look like they just emerged from a barber shop.

Beards Grow Back in Style. Between 1850 and 1870, sideburns gradually crept down gentlemen's cheeks, finally culminating in a mutton chop effect, leaving the chin bare. The term "sideburns" originated from Union Army General Ambrose E. Burnside's illustrious set of side whiskers.

Before 1858, beards were socially acceptable only when worn by artists, writers, and pioneer settlers. The *Knickerbocker Magazine* of 1851 devoted three issues to a tirade against young New Yorkers who had begun sporting beards. They were called "A disgusting insult to refined society."

Very few men dared defy conventions of the day. One brave exception was Joseph Palmer, a veteran of the War of 1812 and a butcher-tradesman. When the bushy-bearded patriot moved to Fitchburg, Massachusetts in 1830, he was greeted by jeering townsmen and stone-throwing children. "Shave off your filthy beard you Jew monster," they yelled. Palmer was a God-fearing churchgoer until the local clergy refused to serve him communion. One Sunday morning, Joseph arose and walked up the aisle to the Lord's Table where he helped himself to a cup of grape juice, saying, "I am a better Christian than any of you."

A few weeks later, four men attacked Mr. Palmer and threw him down on the stone steps of the Fitchburg Hotel. They were after his beard and carried scissors to get it. Palmer slashed out with a jackknife and drove the culprits off. Instead of going home, they went straight to the sheriff and swore out a warrant for Palmer's arrest. He was charged with "committing an unprovoked assault," and was thrown in jail when he refused to pay a fine.

While in jail, Palmer was attacked again. This time by five men also attempting to de-beard him. He immobilized two of them and threw the others out of his cell. For this bit of mischief, Palmer was placed in solitary confinement, on bread and water. Before long, a year had passed and letters smuggled out to friends (who included Emerson, Hawthorne and Thoreau) attracted widespread attention from the press. The resulting public outcry forced local officials to free him, but Palmer refused to leave his cell. His chastised jailers gently carried him out on a chair and placed it on the sidewalk.

Joseph Palmer kept his original set of whiskers for the rest of his long life and lived to see the day when all respectable men wore beards.

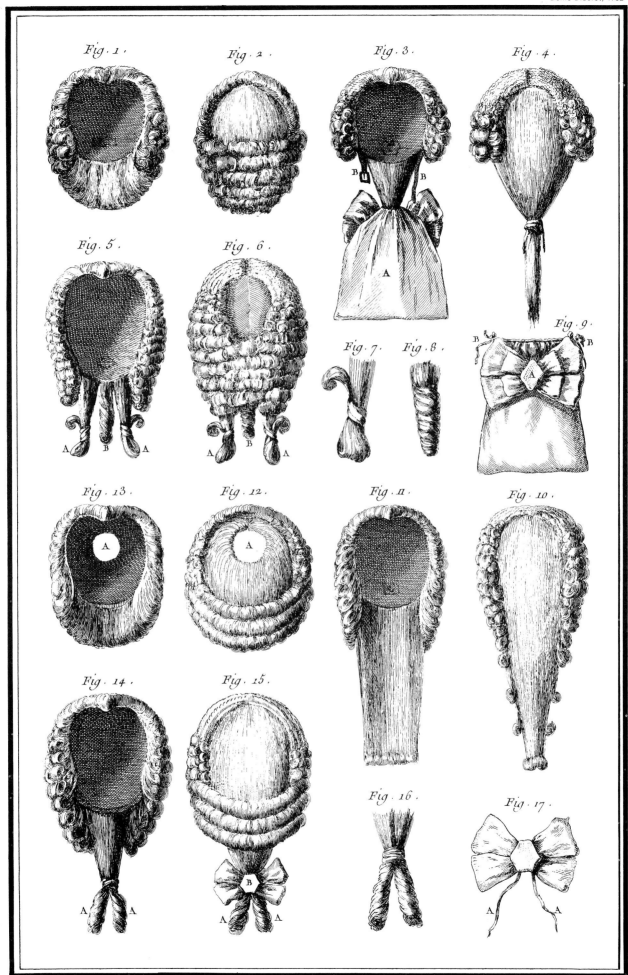

Just a few examples of the hundreds of wig styles available to 18th century squires.

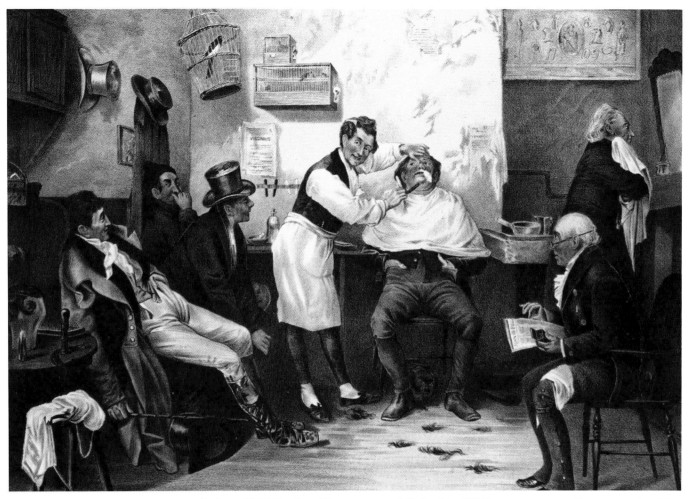

A circa 1800 Barber Shop scene published in 1885.   —*Bettmann Archive*

Out West, it was a whole different story. Gold miners didn't have time to shave, and whiskers were good protection against sunburn and frostbite. By the time the Civil War started, beards and mustaches had become universally fashionable.

The *London Methodist Quarterly Review* had even advocated beards for ministers of the gospel. Alexander Rowland wrote: "The fact that the Creator planted a beard upon the face of the human male indicates that the distinctive appendage was bestowed for the purpose of being worn."

Abraham Lincoln realized the importance of wearing a beard and stayed home to grow one before the election of 1860. However, beard-wearing barely lasted through the Victorian period. Though common from 1858, they had begun to disappear by the beginning of the Gay Nineties.

President Grant sported a short, stubby beard. Rutherford B. Hayes, who served from 1877 to 1881, grew a grey beard that covered his collar. James A. Garfield owned a wonderfully luxuriant growth of whiskers when he was shot on July 2, 1881. Chester A. Arthur sported bushy sideburns and a walrus mustache during his 1881-1885 tenure. Grover Cleveland, who served from 1885-1889, was a well-groomed gentleman with a wide, over-the-lip mustache. Benjamin Harrison, 1889-1893, was the last president to wear a beard. The Victorian age had passed and the nation again became beardless.

Barber Schools Arrive. "In England, America, and all over the civilized world, the decline of the barber was a spectacle for all to see. Barber shops became hangouts, places where low characters assembled. Smutty stories, malicious scandal and gossip of all kinds characterized barber shops. Until a few years ago, a barbershop was a place where men showed their lower instincts and where women dared not enter." So wrote Mr. A. B. Moler in the 1911 introduction to his classic textbook *The Barber's Manual*, which remained in print for 30 years.

A. B. Moler began his apprenticeship in 1889 at the age of 21, under the tutelage of an older brother who had mastered the trade by the time-honored system of on-the-job training. Mr. Moler recounted that he spent the first three years of his apprenticeship engaged in floor-sweeping, neck-shaving and hot-towel dispensing; actually learning little about his chosen trade.

Over the next 10 years, Moler devised a method of training that led to the establishment of the "Moler System of Barber Colleges." Beginning with the main branch which he founded in Chicago in 1893, the colleges spread to every major city in the United States and Canada.

Early barber schools were geared to turn out graduates with marketable tonsorial skills, ready for immediate employment in any shop. No throat-scraping, ear-slashing, lip-scraping, mole-slicing apprentices were

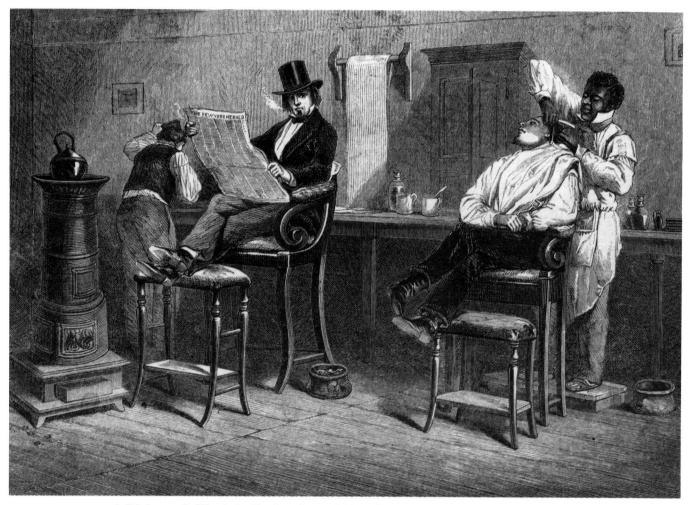

A Richmond, Virginia Barbershop of 1861. Beards were back in style. —*N.Y,. Public Library*

these. However, their instruction was limited to the practical work of shaving and haircutting. Not until about 1920 did barber colleges begin to include elementary chemistry, histology, bacteriology and anatomy in their curriculum. And when they did, they went overboard.

A former official of the Associated Master Barbers of America recalled, "We over-reached ourselves on the professional potential of barbering. Educational standards were established that often defeated enrollment in barber schools. Students were required to know the muscles, nerves, and structure of the head, etc. All of which turned out not to be really necessary to give a good haircut."

Impetigo, scabies, erysipelas, favus, tinea barbae, and pediculosis capitis (head lice) were among the many contagious diseases patrons could bring home from a tonsorial parlor. A second-hand towel, an unsterilized razor, comb, brush, or shaving mug were the obvious transmitters of "Barber Itch."

In the 1880s, chemists began to discover disease-producing microorganisms in everything from surgical dressings to dairy milk. A Parisian doctor by the name of Remlinger grew suspicious of his neighborhood tonsorial parlor and took home the communal alum stick which his barber routinely used as an astringent on razor nicks and dicapitated pimples. Upon microscopic examination of samples from a bowl of water in which the alum stick had been immersed overnight, Dr. Remlinger was amazed to

discover more than 68,000 disease-producing germs, representing a half dozen virulent species.

It didn't take the good doctor long to turn his microscope upon his barber's razor strop, which was used to hone the blade before shaving each customer. He found it to be almost as germ-infested as the alum stick. Dr. Remlinger also condemned barber shop hair brushes as "the most common carriers of diseases causing baldness, and perhaps even cancer."

The Public Was Outraged on both sides of the Atlantic. State legislatures passed laws banning alum sticks and powder puffs! No longer could you use the same hot towel to soften the beards of a dozen customers. A large linen supply became mandatory.

"Sanitary" barber shops began to flourish in every big city. One such establishment in Baltimore made the news in 1897 with its "Revolutionary aluminum-handled razors and brushes," which were sterilized by hot air. Between customers, the barbers in this shop were required to strip to their bare arms and publicly wash their hands and implements in a bowl filled with liquid antiseptic.

In 1916, a couple of entrepreneurial railway employees opened a "Super-Sanitary" barber shop in the New York City Terminal Station. Many others followed what was to be called the new "Terminal Method"; a franchise of sorts. The system included boiling every instrument used, in plain view of the customer, and sealing all brushes in individual airtight cellophane bags. Combs were immersed in a jar of carbolic acid solution.

John Freeauf poses with assistants in front of his New York City tonsorial parlor. Circa 1880. —*Deb Cooney*

Barber Unions were about 500 years late arriving in the United States. As we mentioned earlier, England had a well established brotherhood of razor knights by the year 1300.

A New York Times article of October 30, 1876 recorded the birth of American barber unions:

> "WAR AMONG THE BARBERS" read the headline. The Tonsorial Artists in This City, otherwise known as barbers, who charge ten cents and upward for a shave, are greatly excited on the account of the increasing number of 'rat shops' whose proprietors charge only five cents. Last evening a new organization, calling itself "The United Barbers of New York and Vicinity," whose members comprise both bosses and journeymen, are opposed to a reduction of prices, held its second meeting. About 60 new members signed the roll, making a total membership of 400. A resolution was passed that members of the society could obtain employment in any shop whose owners are members. The journeymen in the 'rat shops' are to be notified that unless they join our society and pay twenty-five cents dues, they will be debarred from obtaining work in shops run by union bosses.

A year later another meeting was called on the same account. "Rat shops" were still charging half the going rates and proliferating as rapidly as the rodents they were named after. These price wars persisted well into the 20th Century. A journeyman barber, employed in one of the best shops in New York's tenderloin district, said to a Times reporter in 1893, "This whole business is a fraud. We only get $14 a week, and we work fourteen hours every day. We don't get time for anything, except to eat and sleep, at odd hours." (Most shops opened at 9 a.m. and closed at 11 p.m.).

Under the headline "Razor Knights Aroused," Charles A. Prinz, President of the Barbers Protective Association of Rochester, N.Y., was quoted in 1896:

> " We want to legislate the incompetent barbers and the so-called barber colleges out of existence, so that no person can manage or be a proprietor of a barber's shop without passing an examination before a competent board of examiners. The lawyers, doctors, dentists, plumbers, druggists, horseshoers, and even policemen, mail carriers and firemen are required to pass an examination; in fact almost every trade and profession in the land is protected.
>
> Is the barber protected? No! Why not? Simply because the barbers have not had the gumption before to look out for their own interests. But now they see to what it will lead unless something is done to legislate the incompetent barbers as well as the barber colleges out of existence. Years ago it was customary for an apprentice to serve three years at the trade before he was considered a barber. But now the majority serve about six months and then start in business for themselves. What kind of work can such a barber do, or a barber who practices eight weeks in a barber college. They certainly cannot do good work, consequently they must cut prices.
>
> At this rate, how long before the whole country is overrun by cheap barbers' shops and the good barbers will have to go out of business or else cut their prices accordingly. This must be prevented by the better class of barbers, who understand their business, banding together for their mutual protection.
>
> The knights of the razor and scissors have been called to arms. All over the State the slogan has been sounded:
> "Down with barber's colleges!"
> "Perdition to the mushroom hair clippers and face scrapers who invade our province with diplomas!"

The next year found conditions unchanged. Immigrant barbers were becoming an even more serious threat to union shops. This article appeared in the January 11, 1897 edition of the Times:

> The barbers of this city want to have a law passed to license barbers, and make them pass an examination before a State Board of Examiners in shaving and hair cutting. They also want to have all schools for barbers abolished. There is a barber college in this city that has been turning out large numbers of barbers. People are shaved free at the schools, and the scholars practice upon the faces and heads of these free customers. This, the union barbers say, is wrong, and they maintain that an apprentice should serve three years in a barber's shop before receiving a diploma as a tonsorial artist.
>
> The union barbers further complain that the Italian barbers have ruined the business by reducing the price of a shave to 5 cents and have the boots blacked in the bargain. Two or three Italian barbers charge only 3 cents for a shave.

Finally, Laws Were Passed. The first barber licensing law in the United States was ratified by the Minnesota State Legislature in 1897, requiring at least an eighth-grade education and twenty-five weeks of barber school to practice there. Conversely, Ohio barbers went unregulated well into the 1920's (with the exception of Toledo, which had an ordinance that prohibited barbering before 8 a.m. or after 6 p.m.).

The next important milestone occurred in 1924 when the Associated Master Barbers of America were organized in Chicago. This newly formed group began an immediate program to foster uniformly higher standards in every state in the nation.

Over the next several decades each state gradually upgraded its requirements for the certification of barbers. Formal classroom training was increased to a minimum of 1,000 hours, and apprenticeship programs of up to two years tenure were established.

An educational council was established and an association of Barber Examiners was formed. New teachers of "Barber Science" were trained, and in 1931 a standard text book was published.

A new code of ethics was bound upon every member of the Associated Master Barbers. Along with the usual sanitary provisions, the following pledges were posted for customers to view:

● "We want you to feel that you are under no obligation whatsoever to tip. You will receive the same attention whether you tip or not.

● We regard the hair tonics for sale in our shop not as "Hair Growers" or "Baldness Cures," but as legitimate beauty aids.

● The preparations dispensed in this shop, and sold for home use, are all standard merchandise, bearing the original manufacturer's label. They are undiluted and guaranteed to be free from injurious ingredients."

1890's Mining Town Featured Tent-covered Saloon and Barber Shop. —*Nevada Historical Society*

Prohibition and the Barber Shop. Why are we writing about saloons in a book about barbers? Because the first business building erected in any town along the path of the Westward Movement was almost always a saloon. It served many functions, including social club, church, court house, and very often a corner was curtained off for tonsorial operations.

Also worth mentioning is the fact that more "barber shop" singing took place in saloons than in haircutting parlors. It took a few beers and at least four bleary-eyed harmonizers to strike up midnight refrains that usually included a tribute to someone's mother, e.g.: "With a smile she always greets me, from her I'll never part. For, lads, I love my mother and she's my sweetheart." (See our snappy chapter on Barbershop Quartets for more on this subject.)

Besides being a cheap flavoring agent in bathtub gin, hair oil also played an important part in bootleg economics. We will cover that subject shortly, but first a little background on a political movement that dried up the country for thirteen years.

From 1920 to 1933, a grand social experiment took place which touched (or tainted) the lives of every citizen in America. The passing of the 18th amendment was a crowning achievement for temperance and prohibition forces who had been working toward the goal since 1870.

Between 1878 and 1898, per capita consumption of alcohol had risen from 8 gallons to 17 gallons a year. In 1898, Americans swilled down a little over a billion gallons of beer, wine and spirits. Farmers soon figured out that their corn and rye crops could be more easily sold in liquid form than at far away grain markets. In the East, where apples outgrew corn, hard cider was the home-brewed favorite.

Everybody drank, even Methodist preachers took a hot toddy to loosen up before Sunday morning tirades.

Entire towns grew up around liquor outlets, especially in the new territories.

During the final days of legalized drinking, beer had become as much a staple as wheat or pork bellies. German immigrants of the 1850's had created a huge demand for liquid hops. Breweries were overbuilt and cut-rate prices meant that more bars had to be opened to increase volume and maintain stockholder dividends. Distillers of hard liquor were also expanding at an abnormal rate.

In even the smallest towns, men with little capital and no experience were set up in the saloon business by the big breweries. These new entrepreneurs were looking for an easy living and pleasant companionship without any real investment in money, or community. New saloons opened along Main Street, down side streets, and eventually into residential neighborhoods. They sprouted up across the street from churches, schools and hospitals. Citizens who wished to confine bar-rooms to restricted districts found themselves up against a stone wall. The breweries had bought off City Hall and all the aldermen.

High-school boys were allowed to sit at the bar and little children brought in tin pails to be filled "for Father." In short, beer was sold to anyone who could reach up and place a nickel on the counter. Any suggestion from a relative or employer that a regular customer's liquor ration be cut back to preserve home and hearth, was rudely rebuffed.

But after decades of abuse, citizens rallied to the cry of the W.T.C.U. Things got so "hot" that even moderate after-work drinkers were ashamed to be seen at a bar; taking a drink seemed to be equivalent to setting fire to an orphan asylum.

George Ade, a saloon historian, wrote in 1931, "So keen was the competition that they roped in prospective customers. On Saturday afternoons, they tried to beat the wife and children to the old man's pay envelope. The saloon owners got on the wrong side of the railway companies, the steel mills, and every sort of factory and retail establishment. When the time came to vote on the 18th Amendment, no one dared to play the role of Devil's Advocate."

The fatal flaw of Prohibition was that it was instigated by a vociferous minority. The masses were never convinced of the necessity of closing every barroom, distillery and brewery in the land. They still sipped cocktails at private parties, carried hip flasks to sporting events, and had bottles sent up to their hotel rooms. Rural drinkers could no longer pick up a jug at the back door of the local general store. More often getting a drink meant donning a black raincoat, pulling on a pair of rubber boots and trudging down a dark muddy country road to a midnight rendezvous with the local bootlegger.

Before the act was repealed in 1932, a half-million citizens were arrested and convicted for violating the law. Prohibition was an unparalleled social disaster. It spawned the growth of great crime syndicates and made drinking attractive to many who were normally teetotalers.

Bootleggers used the beauty and barber shop supply trade to secure large quantities of alcohol for resale. (Poisonous *wood alcohol* was the main ingredient in most hair-care preparations prior to the Pure Food and Drug Act of 1906, after which toiletry manufacturers turned to *grain alcohol* as a replacement.) These legitimate manufacturers had governmental permits that allowed them to buy alcohol at a level justified by their gross sales of beauty products.

Those firms that chose to resell grain spirits to bootleggers found ways to doctor their record keeping and make more money on the basic ingredient than on refined hair tonic. One way to foil the Feds was to make bogus hair oil and bribe barbers into keeping huge containers of what amounted to "colored water" on display (labeled as a popular brand), and sell their own homemade concoctions "under the counter." In this way, up to 500 gallons of alcohol a month could be diverted from each barber supply house into the illicit bootleg trade, at about $10,000 cash per transaction.

In the final days of Prohibition, a group of honest hair tonic manufacturers banded together and formed a protective organization which went around to barber shops and tested the contents of display bottles for purity. Even though the group had no legal authority, they managed to intimidate unsophisticated shop owners into dumping over 50,000 bottles during their short campaign. The profit to the "honorable" group came in refilling those big display containers with regular alcohol-based hair tonic. There was still plenty of money to be made in the legitimate trade, where a 65-cent retail priced bottle of hair oil cost only a nickel to produce.

—Michael Griffin

Early 1900s Black Barber had everything but running water (Mug rack indicates some affluent customers, too.)

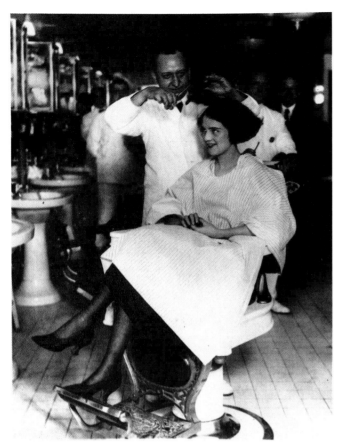

Muriel Redd, a Chicago stage actress, has her hair bobbed before appearing in the show "Tickle Me." New York, Sept. 1920. *—Bettmann Archive*

The Depression Years. The financial collapse of the early 1930's took a heavy toll among barber shops. Not only were banker and stockbroker customers staying away in droves, but 15 million common wage earners were on the dole. In larger cities, over 7 million families were living on incomes of less than $1,500 per year.

My mother was attending a small Oklahoma teacher's college at the time and she recalls "We never went to a beauty shop. The girls would take turns cutting and finger-waving each other's hair. Some women patronized a local housewife who was 'doing hair' in her kitchen. We kept her part time vocation a secret. It was against the law for anyone to cut hair without a license."

To compound the barber's difficulties, beauty salons were beginning to capture a portion of the page-bobbing trade which many women had formerly given to barber shops. In the 1920's and early 1930's, women's haircuts were a very important part of every barber's business. In most towns, the best place to get one's hair trimmed, in the new boyish style, was a barber shop. Beauticians had not yet mastered the graduated neck trim.

Barber supply houses sold almost as many "Hair Bobbing" signs as they did conventional barber poles and *The Barber's Manual* of 1927 devoted six full pages to the fine art of women's hairstyling.

In his 1925 message to a convention of the Associated Master Barbers of America, shampoo magnate Fred W. Fitch admonished the brotherhood as follows:

"Every good barber shop today caters to the ladies trade. They are the chief source of income of thousands of shops. They are bringing *dollars* into the barber shops where formerly only *quarters* straggled in. Barbers who have not taken advantage of the tremendous possibilities in the ladies trade must wake up or fall by the wayside. *The most prosperous shops in America are those that cater to the ladies.* The back numbers are those that consider the barber shop a place for men only—as if a dollar is any less a dollar because you receive it from a woman.

You Master Barbers of America can make no greater mistake than to consider the beauty parlors your enemy. You have admitted the women into your shops; you are installing new equipment and special departments for the women just as fast as you are financially able. Don't you see that your place of business is becoming a beauty parlor, as well as a barber shop? Why not get ready for this change and embrace the opportunity, instead of building a wall around yourselves and becoming shavers and haircutters?"

The Japanese bombing of Pearl Harbor on December 7, 1941 brought an end to the long Depression, but it also removed most men of prime hair-growing age from the civilian population. Military recruits received a hasty scalping upon entering boot camp and army barbers kept all haircuts under the required 1½-inch limit. By the end of the war, many civilian haircuts mirrored military styles. Butches, crew-cuts and flat-tops were added to the tonsorial artist's bill of faire. Also popular in the post-war period were duck-tailed shams, pompadours, and permanent waves. Hair tonic, butch wax and wave-setting preparations enjoyed healthy sales for the next two decades.

A Foreign Invasion. In the spring of 1964, The Beatles, a mop-haired British singing group, arrived in New York and appeared on the Ed Sullivan T.V. show. Teenage girls swooned and teenage boys quit going to their barbers. The resultant decline in the haircutting trade made the Great Depression and World War II pale by comparison.

Hairy young hippies were turned away from the gates of Disneyland and also denied entry into Mexico. Americans were split into armed camps over hair length, and the controversy raged on for nearly a decade. Men were actually hired or fired because of the way they wore their hair. Finally, long male tresses became respectable. Even our pot-bellied 45-year-old banker wore his hair in shoulder-length locks during the 1970's.

Barbers tried to keep their sense of historic perspective. "Surely the trend would soon change?" But no relief came, and shops fell like tenpins. My local barber, Ted, became a sailmaker, a trade he had learned in the Navy.

Women hairdressers, who were more familiar with custom styling, razor-cutting and blow-drying, captured a larger slice of the market (and they often received bigger tips).

Surviving male barbers hastily relettered their signboards to include "Hair Styling," and prices rose with services rendered. Not a few men began to cut their own hair, or invite their wives or girlfriends to learn the art. "Togetherness" took on a whole new meaning, and the last bastion of the American male fell without a whimper.

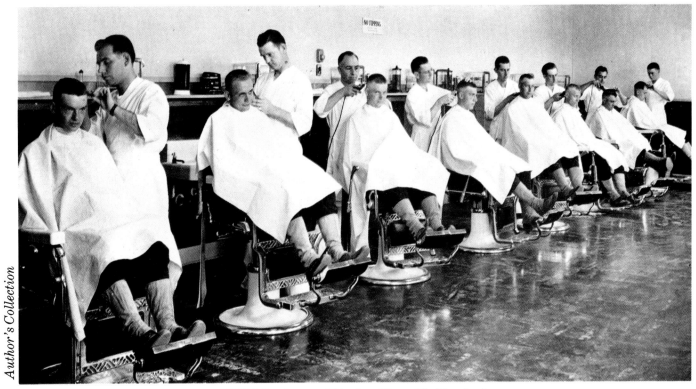

WWII Regimental Barber Shop, No Tipping!

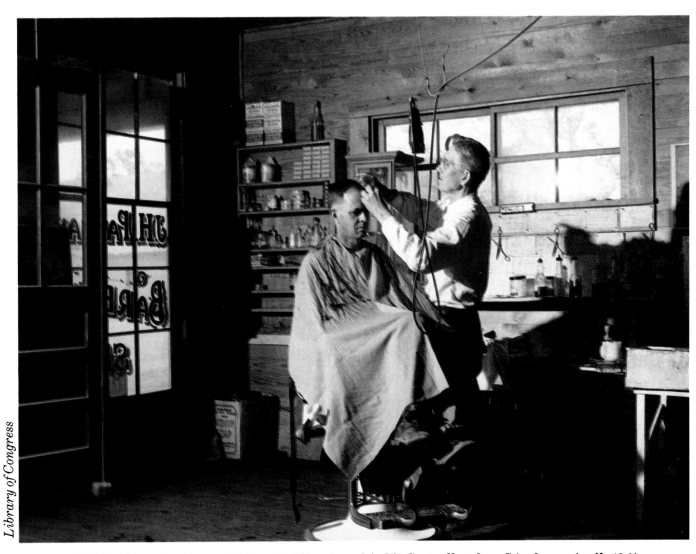

J. H. Farham, Barber and Notary Public, at work in his Centralhatchee, GA, shop.   April, 1941.

THE

BARBER'S SHOP

BY RICHARD WRIGHT PROCTER.

With Illustrations by William Morton.

'Trifles light as (h)air.'—SHAKESPEARE.

MANCHESTER:
THOMAS DINHAM & CO.
LONDON:
SOLD BY SIMPKIN, MARSHALL, & CO.
1856.

THE BARBER'S SHOP, 1826–1856

By Richard Wright Proctor

"Walk into their shops, and see
What witty fellows these shavers be."

W. Morton

Books by barbers, about barbering, are quite rare! The half dozen or so we turned up were mostly puff pieces consisting of customer profiles, philosophical meandering, and Victorian poetry. A couple of these finds were turn-of-the-century instruction manuals promoting proprietary products and trade schools.

Richard Wright Proctor's sparkling autobiography, *The Barber's Shop*, published in 1856, yielded some unique historical nuggets well worth mentioning here. In 1826, at the tender age of eleven, Richard was bound over as an apprentice to master barber David Dodd, of Manchester, England. Mr. Dodd was thirty years old at the time and his chief claim to fame was that he had once courted the daughters of two local merchants simultaneously. His humble shop catered to the town's working class and was open from early morning until midnight every day except Sunday, when shaving stopped at the sound of the village church bell.

These four "sample chapters" will nicely serve as an additional introduction to the modern-day barber trade. Nothing much has changed in the last 150 years. Customers still wonder how much they are required to tip their tonsorial artist. And barbers still are called upon to shave the sick, give advice, dispense the news, change the style and color of hair—and make us all feel better about ourselves in general.

Immediately following are excerpts from Mr. Proctor's work of 136 years ago. The accompanying engravings were rendered by his artist friend, William Morton, from actual barbershop window displays of the period.

The Barber's Shop.

A sample from

CHAPTER I.

The Barber's Clerk Takes up the Pen in place of the Lather-Brush.

Barber's Shop has always been a favourite and convenient house of call, in a literary sense, for authors of every grade and period,—from Don Quixote, with his shaving-pan of brass, to poor Partridge, in *Tom Jones*; and downward even to our own day. It has been a sort of wayside stile, where they have rested and amused themselves.

WHILE lately passing along a public thoroughfare my eye was attracted by a newly-painted sign, bearing this novel inscription,—'Board of Health Shaving Shop. Hair cutting, one penny, shaving, one halfpenny.' Upon drawing nearer to inspect the curiosity, I found the Board of Health rather difficult of access; the steps, ten or twelve in number, descended along the cellar wall, and were barely half-a-yard in width. This unfavourable situation seemed a sufficient apology for reduced terms. I afterwards learned, to my surprise, that the proprietor of this singular establishment had opened various branch concerns, where journeymen were hired to operate. I can sympathise with these journeymen barbers at half-price shaving shops, knowing as I do that few masters, even at the usual trade charges, can now support their families by the profits of the business. Most of them have been compelled to adopt auxiliary aids. You will find them as toy sellers, dealers in periodicals, news vendors, theatrical agents, cigar merchants, and chapmen in general. I have myself been addressed, though jocularly, as hair cutter, librarian, bookseller, umbrella maker, perfumer, and poet! Indeed, a portion of the epitaph, which Tim Bobbin wrote for himself, but which is not to be found upon his gravestone in Rochdale churchyard, will apply to the majority of our fraternity; and with a due allowance for that diffidence which is so apt to depreciate its own worth, might be generally adopted as the barber's epitaph:—

> 'A yard beneath this heavy stone,
> Lies Jack-of-all-trades, good at none:
> E whoo-who-whoo, whot whofoo wark!
> He's laft um aw, to lie i'th' dark!'

The customers of the old-fashioned barber's shop are now found in three divisions, like a general's army. The right wing has sheered off to get its hair cut for a penny; the centre has marched into the threepenny saloons, to be clipped and curled; the *left* wing being all that remains to the original twopenny hair cutter. Smart, cheery places, brilliant with gas, and redolent of rich perfume, are the modern shampooing saloons, where the services for which sixpence was charged in former days are now pleasantly rendered for half that sum; and where hair is cut not only well, but wisely, so that it will need cutting again in a fortnight. Success to the trade! This is the way to make it flourish.

Since wigs have been discarded by all who can do without them; since powder has been banished, except from the stage; and since even ladies' fillets have ceased to be the mode;—Othello, comparatively speaking, has had little legitimate occupation for his nimble fingers: more especially since valets and ladies' maids have usurped the office of the hair dresser.

At a meeting called to challenge the incursion of a cut rate barbers I was tempted to urge the following:

"Adopt my amendment, and you shall win, at little cost, a character with the public for being vastly generous. Gentlemen, we all have one or more patrons peculiarly fitted for this service: friends who ought to bring threepence instead of a penny for each shave. Surely, these will make beautiful halfpennyworths! We must prevail with them, as a special mark of favour, to transfer their kindness just for the occasion. Labourers with a week's growth of bristle, improved by stone-clippings, brick-parings and mortar-dust; chimney-sweepers, unwashed; stooping old men, who require much time and caution to do justice to their deep wrinkles and fleshless jaws: these are elements of success ready to our hands; why should we not use them, and conquer pleasantly? But as even the best remedy is occasionally found defective in obstinate cases, I will strengthen, like Dr. Buchan, my first receipt with additional doses. We must send also a few of our better-class customers; those who require a fresh cloth spread over their apparel, in addition to soap and water, a spotless towel, comb, hair brush, clothes brush, shoe brush, a little oil or pomatum, and other attentions which I need not enumerate. Persuade these fastidious gentlemen to favour our enemies with a call; and when all their requirements are satisfied, let them ask, as is usual with them, 'What is to pay?' Tonsor will leave the recompense to their generosity: they will not approve of generosity; they will prefer exact dealing; and will again inquire, 'What *is* the charge?' Of course, the charge is one halfpenny, as specified in the window, and the crest-fallen shaver will duly receive it. Further, we can personally visit the shops where we are unknown, and shrink from every razor placed upon our faces; we can request our victims to draw the saw over the thumb-nail, or improve the edge on the strop; and even promise to wait while they sharpen it upon the hone. We can alter our tactics by complaining of the water being too hot, or too cold; either scalding or freezing will suit us, according to the weather; and we might make an excellent wind-up by placing a sovereign on the counter, and desiring the half-penny to be taken out of that. The poor Pilgarlicks must then rush out for change, and we could stand smiling on the door-step while they raced along the street from end to end, perhaps, in search of silver for gold. If the renegades stood their ground one week under this battery of comicalities, call me no Solomon. They would assuredly fly by night, to California, or elsewhere, for a quiet existence; and morning would show us no trace of the fugitives."

My comic scheme was not adopted; possibly because it was only conceived, never brought forth. The meeting entertained the more serious proposition; the trade acted upon it, and signally failed.

The Barber's Shop.

A sample from

CHAPTER IV.

Chequers the Sunshine with a few Shadows.

ROWLAND'S MACASSAR OIL

HEIFFOR'S ARMY RAZORS

HAIR DYE

CAN ANYTHING be perfect in creation? Verily, as George Fox would have affirmed, it appeareth not. The hair-dresser's window points to the same conclusion. The bald head comes appealing to the wig, the grey whiskers to the hair-dye; and they suggest, as plainly as ever bachelor hinted to maiden, the mutual advantages to be derived from an union. Bare cheeks find here the bushy appendages they require; while the tuft, the imperial, and the moustache, are also at the service of the vain.

VANITY and necessity are alike patrons of the hair dresser's shop: the poor come to us with their wants, the rich with their fantasies. Yet even this elysium of a business, this merry-go-round of trade, has its peculiar annoyances. Occasionally, a strange customer takes possession of the chair, and presents a beard that you would not shave for a shilling; but there is no escape; although you may be master of the place, you are a servant of the public; you must 'do the deed,' and for a penny. Almost invariably these choice specimens drop in upon your meals, or interrupt your conversation with some particular friend. Sometimes the unwelcome visitor is a miserable old creature, so bent with years that your back is almost broken by stooping to his chin. You see his forlorn condition, and pity forbids you to be harsh or inattentive. But pity cannot prevent you from sickening at the three weeks' produce, matted and dirty, which bristles beneath your hand; neither can it restore one particle of interest to the unfinished meal you were enjoying when your precious patron entered. Or it may be that a coarse clown reels into your shop, full of drink and insolence, and ere you have completed your operation, pushes you aside, that he may emit the fulsome contents of his stomach over your neatly-sanded floor.

Shaving festered and broken heads, and operating at the homes of the fever-stricken and the deceased, formed an unpleasant branch of our calling, which could not in all cases be safely followed. The relatives of the afflicted, aware of our scruples, sometimes concealed the real nature of the disease, substituting a trivial complaint. I shall not readily forget being awoke at four o'clock one morning in winter, during a sweet dream and a heavy sweat, to shave an acquaintance who had just died. He possessed a strong black beard that was difficult to manage even whilst its owner was living. He was stretched upon the bricks of a damp cellar, and, in addition to kneeling, I was compelled to bend over him almost to the earth. The customary cordial to ward off the offensive smell was not given to me on that occasion, and before I had finished my task, I became sick at heart. It was long ere the stench entirely lost its effect upon my system, though the matter would doubtless be treated as nothing, in the experience of a medical man.

On various occasions old David bordered upon adventure in this department of his trade. One night in particular found him called upon to shave a dead stranger, distant about half a mile. On entering the house to which he had been directed, he perceived six or seven aged crones smoking and canting around the fire. When he named his business they handed him a light, telling him to ascend three heights of stairs until he reached the garret, where he would find the object of his search. There he found it, sure enough. A poor suicide by hanging lay heaped in a corner of the dismal room, the noose marks showing upon his neck.

Next our barber's shop is revealed in the full flow of its business, at eleven o'clock on a particular Sabbath morning. It was the first Sunday after the news had reached England of the battle of Navarino (October, 1827). The press contained a full and especial account of every round, decisive blow, and scientific manoeuvre, together with a fine flourish at the glorious (?) result. James Clarke was reading the news aloud. He was a quick and distinct reader, yet the task, with occasional questions and episodical remarks, occupied him five mortal hours, until he grew hoarse and husky. Still he persevered, and each shorn customer instead of departing to make room for the next, lingered over the narrative. The place was crowded, of course. Master and I continued to mow and to listen, without the least thought of danger, or of service-time: when suddenly the door-way became darkened by churchwardens, beadles, and other officials. During a few moments all was surprise, trepidation, and silence. 'Hollo! what is this?' exclaimed the first officer, boasting the largest silver-headed staff; 'one, two, three, four-r-r: no less than eighteen people, upon my conscience!' 'Why,' returned David, innocently, 'what o'clock is it, sir? I'm sure I was not aware that it was so late.' 'How could you fail to be aware, when the church is not twelve paces from your door, and the bell has been ringing half-an-hour, loud enough to deafen you? Besides, you continue shaving, even before our face. We must make an example of you, sir. Beadle, take down the name.' They departed, and we culprits breathed more freely. One who had had just time to conceal himself, then crept out of the pantry, with the striped cloth around his neck, and with the lather mildewed upon his chin. In a little while the sea fight was won, and the group of sinners took the steps together, being duly edified by three strong boys chivalrously thrashing a weak one in Navarino Bay. The religiously-disposed were at the same moment coming out of church. We had a friend in the chief warden, notwithstanding his assumed severity, and we escaped the rigour of the law. He lived within a few doors of our establishment, and was a regular Sunday morning visitor. It was not an unusual thing with him to smile a warning on rising from the public chair, hasten to church, and recross almost immediately, in the stateliest manner, at the head of his official train. Poor Farmer! He was an easy confiding man and the world dealt with him unfairly. Was there ever a character of this description—simple and trusting—that found not some viper, some harpy, male or female, to sting and prey upon him? From the position of a wealthy grazier, he descended in the scale of fortune until he became a butcher's assistant.

The Barber's Shop.

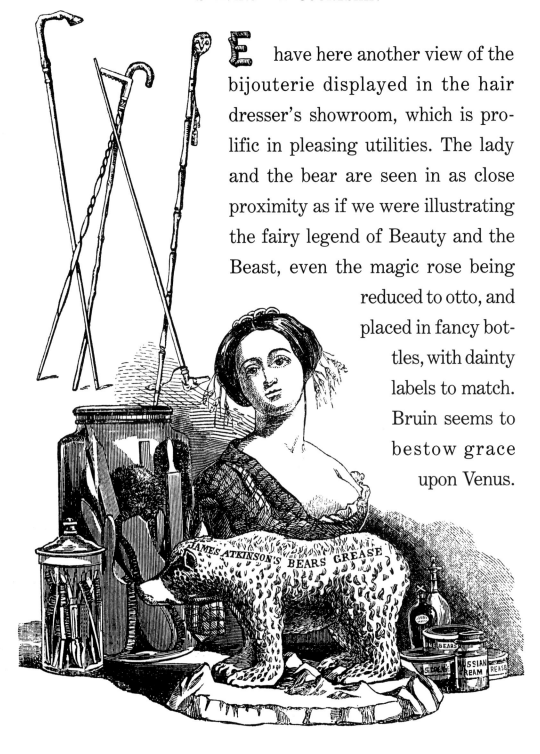

E have here another view of the bijouterie displayed in the hair dresser's showroom, which is prolific in pleasing utilities. The lady and the bear are seen in as close proximity as if we were illustrating the fairy legend of Beauty and the Beast, even the magic rose being reduced to otto, and placed in fancy bottles, with dainty labels to match. Bruin seems to bestow grace upon Venus.

WHILE rivalries are increasing, and terms lowering, even in our cutting and curling saloons, the taste and emulation shown by our leading professors are more conspicuous than heretofore; greater efforts being now made to captivate the copper than were formerly envinced to win the silver coinage. One advertises real heads of hair—not wigs!—which defy detection or successful competition, for thirty shillings. People may shortly be expected to get their heads shaved, in order that they may make experiments of the promised felicity offered at so cheap a rate. The experiments may be tried with safety, for if they fail, applications have only to be made to a neighbouring genius of our trade, who will restore the natural crops within the space of a few hours. It is worth while to listen to the latter gentleman as he speaks of himself and his marvels. His witty rhyming advertisement—his wonderful Tale of a Tub—is here unavoidably omitted, because I have received no commission to insert it in these pages. I cannot, of course, introduce it for nothing, even for a fellow-tradesman, when any manager of a theatre would charge ten guineas for allowing it to be laughed at in his pantomime.

The new-system men are spirited advertisers. They profess to suit the times, and to sympathise with bad trade. They also indulge in sarcasm, and sneeringly disclaim any connexion with the adjoining *butchers* of the association. Their novel expedients to create custom will be better understood after reading the following copy of a placard which was posted on the walls of the city:—

'To be given away a New Hat—or the value in money—every week, to the customers frequenting A. B.'s original city halfpenny shaving shop. [Here follows the address, which I prudently omit, lest my own patrons should be tempted to go.] A. B., prize hair cutter from Dublin, begs leave to announce to his friends and the public in general, that every person calling at his establishment, may have a superior shave for one halfpenny, or their hair cut, in first-rate style, for one penny; and a chance for the New Hat free of expense.'

Sometimes the inducement was varied to a leg of mutton, or a small round of beef. Should I ever follow the example of the elder D'Israeli, and write a book on the Curiosities of (not Literature, but) *Shaving*, I shall be inclined to place this modest prize barber, with his halfpenny hat, upon the first page. The legal shops started in opposition could not be maintained. The 'knobstick' journeymen who were bribed to leave town, returned in a few days to pursue their mischievous courses. The half-price concerns increased in number, rather than decreased; and the evil now appears to be established.

The name in the above card is introduced because my story of our Barber's Shop would be very imperfect without a pen-and-ink sketch of its master, 'Old David.' Old he was not, in reality,

though generally called so, for he died at the age of forty-six. Yet the appellation was justified, for David Dodd was one of those strange characters we occasionally meet with, whose existence knows no summer; their spring-time disappears, and immediately the soberness of autumn sets in, without any apparent interregnum. In his latter days, his boon companions styled him Doctor Dodd, after his celebrated namesake; later still, retaining only his mock title, he was briefly addressed as Doctor.

A wise division of time, the philosophers tell us, will enable a man to accomplish much; and there appears to be truth in the remark, for it enabled my master, in his early manhood, to pay his court to two young women at the same period. He had, like Captain Morris, of convivial memory, a great store of love in his breast, and finding one shrine insufficient for his devotions, he kindled two flames with the torch of Cupid, and kept them pleasantly burning. I cannot say whether many youths are equally wicked and selfish though it is to be hoped not; nor can I tell whether one performance charmed both audiences,—whether the actor merely repeated his part, with variations—or whether, after delighting the baker's daughter on the Monday night, an entirely new farce, fresh scenery, decorations, and the like, were requisite to please the shoemaker's niece, on the Tuesday. All this is now a buried secret, with mould and grass and flowers lying over it, for my master has long ago returned unto dust, and his grave was never pressed by a stone. When his double courtship ended, and he decided on marriage with the shoemaker's niece, the baker's daughter rather speedily followed his example, by wedding her father's foreman. The honeymoon over, my master sought out a likely shaving place, and, as his exchequer forbade him to be ambitious, he took a cellar, in a wide front thoroughfare. While arranging his curls and combs, his blocks and razors, he chanced to look across the street, and whom should he espy but his rejected sweetheart. She was standing, as mistress, in the doorway of a large provision store. It did not take David long to find another location.

The Barber's Shop.

'EASE HER! STOP HER!'
Steam Packet Call.

NOWING when to stop is an important part in writing as well as in speaking. In either case enough is better than a feast. As regards the barber's shop, its clerk or its customers, I have little more to say, at present; and may ease or stop my story as soon as I choose. The sooner, because I have no hero to punish or reward, no heroine to poison or marry, by way of pointing a moral. I remember also that a first visit, either in print or in person, should never be prolonged until the visitor becomes tedious. So short and sweet is my maxim.

THE exterior view selected to adorn the present chapter gives a fair notion of our modern versatility. The sign is happily suggestive, and its clear inference may be thus rendered: So truly do barbers keep pace with Progress, that even the railway cannot leave us behind. The umbrella denotes that we are prepared for rainy days, and the Virginian, for seasons that are smoking hot. The various play-boards nailed against the wall indicate us to be supporters of the drama; indeed, no body of men attend the theatre so well as barbers—on the free order nights. The two poles so plainly discernable, tell what everybody knows, namely, that formerly we were licensed to bleed the lieges freely; but that privilege having been transferred to the surgeons, we cannot now practice the art, even on a pimple, without being punished by loss of patronage. At the third chapter of this book, is given a small exterior with only one pole projecting. That was David Dodd's, and a mort of annoyance, I remember, it caused us. It was a standing jest with the drunken rovers of the neighbourhood, for one of their number to run away with the pole, and for another to bring it back, claiming a glass of ale for his honesty and trouble.

Had I chosen to dive like Rollin, into ancient history, and so trace my subject to its source, even into Paradise, I might have commanded a range long enough to raise the envy of Mr. Warner. From now to Adam! what a vista of beards for the mental eye to scan, backward, backward, through dim ages, until the prospect closes in (h)'airy nothing.' But my chief business, as already expressed, lies with the moderns; so I will leave to antiquarians such obsolete implements of our trade as the Wooden Candlestick, the Basin, the Chafer, the Chafing Dish, and the Crisping Irons. All these belonged to the era of the flying barbers, when shops were few, and gentlefolk were trimmed at home. The hand basin and the soap ball were in use in England to the end of Oliver Cromwell's protectorate; but shortly after the restoration they were thrust aside by the shaving-box and brush, which, together with perriwigs, were introduced to us from France. About the same period the ancient Lute ceased to be kept as a diversion for waiting customers. Its place is now supplied in some shops by the violin, in others by the draught board, and in all by the newspaper, or magazine; though our best beguiler of time is conversation. The opening question is not now, 'What is the news?' but 'What do you think of the news?' for nearly every visitor has his cheap broadsheet to feast upon at home, and consequently is almost as familiar as ourselves with current topics. When newspapers, without supplements, were published at sevenpence each, the case was somewhat different.

The barber's shop thus aided by France, had previously been enriched by Italy. In the reign of Queen Elizabeth the Earl of Oxford brought from that sunny clime the whole mystery and craft of perfumery, and costly washes. These elegant materials enabled the most talented and aspiring members of our trade to become essentially artists, and latterly self-styled professors. They have not, so far as my knowledge extends, erected a professor's chair in a college or hall of their own, but they may yet do so. These are our rich relations, as it were,—the butterflies of our caterpillar family. Or course we are very proud of them, though they are far from being proud of us. The chief perfumers have long ago discarded the barber's homely pole, his name, and I fear, himself, as being too common and unfashionable. Yet why should we blame them for so doing? Each to his element. The exclusiveness affects the barber less than it affects the pole, which seems to be in a transition state at present, and some future Gibbon may chronicle its decline and fall; while some future 'Old Jacob' shall store it in his curiosity shop, along with the telescopes, the Cremonas, the masks, the swords, the pistols, and other relics of a then bygone age and fashion. This prophecy will not, however, be fulfilled in my day; notwithstanding the pride and innovation which threaten its destruction, the party-coloured pole will erect its head, singly and in pairs, much longer than I shall erect my own cranium.

During the reign of Charles II, the hair of ladies was dressed and arranged with the nicest art, and the effect was frequently enhanced by artificial ringlets, called 'heartbreakers' and 'lovelocks:' not inappropriate names, as many a beau found to his cost in Ranelagh, or Vauxhall, when the gay belles were promenading with those graceful appendages drooping over their blooming cheeks. Here would my pen be fain to loiter, but it must hurry onwards, merely addressing to the 'heartbreaker,' in passing, the words which Moore addressed to the last rose of summer:

'Since the lovely are sleeping,
Go sleep thou with them.'

The gentlemen of those times did not, it would seem, keep pace with the ladies in their luxuriant display of hair, for the beard dwindled into whiskers, and became extinct in the reign of James II.

Although hair as a subject of writing or controversy, is of the lightest, and should invariably be lightly and pleasantly treated, it has sometimes given birth to bitter thoughts leading to fatal consequences. In the Anecdotes of Fashion it is recorded that when Louis VII., in obedience to the injunctions of his bishops, cropped his hair and shaved his beard, Eleanor, his consort, found him, with this unusual appearance, very ridiculous, and soon very contemptible. She revenged herself as she thought proper, and the poor shaved king obtained a divorce.

62 YEARS IN A BARBER SHOP

John M. Todd, 84 years of age, 1905.

What was it like to operate a barbershop in Portland, Maine from 1845 to 1905? When I saw John Todd's tonsorial memoirs advertised in an antiquarian bookman's catalog I was sure I had hit paydirt at last. *This was probably the only Victorian barber's autobiography ever published in America.*

When the book arrived I was dismayed to find nothing at all in the first 300 pages that offered any insight into the razor-wielding profession. Finally, on page 301, gold appeared in the form of a tacked-on chapter entitled "Barber's Stories."

The rest of this 324-page volume was devoted to the writer's boyhood on the family farm and his early years at sea. Also included were chapters on hypnotism, spiritualism, socialism, philosophy and religion; as well as countless anecdotes and poems, and the biographies of many of Maine's leading citizens.

John M. Todd was born into the slave-like poverty that was rural New England in the early 19th century. His father, a sea captain, lost everything in the War of 1812. From then onward, his father's wages never exceeded seventy-five cents a day. That was not enough to support the family of eight which remained constantly in debt. At one point, Mrs. Todd had to pay off a local merchant with the family's only milk cow before leaving town.

In 1835, at the age of fourteen, John shipped on board the schooner Fairdealer, which hauled potatoes from Yarmouth, Maine, to Boston. Several years of adventure and depravation followed.

At seventeen, he commenced an active life's work "against slavery of all kinds and especially against the slavery of dissipation with rum and tobacco," (John Todd was the only man in the state of Maine whose name appeared on all three temperance pledges of 1829, 1840 and 1870.)

In 1842, Mr. Todd left the sea to become a blacksmith in the town of Bath. There he learned the trade of shoeing horses and repairing carriages. He also took up Mesmerism (hypnotism), which was then attracting widespread public attention.

After two years of working over a red hot forge all day (and mesmerising young ladies at night), John Todd moved to the city of Portland. "In December of 1844 I went to work at the hairdressing business of Mr. Charles E. Bennett. In 1845, at the age of twenty-four, I opened a hairdressing room of my own in a building on the corner of Middle and Exchange streets, and remained at that location for forty-eight years, and then moved to Temple street where I am now doing business."

Here is that final fascinating chapter from John M. Todd's autobiography, *Sixty-two Years in a Barbershop*, published by the William W. Roberts Co., in 1906.

HAIR CUTTING STYLES 1830–1900

"In 1830, when Gen. Andrew Jackson was president of the United States, the style of wearing the hair was to comb it back from the forehead, no parting, but short, for Jackson wore his that way; that was the fashion for several years, called the Jackson style. Then came the style called the "soap locks," that was to cut it short on the back of the head up to the crown, but leave it long in front of the ears and let it grow long own on each side of the face; I have seen some boys who let it grow so long that they could tie it under their chin, many of them did so for sport, for at a little distance they looked like whiskers. This was in the thirties and early forties.

Then the style changed to the half-shingle, that is, we let it grow quite long all around, and many ladies used to have their hair cut short and then have it curled all over their heads; the men and boys had theirs curled also. I have stood many an afternoon and evening, when there was to be a ball or dance, and curled the hair of both sexes. After that the style was to part the hair on both sides of the head and roll it, the whole length of the head, over the fingers or with the curling iron. This style was called the topknot style, and it used to take a great lot of bear's oil, or perhaps a bear with a split hoof, better known by the name of pig's oil, to grease the hair in those days, for, in addition to the topknot, we had to roll the hair under all around the back of the head.

The hair was left long, down to the coat collar, and I have seen the grease drop from the hair onto a nice velvet collar when I sat in church and saw some foolish dandy trying in this way to rival some competitor in the greasing line. The best barber in town, in his estimation, was he who would put on the most lard or "bear's oil, at twenty cents a gallon, perfumed with bergamont and lemon," and when they bought a bottle of six or eight ounces they would pay from fifty cents to a dollar for it, another proof of "where ignorance is bliss 'tis folly to be wise."

Then came the style of 1850, when the hair was worn quite long, still called the half-shingle, parted behind and combed up over the ears. It was a fine dress style, but it was quite a job to do it well, and with some heads of hair it was almost impossible to do a good job, for some hair was so stiff that, however hard you might try to do a good piece of work, it was bound to stick out like a sore finger. That style remained longer in fashion

than any style I ever knew, when it was changed to combing the hair back of the ears; then the old Jackson style returned once more, under a new name, called the pompadour, that is, combing it up in front.

This style did not remain long, and then came the excelsior, or the highest, as now practiced, when every man and barber has become a law unto himself, has no standard of art, go as you please, grab the clippers and cut it all off whether the customer wants it or not—any hostler could do it as well. But, notwithstanding, hair-cutting is an art, for every artist tries to represent nature. Now, what is the standard of art aimed at by every true artist? When an artist attempts to paint a tree he goes out into the woods to find a perfect tree and then tries his best to represent it on canvas, and he who comes the nearest in doing it is the best artist. So it is with hair-cutting, for the standard of the art is a child's hair that has never been cut, and he who best represents it on the human head is the true artist.

Hair is given for use as well as ornament, but now it is not used much for either, for it is generally cut off. O, how I have trembled sometimes, when men who are much exposed to the inclemency of the weather take my chair, especially on a cold day, and say, "Take your clippers and clip off my hair." I never fail to beg him not to have it done, for I know of more than one who have lost their lives by so doing. So much for its use. Now as an ornament. Have you ever noticed, when admiring the ancient paintings and sculpture of the great artists of Greece and Rome, that you see no bald heads there to represent beauty? Without hair there can be no expression given to the human face. Man should wear his hair the length that beautifies him most, and not have so much cut off at any time as to change his appearance so much that every friend who meets him asks if he has had a fever, or what has changed him so.

The late John Neal, one of Portland's greatest critics on art, used to say to me, "John, if you cut my hair so short that anyone will notice it, you shall never cut it again," and he had it cut every two weeks.

SOME TONSORIAL RECORDS

"Your next, a shave or a hair cut," shouted a barber on Fore street, as a frizzly haired suburban with two inches of whiskers flopped into a chair. "Well, I reckon as how it will have to be both, if you get them ere spears off my face," and so it came to pass, a shave and a hair cut. Only one of many incidents in the thrilling and eventful life of the man who wields the razor. The Portland barbers, genial, generous whole-souled creatures of about two hundred and sixty in number, are more or less record breakers, some might say barbers lie easy, unlike the head that wears the crown, but mind you these are affidavit statements. Records, ye gods listen and hear.

How are thirty-two seconds for a starter, yet Reginald Carles, the elongated blonde at the Congress Square, claims to have performed this feat once over, not counting lathering.

Luke V. Whalen, the only official minute barber in the city, swears that by all that is green on earth that he lathered and shaved a man over twice in just one minute, and that the sum total of his earnings on one third of July was nineteen dollars and thirty-five cents, working up to two o'clock Sunday morning, and "you tell that thirty-two-second fellow," said Luke, "I'd like to meet him down back of some old barn some dark night." George N. Rich says he has got the figures to show that he shaved ninety men in one day and that he also took in fifteen dollars on Saturday. G. A. Waite shaved three men and cut one man's hair in twenty minutes. Henry Mayo, thirty years in the business and one of the lightning manipulators, once shaved a man and cut his hair in seven minutes, and took sixteen dollars and fifty cents on a Saturday. But here's one all hot, grab it before it cools, Fred Morrill, in his palmy days was one of the quickest barbers the sun ever shown on, once shaved a man at four hundred and ten Congress street in time to catch a street car that was at the head of Pearl street when the man entered, the shop and the man he shaved was Billy Moxie of the mailing department of Union Station, who vouches for the fact.

But speaking of tonsorial feats, A. O. Kenny, the young hand-

some barber at the West End, successfully shaved a man on a wager while riding on a tandem bicycle at Kebo Valley Park at Bar Harbor last summer. Samuel DuLaksi turns them off at the rate of one in four minutes. W. A. Orr shaved and cut a man's hair in seven minutes. F. E. Rollins claims nine minutes on a hair cut and twelve dollars and forty cents on a Saturday. A DuChesne can turn them out easily on a two minute basis. Said he took fourteen dollars and sixty-five cents on Saturday without straining a muscle. A. U. Aubbins at the West End has a record of a minute and a half and has done a shave and a hair in eight minutes. D. C. Hutchins, the magician barber, often shaves a man a minute by way of recreation. J. N. Pooler has removed the hair from the faces of eleven men in one hour. George W. Damm once shaved, with a boy to help him lather, seventeen men in twenty minutes.

R. B. Carpenter, the adonis of the profession, once pulled out a hair of a certain butcher's face fourteen inches long and the butcher is still using the same face. Mr. Carpenter is a razorial connoisieur. J. C. Gray, on Munjoy Hill, while in Chicago use to round them out at the rate of twelve men an hour. W. C. Bertrand, the winsome blonde at the Preble, one of the two duplex handed artists in town, has removed the whiskers and curtailed the cranial adornment in just eighteen minutes synchronized in Washington D.C., time.

One of the long renowned tonsorial artists, who has been in the business sixty-one years, the same man who twice cut Jeff Davis's hair, and who has, perhaps, shaved more of the distinguished men of Portland than any other barber, has two customers now who have been with him over fifty years. He has taken forty dollars in one day, with four men beside himself. His record is fifteen dollars and fifty cents in one day, and in the year 1874, his receipts, with four men, were five thousand and fifty-one dollars. There were not over twenty barbers in Portland at that time.

J. C. Moxcey has been plastering the lather on the human face forty-five years, and it is estimated that Mr. Moxcey and the razor have traveled in the aggregate over seven hundred and eighteen miles over human faces. In his younger years no more alert barber stood by the mug.

One of the most remarkable barbers in the city in point of service and in feats performed is Luke V. Whalen, who has seen forty-five years of barbering and blacksmithing combined. He is sometimes called the father of barbers, and was known far and wide as the swiftest in the business. He has graduated a larger number of apprentices than any other wielder of the razor in

these parts. Boys who used to work beside Whalen are scattered from Eastport to Denver.

George N. Rich was industriously scraping customers forty-three years ago. Charles Sherry, a progressive and scientific barber, shaved his first man with John B. Pike, thirty-four years ago, and A. Murphy, who keeps canaries for mascots, has seen a quarter of a century of service. J. Orrin Reid, who died recently, had a record of forty-five years in the business. J.P. Welch, one of the most skilled in the city, looms up with a record of seventeen years. Who says barbering does not conduce to longevity?"

Mr. Todd goes on to name every barber who had ever operated in Portland; probably in the hope of selling each one of them a copy of his book. He concludes with some amusing anecdotes and a list of formulas he used from 1845 to 1905.

"It was a bitter cold Saturday night and the people who were out had to keep on the move pretty much all the time to keep from freezing to death. Notwithstanding that the thermometer was nearly down to the zero mark, the usual Saturday night crowd was on hand and the stores and theatres were largely patronized. The clerks were kept busy until closing-up time, and big audiences filled both the Jefferson and the Portland. When the curtain went down at the vaudeville house at 10:20, the people in the audience tucked on their outer garments and rushed down the stairway. A long line of electrics was waiting and all of them were filled in no time. In fact, the electrics did a flourishing business at this particular time.

John M. Todd, when he was in his eighty-fourth year, finished a busy day's work at eleven o'clock and, pulling on a lightweight overcoat and a cap down over his ears, started to walk to his home on Hampshire street. He didn't mind the cold a bit. "Do you say it's cold?" remarked the veteran as he left his shop at the corner of Middle and Temple streets. "This isn't bad at all. I enjoy it. My body never gets cold, and my ears are the only part of my anatomy that is ever affected. They say this is a tough winter, but it doesn't begin to compare with some others we have had here in Portland. Why, in the winter of '72–'73, the harbor froze over so that you could ride down to Harpswell on the ice. For a steady ninety days the snow didn't thaw in front of the post office." I can take my oath to that statement. That was one of the winters when I had my barber shop at the corner of Exchange and Middle streets, where Delavina's cigar store is now located. For a continuous stretch of ninety days the frost was so thick on the windows of my shop that I couldn't look out to the sidewalk. The thermometer once dropped to twenty-eight degrees below.

Mr. Creech, rather a famous artist, came here from Boston and, with a great flourish of trumpets, opened a shop, expecting to carry everything in the barber line by storm; advertised that he used nothing but Damascus blades and Kesan soap, a famous shaving soap—every barber used it, but he was giving a big bluff. There was a well known soap maker in the city who manufactured soft soap and sold it by the barrel. There was also a famous old blacksmith here who, of course, never made razors. The day after Creech's advertisement appeared I came out with a notice that I was doing business at the old stand, still using Mansfield's soap and Averill's blades. Of course, it was intended as a burlesque on Creech. I was well acquainted with him, but did not know how he would take the joke. He met me smiling in a few days and said, "Todd, that was the worst let-down I ever had."

I had an apprentice boy many years ago who was very precocious, with great self-reliance. He had not been in the shop but a very few days when he was anxious to shave someone; he thought he could do it. My men had let him shave them to give him a little practice. One day a coal heaver from Commercial street came in with a very hard beard, full of coal dust, and I wanted to give the boy an object lesson to take the conceit out of him a little. I said, "Jimmie, go ahead and shave that gentleman." He commenced and worked for about half an hour, digging and scraping the man's face until it was as red as a beet; finally, he got through and the man got out of the chair. The boy, fearing that he hadn't given satisfaction, stepped up to him with great assurance and said, "That was a good shave, sir, wasn't it?" The old fellow rubbed his face and said, "It was a fine shave, my lad, but I have suffered damn bad for it."

I had a neighbor, a Mr. Moxcey; occasionally we would play jokes on each other. One Saturday afternoon he was quite busy; a longshoreman, an Irishman, came into his shop with a long and hard beard. Joe did not care to shave him, and thinking to play a trick on me, he said, "I am quite busy and you go up to Mr. Todd's, just above here, he don't have a good deal to do; you would be very likely to get a shave there, and I will pay for it;" handing him ten cents. The poor man went down to the foot of the stairs, stopped and thought for a few moments and said, "Faith, I will go back and get him to shave me, if it takes all day." So he went back and gave Joe the same ten cents he had given him, saying that he would wait all day rather than go back on him, the generous man that he was."

BARBER'S FORMULAS USED BY JOHN TODD, (1845–1905).

Todd's Hair Dye. Formula No. 1: Dissolve two drachms of gallic acid in two ounces of alcohol, add one pint of soft water.

Formula No. 2: Take two ounces of gum arabic, put in a pint of soft water, add twelve grains of gallic acid, when dissolved ready for use.

Formula No. 3: Take one ounce nitric crystalized silver, add two ounces of aqua ammonia concentrated, when dissolved add five ounces of the gum solution.

Formula No. 4: One drachm of sulphate of potash, one ounce of soft water, shake it well.

Gilmans' Hair Dye. Formula No. 1: Dissolve one ounce of gallic acid, six ounces of alcohol and when dissolved add one quart of soft water.

Formula No. 2: Dissolve one ounce of crystalized silver to four ounces of water, add one ounce of gum arabic as thick as it can be dissolved, then add one ounce of ammonia concentrate.

Formula No. 3: Dissolve one ounce of sulphate of potash in eight ounces of soft water.

Directions for using these dyes: Wash out the hair or whiskers clean with soap and water thoroughly and then dry it. Then apply number one with a tooth brush, dry the hair well, then, take a clean tooth brush and apply number two. Be sure to get every spear dry. Then go through the same process with number three with a clean brush.

Todd's Luxsolus Liquid Dye. Formula No. 1: Nitrate of silver, one-quarter ounce; spirits of ammonia, one-half ounce. This is the same as the Capalani Hair Dye (soft water, six ounces). Directions: Moisten the hair with a tooth brush.

Directions for using Todd's Luxsolus (light of the sun) Liquid Dye: Wash out the hair and whiskers clean, dry thoroughly then take a tooth brush and apply the liquid, wet the hair with the dye, be careful not to get it on the skin, if you do wipe it off before it dries.

For removing dye from the skin: Gum of potash, one-half ounce; soft water, one ounce.

Hair Oil. One quart of castor oil, three quarts of alcohol, three drops of liquid of potassa, scented with oil of rose.

Comam Crescre. Three parts of alcohol, one of castor oil, scented with lemon and rose.

Todd's Hungarian Balm. For making ten gallons: Tincture of spanish flies, four ounces; benzoeic tincture compound, two ounces; peruvian bark, two and one-half ounces; borax, two and one-half; rosemary, three; salt, three; glycerine, ten pounds; water, ten gallons; scented with musk and bitter almond filtered through paper.

Aqua Vita. Water, one gallon; tincture of contharies, two ounces; benzoes, two ounces; peruvian park, one-half ounce; borax, one-half ounce; perfume bergumot.

Powder for the face. Pulverized arrow root mixed with rice flowers equal parts.

Cure for humors. Acetic acid, one ounce; one ounce of tincture of muriate iron.

Sea Foam. Rain water, one pint; alcohol, one pint; glycerine, one-half ounce; ammonia, one-quarter ounce.

To prevent hair from falling out. Take an eight-ounce bottle, fill it with water, put it in a table spoonful of sulphur, shake it whenever used and put it on and rub it well in the hair for three night in succession. Do this once a week until the hair ceases to drop out.

Cure for ring-worms. Acetic acid, tincture of iron, or per sulphur of iron, equal parts.

Cure for humors. Sure cure for what is called the barber's itch. Acetic acid, one ounce; tincture of muriatic iron, equal parts. Directions for using: take a feather or a stick and dip it into the liquid and moisten the sore with it a few times. Don't drink it, it is poison.

"In 1846 and '47 when the Mexican war was being carried on, General Twiggs was in the fight. He was troubled with a bad sore of the scalp. The doctor prescribed as a remedy lax-sulphur and sugar of lead. Wherever it came in contact with the hair it restored it to its original color. The account of it was given out in the newspapers and a druggist put it up and called it "Twiggs' Hair Dye," and it had a great run. I sold much of it until I became satisfied that it was injurious to the health, for sugar of lead is a poison and I have never seen any hair dye that took from ten to thirty days to change the color of the hair that did not contain sugar of lead."

Author's Note: These early formulas are reproduced here for reference only. They could be very injurious to your health.

PRICE LIST OF
HAIR DRESSERS' SUNDRIES.
1882-83

PRACTICAL CUTLERS,
(OVER THIRTY YEARS' EXPERIENCE)

349 Washington Street, Boston, Mass.

Importers, Manufacturers and Dealers in

Cutlery, Fancy Goods and Hair Dressers' Sundries.

OUR TERMS ARE STRICTLY CASH

Or C. O. D. (cash on delivery) with addition of express charges for collecting and returning the amount to us.

When possible, forward amount of bill when ordering, and thus avoid the expense and annoyance of collection charges. Money may be sent with perfect safety by cheque, payable to our order; by registered letter; post office order, or by money order system of American Express Company; or small amounts may be sent in common letter with reasonable safety, in one or three-cent postage stamps. Customers at a distance, when they do not send full amount, should always send a reasonable amount with their order, as a guarantee of good faith.

We do not warrant that our razors or any other goods will meet the peculiar wants of the purchaser; but any article bought of us will willingly be exchanged, if returned to us *unused.*

PLEASE PAY PARTICULAR ATTENTION TO THIS DIGEST OF POSTAL LAWS.

We can send by mail to any part of the United States or Territories, Shears, Razors, Hones, Combs, Strops, Brushes, or other articles too numerous to mention. *Fluids or Glass* ARE NOT MAILABLE.

The rate of Postage is one cent (*pre-paid*) for every ounce or fraction of an ounce, and the package must not exceed four pounds in weight.

Packages can be registered for ten cents each additionally, and thereby have perfect safety and delivery guaranteed.

When sending Shears or Razors see that the points of the Shears are thoroughly protected by a cap of paper, metal or cloth, and that the Shears or Razors are carefully *tied* up in paper or other suitable material, and put in a pasteboard or other suitable box, so as to render it impossible for them to injure other mail matter.

DO NOT SEAL OR ENCLOSE ANY WRITING

In the package, as it thereby becomes liable to full letter postage. *But,* you are allowed to put your name on the outside as a means of identification This should always be done, to avoid mistakes.

When ordering Goods, look at price in Price List, add *enough* for postage, and send full amount by mail, post office order, or registered letter; the last two are perfectly safe. Be sure and send *enough. We will always return any balance.*

We give the following as samples of average cost of postage *to and from any part of the United States :*—

One 7-inch Razor Hone,	.	20 cents.
" Requisite Strop, large,	.	6 "
" " " medium,	.	4 "
" Horse-Hide or Canvas Strop,	.	2 to 4 "
" dozen Dressing Combs,	.	10 "
" Comb,	.	2 to 4 "
" sample stick of Turkish Cosmetique,	.	2 "
" dozen Turkish Cosmetique,	.	13 "
One-half dozen Moustache Wax,	.	5 "

THE CANADIAN POSTAL LAWS

Provide that " actual patterns or samples of merchandise, and having no intrinsic value in themselves," may be sent to and from *Canada* at a uniform rate of *10* cents for each package not exceeding *eight ounces in weight.* All new goods are liable to be detained at custom house for payment of duties. New Razors, Shears, etc., are subject to duties.

We have a great deal of trouble with mail packages *going to* Canada, and would advise our customers to have *all goods* sent there by express.

We advise our customers to avail themselves of the advantages offered by the **MONEY ORDER SYSTEM** which has just been adopted by the **AMERICAN EXPRESS COMPANY,** by which orders can be made payable to us from any of the 4000 offices of the Company in the United States, at the following rates : **For $1.00 to $5.00. 5 cents ; over $5.00 to $10.00, 8 cents.** "THE CHEAPEST, SAFEST AND MOST CONVENIENT MONEY ORDER SYSTEM EVER ADOPTED."

THE AMERICAN EXPRESS COMPANY

Have also made arrangements by which they can send to or from any of their 4000 offices, and by which they can *pro rata*, or send at one charge, small packages, not exceeding seven pounds in weight, to or from places where they have no office, but which are controlled by the Adams; United States; National; United States and Canada; North Pacific; Delaware' Lackawanna and Western; Union; Baltimore and Ohio Express Companies; at their offices, and with the Pacific and Wells, Fargo & Co Express Companies, on all "all-rail points" controlled by them east of Ogden, Utah.

By this arrangement the express charges are about as follows :—

1 pound package,	. . . . .	25 cents.
2 " " according to distance,	25 to 30 "
3 " " " "	25 to 40 "
4 " " " "	25 to 60 "
5 " " " "	25 to 75 "
6 or 7 pound package, " "	25 cents to $1.00.

In sending goods, either by mail, express, or freight, if entrusted to us we will exercise our best judgment on all points.

AMES & STUART, Printers, 58 Federal Street, Boston.

ATOMIZERS.

'BOSTON PERFUMER."
90 cents each.

"FAVORITE."
50 cents each.

They are very simple in construction, and can readily be adjusted to throw a light or heavy spray, as desired.

Atomizer Bulbs and duplicate parts of Atomizers at reasonable rates.

AMMONIA.

Best English, 40 cents per lb.; 5 cents per ounce.

BOILERS

FOR BARBERS' USE.

4 qt. Copper			$7.00
6 " "			8 00
4 " Nickel Plated			9.00
6 " " "			10.00

BOILER HEATERS.

NON EXPLOSIVE.

The No. 1 will heat a boiler of ordinary size.

The No. 2 can be used with one or both wicks.

No. I. Price, $2.50.
(Has one 4 inch wick.)

No. 2. Price, $4.00.
(Has two 4 inch wicks.)

"CHICAGO"
BENCH BOTTLES.

BLUE,

GREEN,

AMBER,

OPAQUE,

FLINT

PRICE, 40 CENTS.

BARBERS' CASTER.

An entirely new design. It is heavily silver plated.
Price, including three labeled bottles and one bowl, $6.00.

RUBY
ENGRAVED BOTTLE.

See Ruby Bowl on page 10, made to match this Bottle.

PRICE 50 CENTS.

"BELL BOTTOM" BENCH BOTTLES.

A new pattern. Blue and opal color. The labels are glass, and are set into a recess. Large size hold 16 ounces, and are labeled "Bay Rum." "Cologne," "Shampoo," "Sea Foam," "Florida Water," and "Hair Tonic." Small size hold 8 ounces, and are labeled "Hair Oil."

"STANDARD" BENCH BOTTLES.

Clear glass, with *brilliantly* colored glass labels. Large size hold 16 ounces, and are labeled "Bay Rum," "Cologne," "Shampoo," "Sea Foam," "Florida Water," and "Hair Tonic." Small size hold 8 ounces, and are labeled "Hair Oil."

SHAVING BRUSHES.

"Crown" Bound Brushes.

Black Enameled Handles.   *French Bristles.*

Good Brushes. Have sold them for nine years past. Prices as follows:

	Per doz.	Each.
No. 112, Length 6 inches,	$3.50	33 cents.
No. 19, " 5½ "	2.75	28 "
No· 16, " 4¾ "	2.25	25 "

We have brushes similar in appearance to the above. In them the copper "crown" is dispensed with, but strength is obtained by a peculiar formation of the handle. Prices as follows:

	Per doz.	Each.
No. 101, Length 4¾ inches,	$1.25	13 cents.
No. 102, " 5 "	1 50	15 "
No. 103, " 5¼ "	1.75	20 "
No. 104, " 5¾ "	2.00	25 "

The "Patent Wedge-Fastened" Lather Brushes

(See cut) have black enameled handles. They are a showy, good brush and well adapted for "customers'" use. There are many imitations in the market; we have seen some with a "plug" of wood "as large as your finger" in the middle of the bristles. Prices as follows:

	Per doz.	Each.
No. 130	$1 00	13 cents.
No. 127	.90	10 "
No. 126	.80	8 "
No. 125	.60	6 "
No. 123	.50	5 "

Black Enameled Handle Metal Ferrule Brushes

See cut of brush on top of mug numbered "Champion" Mug, on page 9. Prices as follows:

	Per doz.	Each.
No. 10	$1.00	10 cents.
No. 20	1.25	13 "
No. 30	1.50	15 "

McLAUGHLIN'S

(Murphy, Leavens & Co.,)

Lather Brushes.

GENUINE.

The Old Standard.   **Beware of Imitations.**

		Per doz.	Each.
Black Handles (Copper Bound)	No. 113,	$2.80	25c
" "	No. 114,	3.20	30c
" "	No. 115,	4.00	38c
" "	No. 116,	4.80	45c
Bl'k Walnut Handles, "	No. 7,	3.00	30c
" " "	No. 9,	3.60	35c

BONE AND METAL

CASED BRUSHES

For Travellers' Use.

Rosewood Handle, Horn Ferrule,

French Bristle,

LATHER BRUSHES.

These are the favorite brushes among barbers in the Western States, and are likely to become a favorite here

	Per doz.	Each.
Large size	$3.50	35 cents.
Medium	3.00	30 "
Small size	2.75	25 "

In addition to the foregoing, we have a large variety of common Lather Brushes, in all styles of finish, at prices which we guarantee to be satisfactory.

FANCY HANDLED SHAVING BRUSHES

In Bone, Horn or Wood Handles.

Badger-Hair Shaving Brushes

In extensive variety, in Bone, Ebony, Enameled, and Nickel Plated Handles.

HAIR BRUSHES.

We have fifty or more different patterns of French, English and American Hair, which we cannot well enumerate. Tell us what you would like and we will send you good goods at bottom rates.

"BOSTON" HAIR BRUSH.

We have sold these celebrated Black Bristle Brushes for many years. They are the standard of excellence, and "wear like iron" Prices as follows:

	Per doz.	Each.
No. 332, length 10 inches,	$7.20	70 cents.
No 306, " 9 "	6.40	60 "
No. 279, " 8 "	5.40	50 "

Shampoo Brushes,	Face Brushes,
Hat Brushes,	Nail Brushes,
Dye Brushes,	Bath Brushes,

IN GREAT VARIETY.

NECK BRUSHES.

Black Enameled Handles: Horse Hair, 75c. Bristles, 50c. each. Wood Handles: French dyed (crimson) bristle brushes, 75c. each. Common Bristles, 40, 50, 66c. each.

ERRATA.

This space was reserved for a cut of the "*Britannia Handled, Nickel Plated, Neck Brush,*" Price $1.75 each," and the page kept back to be printed last of all. We now use the space to say that the Post Office Department has just ruled that

RAZORS

ARE

UNMAILABLE,

NO MATTER

HOW PACKED.

The postal laws otherwise remain unaltered, but no doubt the "razor" clause will be amended so as to allow them to be mailed.

CLIPPING MACHINES
For Barbers' Use.

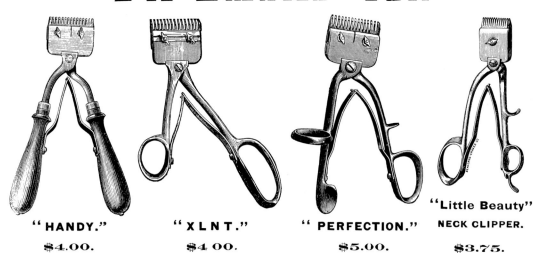

"LIGHTNING"
Clipping Machine.

"HANDY."	"XLNT."	"PERFECTION."	"Little Beauty" NECK CLIPPER.
$4.00.	$4 00.	$5.00.	$3.75.

Can be sent by Mail, Registered, at an additional cost of 40 cents or less.

☞ See Digest of Postal Laws and Express Package Rates on first page. ☜

WE ARE PROPRIETORS OF THE
"PERFECTION" AND "LITTLE BEAUTY,"
ALSO, SOLE AGENTS FOR THE
"XLNT," "HANDY," AND "LIGHTNING" CLIPPING MACHINES.

Price, $30.00.

As will be readily understood by the engraving, this machine is run by motive power, which may be supplied by a boy revolving the large wheel, and thereby (by the belt seen in the cut) giving motion to the small wheels and thence transmitting it to the cutter through the flexible "cable" seen under the arm of the "artist."

With the "*Lightning*" *Clipper* a head has been clipped in one and a half minutes. They are now put in market in response to many enquiries.

For transportation they are packed in a box 20 inches wide by 24 long and 11 deep, accompanied by full directions for setting up and running them.

We have made Clipping Machines for Barbers' use an especial matter of study and experiment, and we take great pleasure in calling attention to the above styles. They are made under our special direction and supervision, and we are confident that, in their various forms, these combine more points of excellence than any other yet in market. The names given them are such as have been used by leading barbers in expressing their opinion of their relative merits. The "*Little Beauty*" is entirely new this season. It will no doubt become an indispensable tool for *Neck Clipping and Trimming,* as it does the work much quicker and better than scissors, cuts nearly as close as a "dry shave," and does away entirely with the danger of "nipping" the neck. The cutting-plates of the "HANDY," "XLNT," and "PERFECTION" are alike in each, and the special merit of one above the other consists in the style, shape and bearing of the handles. They can be used with one or both hands, or if it is desired to leave the hair longer than a "close clip," it can be done easily by clipping over a common dressing comb, or by using *Candrian's Adjustable Clipper Plates.* (See description.)

☞ You can sharpen either of these, and the "Little Beauty," yourself. A Grinding Plate and full directions accompany each machine. They are nicely finished in nickel plate, and in case of need, duplicate parts can easily be obtained.

"HORSE" CLIPPER.
STRAIGHT.
Price, Nickle Plated, $5.00.   Japanned, $4.00.

We have also an excellent Horse Clipper, similar to the above, not so nicely finished, but a GOOD article. Price, Nickle Plated, **$4.00.** Japanned, **$3.50.**

"HORSE" CLIPPER.
BENT.
PRICE, - - - $4.00.

These machines are of the same excellent quality as the "PERFECTION" and "XLNT." The "STRAIGHT" one is made especially for use on horses, but is used by some barbers. The "BENT" is made expressly for "clipping horses' legs as they stand upon the floor."

Sharpening or Repairing Clipping Machines.

In answer to many inquiries, we would say that our usual price for sharpening our machines is 60 cents each, (exclusive of postage or expressage.) We charge from $1.00 to $1.50 for sharpening others. We cannot set an exact price because of the uncertainty of what labor may be needed. Other repairs will be made, and parts supplied, at reasonable rates.

TURKISH COSMETIQUE.

TURKISH COSMETIQUE.

We are originators and proprietors of this "Standard" Cosmetique. It has now been some seven years in the market, and is quoted as the *"Standard of Excellence"* throughout the New England States, and is used by Hair Dressers from Newfoundland to California.

From experience we are assured that a single trial will prove that it is, beyond question,

THE BEST IN USE.

For *Fragrance of Perfume* it stands unrivalled, as well as for its *wearing* and *lasting* qualities as a Cosmetique. It does not "crumble" like Italian Cosmetique, or "grease" like the French, but it "blends right on to the hair," giving it a peculiar silky lustre.

The excellence of this Cosmetique is attested by the fact that numerous weak imitations of it are in market all over the country. Beware of these, and insist on having the genuine.

TURKISH COSMETIQUE.

It is put up in Turkey-red paper wrappers. In size it is a little larger than the small size Italian Cosmetique; but it is much more lasting as it "goes farther" in use.

In addition to the original "Rose" color we now have it in Brown or Black.

PRICE, $1.25 PER DOZ., OR 13 CTS. EACH.

Or sent postpaid on receipt of $1.39 in money or stamps. Sample Roll sent, postpaid, for 14 cents.

☞ It is for sale by our authorized agents, and by the leading druggists and barber supply dealers in the United States and Canada.

☞ Aside from its many virtues as a cosmetique, it has been found to have unrivalled soothing and healing qualities, and is now much used as an application to the face after shaving.

Camphor Ice, Cold Cream, Etc.

HEGEMAN'S CAMPHOR ICE, $1.70 per doz., or 15 cts. each.

CAMPHOR ICE AND GLYCERINE, Common, $1.00 per doz., or 10 cts. each.

COLD CREAM, PATEY'S, English, in pots, $1.75 per doz., or 20 cts. each.

COLD CREAM, LLOYD'S, Rose, English, in collapsible tubes, large, $4.25 per doz., or 40 cts. each. Small, $2.50 per doz., or 25 cts. each.

LLOYD'S EUXESIS, (now much used after shaving,) $4.50 per doz., or 45 cts. each.

"TURKISH COSMETIQUE" is now much used in place of Camphor Ice, etc. Price, $1.25 per doz., or 13 cts. a roll.

COSMETIQUES.

	Per dozen.	Each.
Turkish, (Smith Bros.)	$1.25	.13
Cosmetique des Fleurs, (Smith Bros.,)	1.00	.10
Cosmetique Fixateur, (Smith Bros.,)	.90	.10
Moustache Wax, (Smith Bros.,) in rolls,	1.00	.10
Coudray's, No. 940, genuine,	1.25	.13
Pomade Hongroise, (Coudray's,)	2.75	.25

BEWARE OF

MOUSTACHE WAX

SMITH BROTHERS,
349 WASHINGTON ST., BOSTON, MASS.

IMITATIONS

$1.00 per doz., or 10c. each.

The following letter from Prof. Wm. Roberson, (since dead, but at that time) proprietor of the largest hair dressing establishment in the world, explains itself:—

SPARTA, WIS., August 19, 1877.

Messrs. SMITH BROTHERS,
349 Washington Street, Boston, Mass.

SIRS:—Please send to my address, 615 Washington Ave., St. Louis, two dozen of your Moustache Wax, such as you send to R. J. Stockton, Merchants Hotel, Barber Shop, St. Paul, Minn. I saw it there in use a few weeks since, and think that it will suit me. If it meets my expectations I will order more. Send this as soon as the 1st of September, as I will be at home at that time. Send it C. O. D.

Respectfully,   WM. ROBERSON.

SMITH BROTHERS'

EXTRA FRAGRANT

COLOGNE.

Price, $6 00 per gallon; 75 cents per pint
Trial bottle, 15 cents.

We have during the past year introduced with gratifying success this most *fragrant and lasting Cologne.* Quality considered, it is the cheapest Cologne for barbers' use in the market.

TRY IT! YOU WILL LIKE IT!

COLOGNES, FLORIDA WATER, ETC.

Cologne. Hoyt's German, large, $7.50 per doz.; 70 cts. per bottle. Small, $1.70 per doz.; 15 cts. per bottle.

Florida Water. Murray & Lanman's, $5.75 per doz.; 50 cts. per bottle.

Lavender Water. Lubin's, Amber, $10 00 per doz.; 90 cts. per bottle. Lubin's, Pale, $8.00 per doz.; 75 cts. per bottle.

Coudray's (French), $5.50 per doz.; 50 cts per bottle

The above cut represents the Attachment. The elevations at the end of the teeth of plates project over the teeth of Clipper, as shown in cuts of side views, and thus perform the service of a *perfect comb or guide,* to bring the hair into proper position to be cut. The plate is so constructed that it is firmly held to the Clipper, and can be easily attached or removed.

We are Sole Agents for the New England and adjoining States and Canada for

CANDRIAN'S

Adjustable Clipper Plates.

We have personally examined all other adjusting devices yet in market, and have been obliged from our own judgment and testimony of experts to pronounce them as being worthless for the purpose intended. There is nothing *"sure"* about them, you *can* cut the hair *"any* length" with them, but cannot rely on having *the* length desired, as the hair will "run" and "double up" between the combs or the so-called "adjusting device"—thereby leaving the hair uneven.

Candrian's Adjustable Clipper Plates

ARE A SURE THING.

They are made to fit the "PERFECTION," "X L N T," "HANDY," and other one-hand Clipping Machines. In ordering, *be sure* to state what make your Clipper is, and the number of teeth it has.

Price of Plate: { No. 1, which cuts the hair ⅛ inch long } { No. 2, which cuts the hair ¼ inch long } { No. 3, which cuts the hair ½ inch long } $1.00 each.

Sent by REGISTERED Mail on receipt of Price and an additional 3 cents per Plate, and 10 cents for the package

Full size side view of Clipper with No. 1, plate attached. The space between the upper and middle dotted lines represents the length of hair cut by the Clipper alone, being one-eighth inch. The space between the middle and bottom dotted lines represents the length of hair cut by plate, making one-fourth inch together.

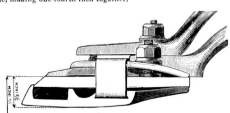

Full size side view of Clipper with No. 2, plate attached. The space between the upper and middle dotted lines represents the length of hair cut by Clipper with No. 2, plate attached, being three-eighths inch. The space between the upper and *lower* dotted lines represents the length of hair cut with No. 3, plate attached, being one-half inch.

COMBS.

COMBS.

HAIR DRESSING COMBS, 1 INCH WIDE.
25 Cents each. $2.50 per dozen.

HAIR CUTTING COMBS, 7-8 INCH WIDE.
25 Cents each, $2.50 per dozen.

"NARROW" COMBS, 5-8 INCH WIDE.
With thick or thin backs, suitable for "cutting" or "feathering."
25 Cents each, $2.50 per doz.

"ALL COARSE" TOOTH COMBS.
Widths and Prices as above.
ENGLISH "QUILED" THICK BACK COMBS. Styles as above.

			Per Doz.	Each.
Wide,	. . .		$4.00	40c.
Medium,	. . .		3.50	35c.
Narrow,	. . .		3.00	30c.

ELECTRIC HAIR DYE. BLACK.

DIRECTIONS FOR USE.—*Usually*, no preparatory washing is needed, but if the hair is *very* "greasy" it will be well to wash it well with shampoo or Borax water, which then wash off and dry the hair a little; then apply the preparation in the large bottle, being particular to apply it to all the hair. Then apply the preparation in the small bottle, and wash off in clear water. On some hair a weak solution of Sulphuret of Potass may be used advantageously, *as a third preparation* to "set" the color.

PREPARED BY
SMITH BROTHERS,
Manufacturers and Dealers in
TOILET ARTICLES,
Washington St., Boston. Mass.

SMITH BROTHERS' ELECTRIC HAIR DYE.
BLACK.

In Boxes containing both preparations and full directions. Price, 50 cents per box to the "trade," or 75 cents retail.

Dye Combs.—$1.25 per doz.; 13 cts. each.

Dye Spoons.—35, 25 and 20 cts. each.

COMBS.

All our Barber Combs are made expressly to our order. In the various processes to which the horn is subjected in the factory we insist that every care shall be taken to preserve the "life" of the horn—that it shall not be burned out with heat, nor eaten up with chemicals—and that no pains shall be spared to ensure the combs being of the

BEST QUALITY IN EVERY RESPECT.

Our aim is QUALITY AND CHEAPNESS, as far as is consistent with quality.

HONES.

YELLOW HONES, BEST SELECTED.

7 inch each,	$2.50	$2.00	$1.75	$1.50
8 " "		4.00	3.50	and 3.00
9 " "		5.00	4.50	" 4.00
10 " "		6.00	5.50	" 5.00

Common coarse Hones at nominal prices, VIZ : 50 cts., 75 cts., $1 00 and upward, according to size and quality.

BLUE WATER HONES

Are nearly all alike in grit : "they cut slowly, but put on a very fine edge " Prices as follows :

Water Hones and Rubbers,	$2.00	$1.50
Extra Rubbers, . . .	25 cts. each.	

We have welcomed, tried and thoroughly tested all the various new kinds of hones as they have been brought into the market, but are sorry to be obliged to say that we have found none which have the *lasting qualities* which characterize the above.

YELLOW OR BLUE
German Hones.

Of these we carry the largest assortment of Razor Hones in the United States, from which we will honestly try to select just such as our customers desire, and at reasonable prices. When ordering, tell us as explicitly as possible, what lubricant you use ; what grit you like ; and, when possible, send your old hone, or a reasonably large sized piece of it, to compare by.

SEE NOTICE OF
Postal and Express Arrangements
ON FIRST PAGE.

COMBS.

CLIPPING OR NECK COMBS.
VERY THIN.
25 cents each. $2.50 per dozen.

TAPERING CLIPPING COMBS.
A NEW PATTERN.
25 cents each. $2.50 per dozen.

TAPERING, AMERICAN PATTERN.

1⅛ in. wide at coarse end,			30 cents each, $3.00 per dozen.
1 " " " "	25 "	2.50 "
⅞ " " " "	25 "	2.50 "
⅝ " " " "	25 "	2.50 "

TAPERING, FRENCH PATTERN.

1¼ in. wide, at coarse end,			40 cents each, $4.00 per dozen.
1 " " " "	35 "	3.50 "
⅞ " " " "	30 "	3.00 "

Dye Combs.— $1.25 per dozen, or 13 cents each.

"Natural" Brown HAIR DYE.

DIRECTIONS FOR USE —Wash the hair thoroughly with Borax water, and wash off clean. Dry a little; then thoroughly saturate the hair with the preparation in the large bottle; dry a little, or thoroughly, then apply the preparation in small bottle. Wash off in clear water. The result will be a "natural" brown color.

PREPARED BY
SMITH BROTHERS,
Manufacturers and Dealers in
TOILET ARTICLES.
349 Washington St., BOSTON, MASS.

Smith Brothers'
"Natural" Brown Hair Dye.

We have succeeded, after much trouble and expense, in manufacturing a Hair Dye which dyes a "Natural" Brown. It is put up in boxes, with full directions. Price 50 cents to the "trade," or 75 cents retail.

READ.

LINDSAY, ONT., Feb. 17, 1882.

The Clipper that you sent me some time since has given me such good satisfaction that I have concluded to give your razors a trial. Send ——

C. ORZEL.

HARLAN, IOWA, Dec. 19, 1881.

As I always dealt with you while in the East I find it hard to give you up; although I can get goods nearer they do not fill the place of yours. Send me ——

J. B. LYON.

BINGHAM, IOWA, Feb. 4, 1882.

Some time ago I ordered a horse hide strap of you, and I liked it very much, but I sold it to a brother barber. Please send me another by return mail. I enclose money.

W. H. WILLETTS.

WEST OAKLAND, CAL., May 18, 1881.

Send me $5.00 worth of your Turkish Cosmetique. You know me as an old customer in New York State.

J. JENNERY.

PETERSBURG, VA., July 5, 1881.

The clipper and scissors came to hand and acted splendidly.

MOSES STITH.

CONCAVING,

SHARPENING AND REPAIRING.

All our Concaving, Grinding, Sharpening and Polishing is done on the premises, by our own workmen, and is supervised by our senior partner, who has had over thirty years' practical experience as a cutler.

PRICES AS FOLLOWS:

Razors, *full* concaved,	. . .	50 cents each.
" 3-4 "	. . .	35 "
" half "	. . .	25 "
" plain ground,	. . .	15 "
" re-concaved,	. . .	15 to 25 cents.
" re-handled,	. . .	25 cents each.
Shears sharpened,	. . .	15 "
New screw,	. . .	10 "

When sending or ordering carefully read **Postal and Express Arrangements on First Page.**

ERRATA

Customers in **Ontario** are informed that the *pro rata* Express Parcel Arrangement is not yet in operation there.

READ.

MERRIMAC, MASS.

I sent a lot of blades to you yesterday, and here are five more. I want them concaved thin and square pointed. Your work suits me better than any

N. M. RICKER.

TAWAS CITY, MICH., Nov. 18, 1881.

I send you nine razors to concave. I enclose $5.00 in this letter.

E. CARSON.

TAWAS CITY, MICH., Mar. 6, 1882.

I send you two razors; please give them a full concave. The last sent you were very nicely done.

E. CARSON.

MECHANICS FALLS, ME., Feb. 27, 1881.

Please send me three of your best razors (one dollar each.) I do not say what kind, but rely on your judgment. I want them for my own use in my shop; also send ——
Enclosed find $5.00.

JOHN F. BRIGGS.

MEREDITH, N. H., June 10, 1881.

Please send me ——. I have sent you a few small orders before which have received prompt attention and given good satisfaction.

F. B. WILSON.

Barbers' Tool Bracket.

The Tool Bracket is ebonized and gilded, or made of black walnut, engraved but not gilded. The back of the razor rack is of velvet. The panel, seen immediately below the razor rack, is on hinges, fastened at the lower edge, and can be let down, making a shelf for combs. A leather strap is provided, behind which the combs are placed to keep them in position when the panel is up, as seen in the engraving. The neck duster and face brush are held in place by spring clamps, into which they can be pushed with the greatest ease. No time is lost in hanging them up, as is often the case when a neck duster is hung with a string on a hook. If a shaving paper case is wanted, we can put one in place of comb shelf, at the same price.
When ordering be sure to state whether ebony or walnut is wanted

PRICE, $2.50.

WE ARE

SOLE AGENTS

FOR THE

New England States

AND

CANADA

FOR THIS

NEW AND USEFUL

ARTICLE.

THE INVENTOR

IS A

Practical Barber.

Williams' Patent Shaving Cup.

PATENTED JUNE 22, 1880.

As will be seen by the cut, the improvement consists in providing a cup with a bottom supplied with a number of small pegs.

The soap is to be pressed hard down upon these pegs, thereby holding the soap firmly, until it is entirely taken up by the brush.

The inventor claims that by its use you can save **50** per cent of your soap:

As The pegs hold the soap so firmly that it does not break up when worn down thin.
The water cannot get under the soap and soak it soft and useless.
The brush has a ready action on the soap
There are no waste pieces coming from this cup, continually stopping up your waste pipes.

The Cup is made of Hard White Metal, and warranted Triple Plate Silver.

PRICE, $1.25. A DISCOUNT ON ONE-HALF DOZEN OR DOZEN LOTS.

MEDIUM SIZE.

BEST FRENCH CHINA MUG.

(The above is "life" size, as nearly as is possible to show by a drawing.)

Price for Mug, including name, dash, and three gold bands, as above, 75 cents each.

LARGE SIZE.

BEST FRENCH CHINA MUG.

(The above is "life" size, as nearly as is possible to show by a drawing.)

Price for Mug, including name, dash, scroll work, two light and one heavy gold bands on top edge, as above, ... $1.15 each.

MUG
DECORATING
A SPECIALTY.

China Mugs Ornamented to Order

With Names, Numbers, Monograms, or any Style or Design of Ornamenting.

☞ All the decorations and ornamenting are burned on to the mug.

☞ The gold used is the best "Burnish" Gold, therefore time (usually a week) is required to have the work done properly and with due regard to its durability.

☞ "Bright" Gold is less durable, but is used by many decorators, because by so doing they can do the work quicker, and with more profit to themselves.

☞ When ordering *be sure* that the names are spelled correctly, otherwise we will not be responsible for errors. Write the names in a full round hand, or in capital letters thus: "SMITH BROTHERS," "J. W. S.," etc.

The following will give a general idea of leading styles and prices of ornamented mugs. The prices vary according to kind of mug and amount and style of ornamenting: —

Large size,		with gold bands, 5-8 inch wide colored top band, gold name and scroll work in front, and cluster of flowers on each side	$2.00 each.
"	"	with four gold bands, wide colored top bands, and gold name	1.25 "
"	"	with gold name, scroll work, dash, three bands, heavy gold band on top edge, (see cut)	1.15 "
Medium size,		with three gold bands, maroon or other color on body of mug, white shield in front, gold name and colored flowers	1.50 "
"	"	with gold name and scroll work in front, three gold bands and heavy top colored band and cluster of flowers on each side	1.50 "
"	"	with gold name, scroll work, dash, three bands, heavy band on top edge	1.10 "
"	"	with gold bands, heavy color band, colored flowers and gold name	1.00 "
"	"	with gold name, three gold bands, two color bands and spray of roses around name	.85 "
"	"	with gold name, three bands, and gold ornamental dash below name, (see cut)	.75 "
"	"	with gold name and three bands	.63 "
"	"	with gold name only	.60 "
Smaller size,		same style as cuts, with gold name and three bands,	.60 "
"	" " " " " "	top band,	.55 "
"	" " " " " " " "	only	.50 "

"REQUISITE" SHAVING MUG.

White Stone China Ware with three gold bands, as above.............$6.00 per dozen, 60 cents each.
With bands as above, and sprays of colored flowers on both sides and gold name..........$1.25 "

NUMBERED "CHAMPION" SHAVING MUG.

(Patented December 18, 1877.)

This style is manufactured with numbers on expressly for barbers' use. They are made of Stone China Ware, and have three gold bands in addition to the numbers. Numbers run from 1 to 12, 1 to 25, 1 to 36, and 1 to 48. Price, $3.50 per dozen.

"REQUISITE" SHAVING MUGS.

We are patentees and proprietors of these now celebrated mugs. We supply them to barbers and also put them up for the market in various kinds of material and styles of decoration. They are soaped and boxed up in half dozens, and are largely sold by the druggist, fancy goods and cutlery trade. Prices as below:

White Stone China with assorted colored flowers and gold bands. Price, $6.00 per dozen, 60 cents each.

WHITE OPAL WARE

Price, $4.50 per dozen or 40 cents each.

We are also patentees and proprietors of the "Champion" Shaving Mug. As may be seen by the cut, the improvement consists in providing a 'thumb rest, or hollow, or "saddle," in which the brush may be laid and the bristles thereby be kept straight. It is one of these "little" "simple" improvements which is appreciated the moment it is seen, and which causes people to wonder why it has not been done before. We are placing these mugs in market in various kinds of ware and styles of decoration, and soaped or empty, to suit the different lines of trade who use them. Prices and styles as follows:

White (opal) ware, (see cut) soaped and boxed, per dozen, $2.25
" " " " empty, " 1.75

"CHAMPION" SHAVING MUG.

(Patented December 18, 1877.)

"TOILET" MUG.

White Stone China Ware, handsomely decorated, (without soap,) $4.00 per dozen, 40 cents each. As will be seen by the cut, this mug is adapted for use either as a shaving mug for gentlemen, or as a tooth brush or toilet mug for ladies.

"POPULAR" SHAVING MUG.

These Mugs are made of opal (white) ware, are of our own design, and are soaped, labelled and boxed in half dozens, ready for retail trade. Price, $2.00 per doz. "Popular" Shaving Mugs, empty, for barbers' use, $1.50 per dozen.

OILS AND PREPARATIONS FOR THE HAIR.

Per gallon.

Castor Oil, **not** perfumed, (per 5 gal. can) ⎱ at market
" " " (per gal.) .... ⎰ rates.
No. 6 Oil, extra perfumed, ...$2.50
No. 5 Castor Oil and Alcohol, well perfumed,........ 2.25
No. 4 Castor Oil and Salad Oil, " " 1.25
No. 2 Oil, extra perfumed,.......................... 1.25
No. 1 Oil, well perfumed, ... 1 00
Sea Foam,... 2.00

When cans or bottles are not sent with orders we supply new ones at low rates We do not loan bottles or cans.

☞ Oils and materials for preparations are *extremely* liable to market fluctuations. We shall lower the prices when possible, and only advance when compelled to.

Brilliantine, for Glossing the Moustache and Whiskers, in 2 oz. bottles, $3.25 per doz., or 33 cts. per bottle. 1¼ oz. bottles, $2 00 per doz., or 20 cts. per bottle.

	Per doz.	Per bottle.
Carboline,.............................	$8.00	.70
Egyptian Secret,.......................	6.25	.55
Hair Vigor, Ayer's..................	7.00	.63
Hair Renewer, Hall's Sicillian,..........	6.75	.60
Purity, Hursell's,......................	3 50	.33

OILS, ESSENTIAL, WARRANTED BEST QUALITY.

	Per oz.		Per oz.
Almond, (Mirbane,)..	$0.10	Cloves,..............	$0 25
Bay, best,..........	1 00	Geranium,Rose,French,	1.25
Bergamot, ...	.25	Lavender Fleurs,......	.15
Cassia,............. ...	.10	Lemon,..............	.25
Citronella,........	.15	Lemongrass,..........	.15

☞ Any of the above Oils supplied in any quantity at market rates.

Combination Oil, No. 1, excellent for perfuming cotton seed oil, 25 cents per oz.

Combination Oil, No. 5, for castor and alcohol, 25 cents per oz

Other Oils used by hair dressers supplied at lowest rates.

Nitrate of Silver. Best, $1.00 per oz.

Poles. Barber Poles, any size or style, made to order.

Powder or Sponge Bowls.

Made of

CRACKLED GLASS.

BRILLIANT AMBER

or

CANARY GREEN

COLOR.

Price,............50 cents.

RUBY ENGRAVED

BOWLS.

Price,..........50 cents.

Plain Colors:

BLUE, PURPLE, GREEN,

AND

Clear Glass.

Price, 25, 30 and 35 cts. each.

Powders. Toilet Powder.

"Extra Perfumed Toilet Powder."

It is the best we have ever seen. It gives universal satisfaction to our customers and to their patrons, and the report is made to us that the fragrance is a subject of remark whenever the powder is used.

"It is saturated with the finest odors, extracted direct *from the flowers*. and as it is put up in tin cans it retains its strength, and is, therefore, much preferred to the French Powder, put up in packages."
Price, 1 lb. Cans, 50 cts. each ; 1-2 lb. Cans, 30 cts. each.

	Per doz.	Per pkge.
Lubin's French, genuine,	$1.75	.15
Rogers and Galley's, French,	1 25	.10
American, Common,	.60	.06
Magnesia, Irish. in 2 oz. packages,	.80	.08

Puff Boxes. Various styles and prices.

Puffs. 15, 25, 35 and 50 cents each.

Pyrogallic Acid. Best imported, 85 cts. per oz.

RAZORS.

BEST QUALITY. **FULL CONCAVED.**

LARGE, MEDIUM, OR SMALL SIZES.

☞ ALL AT A UNIFORM PRICE OF $1.00 EACH. ☜

THESE PRICES TO BARBERS ONLY.

Our assortment comprises selected Razors of the following brands:

SMITH BROTHERS.	WADE & BUTCHER.	JOHNSON.	ROGERS.
" SPEED "	" BOW "	" HAMMER."	ELLIOT.
DIAMOND SPEAR.	WOSTENHOLM.	SELLERS & SONS.	"BENGALL."

" PIPE," etc.

We have now had the " Smith Brothers'" Razors some twelve years in the market, and have spared no pains to have them "right." We select the following from among many testimonials we have received in regard to them :

ALTON, ILL., Jan. 4, 1879.

SMITH BROTHERS :—DEAR SIRS,—Please send me two (2) of your "Smith Brothers'" Razors. Please send me two that are right *hollow, thin*, and have a *light ring* to them if you *touch their point or edge* (an E flat sound)—one not too hard or too soft. Enclosed you will find money. Send in haste. Read over my last letters ; I have patronized you gentlemen before ; please give satisfaction once again.
I remain, yours truly, A. J. KINGSLEY.

ALTON, ILL., Feb. 3, 1879.

SMITH BROTHERS :—GENTLEMEN,—I received your razors three weeks ago, and am very much pleased with them indeed. They are as *true* as steel can be, and as light as a feather ; and for the edge—why, they keep a uniform edge as long as they are used   I doubt if there are two better razors in the city of Alton than mine. With best respects for Smith Brothers, Cutlers, until some future day,—for I will want some more later,—I remain, your very pleased and delighted customer, A. J. KINGSLEY.

LOWELL. MASS., March 31, 1880.

SMITH BROTHERS :—GENTLEMEN,—It gives me great pleasure to inform you that the [12] Smith Brothers Boston Razors, which were presented to me by my customers, have been thoroughly *tested* by me, and *every one of them is excellent*. I also know of others of your razors that the owners deem invaluable
Very truly yours, E. H SOPER, Merrimac House.

ROCKLAND, MAINE, April 3, 1880.

SMITH BROTHERS :—GENTS,—Please send me three of your medium sized razors I have a number of them in my shop, which have been in use four or five years, and they are the best I have found in some twenty-five years' experience as a barber. Yours, truly, FRED. G SINGHI.

SALEM, OREGON, Jan. 2, 1882.

Please send me two more of your Smith Brothers' Razors. The one that you sent me is the best I have ever used in all my experience as a barber. J. V. RONCO.

ADAMS, MASS., May 2, 1881.

Please send me one of your razors. Send me a good one that will stand the test as well as the last one you sent me. A. H. C. POMEROY.

We are Special and Sole Agents for this vicinity for the

"SPEED" AND "DIAMOND SPEAR"

RAZORS.

We have sold the "SPEED" Razors for several years past, and invariably have the most favorable reports in regard to them.

We have had the "DIAMOND SPEAR" Razors now some three years in market ; they are steadily growing in public favor.

Prices and sizes as above.

BARBER SHEARS.

There was a time when we could sell the leading makes of Barber Shears without fear of their being any thing but "all right" But that was years ago. Of late days the manufacturers' aim seems to have been to see how many they could "rattle out" in a given time, paying no attention to quality of steel or temper. The result has been dissatisfaction to the barber and blame to cutlers who attempt to put them in order, and the cause of endless complaints that "that was a poor grind last time. the edge did not last a week," etc. To obviate this we have had goods made especially for us, with varying success but not entire satisfaction. We are now having made, and will shortly have in market, a lot which we have reason to believe will be about as they should be in quality and temper, and we take great pleasure in calling your attention to them. They will be hand forged and welded, and tempered with great care, and have steel rivets.

☞ Prices as follows : Smith Brothers' *nickel-plated handles*, sizes, large, medium, and small ; prices, $1.25, $1.50 and $1 75 per pair.

Smith Brothers' japanned handles, small sizes ; prices, $1.00 and $1.25 per pair.

Left-Handed, japanned, $1.75 per pair.

Heinisch's First Quality ; three sizes ; 75 cents, $1 00, and $1.25 per pair.

☞ We revise all new shears, and see that they are in working order before selling them.

STRAPS.

HANC.

Russia Leather, Extra Thick,.................................$1.25
Russia Leather, pressed and prepared,....................... . 1.00
Russia Leather, common finish,.................75, 50 and 40 cents each.
Horse Hide, (prepared,)......................................50 cents.
Canvas, (prepared,)..50 "

If to be sent by mail, 4 cents extra.

50 cents each.   HORSE HIDE   By mail 54 cts.

OUR CELEBRATED HORSE HIDE STRAPS

Have now been in market the past eight years. They are prepared ready for use, and give universal satisfaction. We sell them at wholesale all over the country, and their celebrity has caused many imitations to be put on the market. If you do not buy direct from us, or our authorized agents, see that our brand is stamped upon them, without which none are genuine.

"REQUISITE"
RAZOR STROPS.

Ruinous trade competition has, during the past year or two, led some of the old Standard Razor Strop makers to so far forget themselves as to put their own names on to poor trashy goods; as a result their labels are no longer a guarantee of quality.

To protect ourselves and our customers, who, when they order, expect us to send them a *first quality* reliable Strop, we are having such made, and herewith call attention to them below. They are of guaranteed excellence and, quality being considered, very low in price.

S.B RAZOR "REQUISITE" STROP
SMITH   BROS.

	Per doz.	Each.		Per doz.	Each.
17½ inch,...........	$13 50	$1.25	12 inch,............	$6.50	$0.60
13½ "	7.00	.70	10 " travellers' size,	6.00	.60

SPONGES.

Mediterranean Sponges,...............$1.50 per dozen, or 15 cents each.
Florida Reef Sponges,..................$2.00 per lb., or 3 to 5 cents each.
Sheep's Wool Bath Sponges,................15, 25, 30 cents and upwards.

SPONGE BOWLS.

Various colors,.......................................25 to 50 cents each.

SHAMPOO SPRINKLERS.

Various styles,............................... ....75 cents and upwards.

RUBBER HOSE.

Double Thick, for Shampooing,.......................25 cents per foot.

SOAPS.

SHAVING. We are sole agents for the New England States and the Dominion of Canada, for the celebrated

"KENTUCKY"
Shaving Soap.

For description and price see extended notice.
WILLIAMS' BARBERS' BAR SOAP is now put up in round and square bars, solid, or cut up in cakes, six to the pound. We supply it at lowest prices, viz:—$2.70 per box of 10 lbs., or 30 cents per single bar.
EUXESIS, LLOYD'S GENUINE, $4 50 per dozen, 45 cents each.
SHAVING STICKS, PEARS' GENUINE, $2.75 per dozen, 25 cents each.

Other shaving compounds at lowest rates.

Medicinal and Toilet Soaps.

	Per doz.	Per cake.		Per doz.	Per cake
Cuticura,..............	$2.00	.17	Constantine's,........	$1.50	.15
Carbolic, Buchan's,....	2.00	.20	Tar, Packer's,........	1.60	.15

Sulphur, Glenn's,, $2.00 per doz. .20 per cake.

TOILET SOAPS.

Castile Soaps, American and Imported. Pumice Soap, Cashmere Boquet, Transparent Soaps, etc., etc., at low prices.
Mayflower Soap, 6 oz. cakes, excellent for the wash-stand, 75 cents per dozen, or 8 cents per cake.

WE ARE SOLE AGENTS FOR THE
New England States & Dominion of Canada
FOR THE

It is put up in full weight 1 lb. square bars.

1 lb. round bars, (6 cakes to the bar.)

Price, $2.20 for 10 lb. box, or 25 cents per lb.

This soap is made in Covington, Kentucky. Some five years ago we thoroughly satisfied ourselves in regard to its quality, and accepted the Sole Agency for the New England States and Canada, and proceeded at once to introduce it to the attention of our customers. Our success has been most gratifying, and the soap has attained a high reputation and its sales are steadily increasing. We could obtain almost unlimited extended testimony in its favor, but we do not deem it necessary, as the following lines, selected from many testimonies which have been sent to us, give it in a "nutshell":

"THE PERFUME IS EXCELLENT."

"THE LATHER IS SUFFICIENTLY LASTING BUT IS NOT GLUTINOUS."

"It makes a Fine, Smooth and Penetrating Lather, and does not Irritate the Face."

"NEITHER DOES IT SLIME IN THE MUG."

TO HAIR DRESSERS

GENTLEMEN :—

It is entirely in our power to always make this soap of a uniform quality. Its superiority you will find BY A TRIAL. We have an abundance of testimonials from all parts of the country which speak in its favor; but judge for yourself — TRY IT.

HECKMAN & CO.

"PROVE ALL THINGS; HOLD FAST THAT WHICH IS GOOD!"

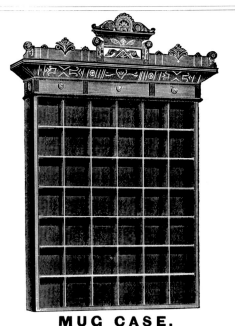

MUG CASE.

With 42 Holes..$11.00

THIS WORK-STAND

Is 3 feet 6 inches in height, and is made of black walnut, handsomely ornamented with moulding and *richly gilded* engraving. The drawer with the two drop handles is intended for the barbers' tools. The second apartment, provided with a self-closing spring door, with one drop handle, is for *clean towels* and shaving papers, and the two lower apartments are intended for the *used* towels and papers.

Price,................................$10.00

WORK-STAND OR BUREAU.

As will be seen by the cut, this Work-Stand has three small drawers at the top, and two spring doors below.

Price,........................ ....$12.00

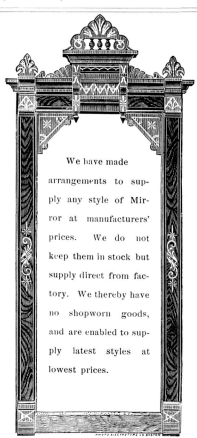

We have made arrangements to supply any style of Mirror at manufacturers' prices. We do not keep them in stock but supply direct from factory. We thereby have no shopworn goods, and are enabled to supply latest styles at lowest prices.

TWO-DRAWER
Looking-Class Bracket.

Made of black walnut, engraved and gilded, with ebonized beads and panels.

Price,.... ....$4 50

ONE-DRAWER
Looking-Class Bracket.

Made of black walnut, carved and gilded.

Price,........................$3.75

ONE-DRAWER
Looking-Class Bracket.

Made of black walnut, engraved but not gilded.

Price,...., ...$3.50

MUG CASE.

With 25 Holes............... ....$6.00

ONE-BOWL
WASH-STAND.

TWO-BOWL
WASH-STAND.

These Wash-Stands are made of black walnut, and have dished Italian marble slabs.

One-Bowl Wash-Stand, size of slab 1 foot 8 inches by 2 feet 6 inches.   Price...............:....$25.00

Two-Bowl Wash-Stand (see cut), size of slab 1 foot 8 inches by 4 feet.   Price...................... 45.00

46

Clough's Barber Chairs.

They have a cane seat and back, making them very neat and cool.

3.

No. 3 is an Automatic Chair. In use you have only to see that your customer sits well back in the chair, with his feet on the foot-rest, pushing out just far enough to be comfortable for hair-cutting and clear out for shaving. After shaving the customer raises up and leans forward, the chair then goes back to first position again. It can also be easily operated by the workman by moving the foot rest up or down with the hand or foot.

No. 3 Chair, price $32.00

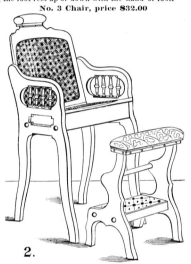

2.

No. 2 Chair is very simple, being at all times in position for hair-cutting. When the shaving position is required just see that the customer sits well back in the chair, then raise the head-rest to the collar, then lift the little catch on the lower part of the back and the chair then goes into position for shaving and goes back when the customer sits up again. The foot-rest is also new, with three different rests for the feet, making all together a very neat chair.

No. 2 Chair, price $27.50

CUT SHOWING
"UNION" METALLIC CHAIR
With the **Reversible Seat** partially reversed.

BARBERS' CHAIRS.

We are Sole Agents for the New England States and Canada for the following Barbers' Chairs:

☞ We sell Barbers' Chairs at Manufacturers' Prices. ☜

BOTTOM PRICES TO BARBERS.

☞ No Discount can be allowed to Furniture Dealers or other Traders. ☜

Terms, STRICTLY CASH, or C. O. D., with addition of Express Charges for collecting and returning the amount to us.

☞ *When ordering* you should send full amount, if possible — we can then send by freight at low rates — you thereby avoid possible excessive express rates and annoyance of collection charges. *When you do not send full amount you should always send a reasonable amount with your order, as a guarantee of good faith.* When sending chairs out of the city we pack "Centennial," "Champion," and "Popular" Chairs in mattings, and charge one dollar extra for the matting, *which we refund* when the mattings are returned *express free* to us. The other chairs come boxed or crated. No charges for boxes or crates. We deliver chairs free to any depot in this city.

☞ *The easiest way to send money* is by Post Office Money Orders, which may be obtained at nearly every county seat, in all the cities, and in many of the large towns. We consider them perfectly safe, and the best means of remitting fifty dollars or less, as thousands have been sent to us *without any loss.* Registered Letters are a very safe means of sending small sums of money where Post Office Money Orders cannot be easily obtained.

"Union" Metallic Adjustable Back and Revolving Seat Barber Chair.

They are very simple in operation; by placing the foot on the treadle (seen under the rear of the chair) the back and arms swing into position shown by dotted lines, or into such intermediate positions as may be desired.

They also, in addition to the adjustable back *have a revolving seat*, one side of which is finished in plush, and the other with perforated wood. The seat is held in position by a spring catch.

Price in Crimson, Green Plush, or Moquette, $50.00

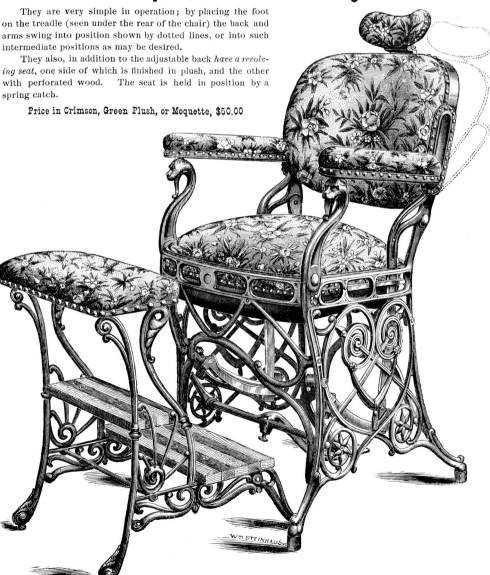

47

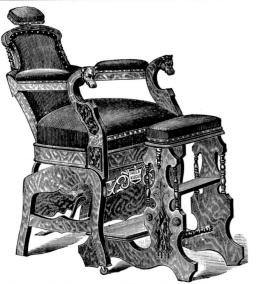

T. A. KOCHS' ARBER CHAIR, NO. 6.

(Patented Feb. 17, 1880.)

Is made of solid black walnut and French walnut veneered panels, very handsomely ornamented and oil finished. The back of the chair is covered with plush. The chair is adjustable to any desired position for shaving or hair cutting, by means of the treadle seen at back part The platform and crossbar of the footstool are covered with sheet brass.

Price, covered with best mohair plush, green, crimson, or maroon, $50.00

CHILDREN'S

HAIR CUTTING CHAIR.

Made of black walnut, with Cane Seat and Back.

Price, - - - $5.50.

T. A. Kochs' Summer Chair.

(Patent.)

This chair is especially adapted for *use in summer*. It makes a very comfortable chair; the cane seat and back can be easily taken out and upholstered, if required; the head and arm rests, also foot-stool and back of chair, are covered with leather. The chair is adjustable to all positions for shaving by means of same machinery as is used on Garden City Chair.

Price, - - - $22.00

T. A. Kochs' Patent Barber Chair, No. 1.

(Patented Feb. 17, 1880.)

Made of solid black walnut, handsomely carved, with French walnut veneered panels. Finely polished and oil finished.

This chair has a very wide seat, and yet so arranged that the operator will experience no difficulty or inconvenience in reaching the face of the occupant from the side. It is adjustable to any desired position for shaving or hair cutting by means of the treadle seen at back part.

The platform and crossbar of the foot-stool are covered with sheet brass.

Price, covered in best mohair plush, green, crimson, or maroon, or moquette, $45.00.

T. A. KOCHS' "GARDEN CITY" CHAIR.

This Chair is new in this market, and is made in the best manner and of best materials. It is as substantial and durable as any Barber Chair in the market. The appearance of the chair is good; the platform of the foot-stool is covered with sheet brass. The chair is adjustable to all positions for hair cutting and shaving.

PRICE.

Covered with mohair plush, maroon, crimson, or green,..............$33 00
Covered with Tapestry Brussels carpet,............................. 28.00

"CHAMPION"
Barber Chair.

As will be seen by the cut, they are similar in appearance to the "Centennial" chair. They differ in various points, and particularly in the adjusting device.

The "Champion" chairs are strongly and neatly built of black walnut and thoroughly upholstered, and we sell them at prices as follows:

Best velvet carpet...... ....$33.00
French plush, maroon, green. or crim-
    son colors,................... 35 00
French plush, any color, carved and gilt
    and nickel-plated movement, ... 40 00
Transportation mattings,........$1.00 extra.

"CENTENNIAL" BARBER CHAIR

We have advertised these chairs since 1876. We have sold *hundreds* of them since, and the universally favorable report from the users is sufficient guarantee of quality. The frames are made of black walnut, and are put together in the most thorough manner. The upholstering is "first-class." The back can be raised or lowered *instantly*, to suit the convenience of the operator, by turning the wheel seen at the back part of the seat. The head-rest oscillates, and can be *instantly* adjusted to the head for shaving, or swung forward so as to " sit a customer *up properly* for a hair-cut." Leading styles and *reduced* prices, as follows:

Best velvet carpet (Roxbury)............................$33.00
Common plush................................... ... 33 00
French plush, green. maroon, or crimson...................... 35.00
Transportation mattings, $1.00 extra. See terms.

We have, also, chairs of above make with less work on the frames and scroll-wheel adjusting device. Price in velvet carpet, $30 00. Tapestry carpet, with ratchet device, $25.00.

"POPULAR"
Barber Chair.

They are of the same general appearance as the "Champion." The frames are lighter; the wood work is not molded, but is otherwise well-finished. They are well upholstered, and the *prices are low*.

Tapestry carpet, with " Ratchet " move-
    ment $25.00
Tapestry carpet, with " Champion "
    movement....................... 27.00
Transportation mattings.........$1.00 extra.

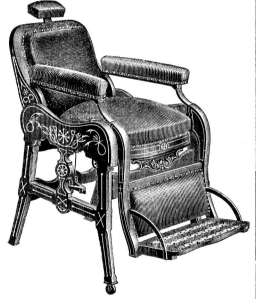

Reclining Barber Chair No. 5.

Price—Covered with green, crimson or maroon
    mohair plush, - - - - - **$47.00**
Cane Seat, - - - - - - 3.00
No charge for boxing.

" No illustration can do this chair justice, it needs to be seen to be appreciated. The frames are made of black walnut, oil finished, and have gilt engraved lines. The adjusting apparatus is almost automatic; the barber has only to press upon a treadle lightly with a foot from either side and the chair will adjust itself; when the desired position is reached the barber releases the treadle, and the chair remains firm; no further action on the part of the barber is needed; as the customer rises after being shaved his weight upon the seat raises the back and lowers the foot-board."

WE ARE
SOLE AGENTS
FOR THE
New England States and Canada
FOR
HENRY ARND & BRO.
THE CELEBRATED
BARBER CHAIR MANUFACTURERS,
ST. LOUIS, MO.

From their extensive line we have selected their

RECLINING
Barber Chairs

As being especially new and desirable and a novelty in this market, and have no hesitation in recommending them as a superior article.

In reference to the No. 5 Chair the Messrs. Arnd advertise to their customers as below. *We should be glad to offer the same terms but cannot*, because our profit is so small that we cannot afford to run any risk whatever in the matter.

" We are so confident of this chair meeting the approval of purchasers, that we propose to ship to any part of the United States upon condition that purchasers not liking the chair after seeing it may return same at *our expense;* provided, of course, that it has not been used, and is properly re-boxed and forwarded to us, we paying *return* freight only."

Reclining Barber Chair No. 9.

HAS CASTERS IN FRONT.

Price—Covered with mohair plush, ... $40.00
" " Brussels carpet, ... 36.00

On this chair the principle of construction and operation, as well as the finish, is the same as the No. 5 Chair. As will be seen by comparing the illustrations, the No. 9 chair is somewhat differently designed, and has no engraved lines, and but a small piece of carving on each side of frame. This chair is also upholstered with the best materials. The foot rest is lined with sheet brass.

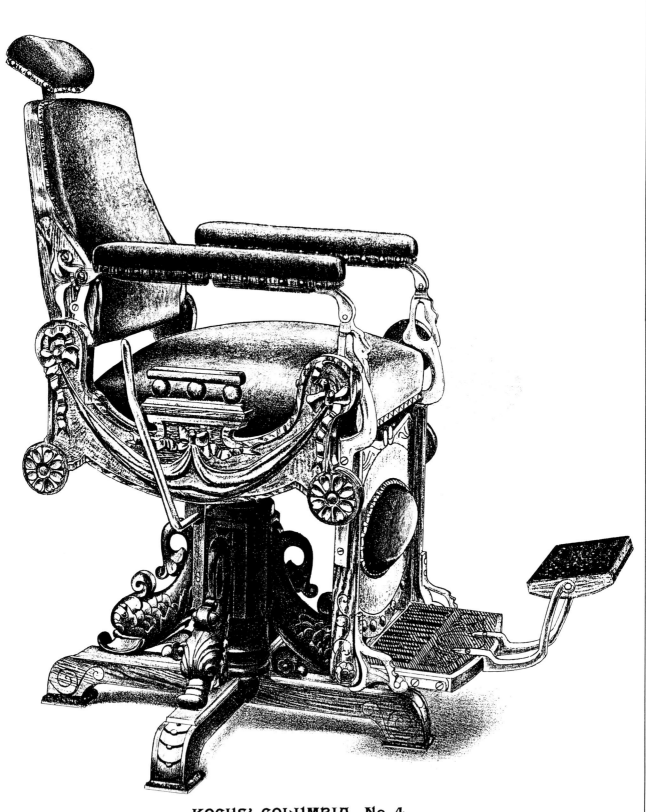

KOCHS' COLUMBIA, No. 4,

REVOLVING   AND   RECLINING   BARBERS'   CHAIR.

Patented Dec. 8, 1891.

Made of Oak (antique finish) only. Price, covered with best Mohair
Plush, Crimson, Green or Old Gold,   -   -   - $65.00.

ANTIQUE BARBER CHAIRS

Barber chairs have been around, in one form or another, since the beginning of the haircutting trade. Those pictured in engravings of the Civil War period were adult-sized high chairs with upholstered backs and separate, unattached foot rests.

These elevated chairs were of a fixed height. They did not have an up and down mechanism, nor did they recline. The customer simply tilted his head back for a shave. Short barbers could adjust their access to a client's head by standing on a wide low box. Mounting a footstool would have been too dangerous for a man or a boy wielding a straight razor.

Among the most successful American barber chair manufacturers was a young German immigrant named Ernest E. Koken. Mr. Koken patented his first reclining chair design in 1881 at the age of twenty-six. The basement under Mr. and Mrs. Koken's home served as their factory. There, by lantern light, the young entrepreneur laboriously turned dozens of black walnut spindles on a foot-operated lathe and cut out pairs of the ornate side supports on a pedal-powered jigsaw. Upstairs, a dining room table served as the pattern drawing department.

Koken called on barbershops during the day, selling his new chairs and hair-care supplies while expanding the shaving mug decorating business which he had established seven years earlier. At the turn of the century, Mr. Koken designed and patented an hydraulically operated chair which was widely coveted by his competitors. The Koken Barber Supply Company sold more than 10,000 of these chairs in 1913.

Other barber chair manufacturers of the period were: Henry Arnd & Brother, also of St. Louis, Eugene Berninghaus, of Cincinnati (who claimed credit for inventing the first revolving and reclining barber chair), H. A. Candrian (makers of the "Union" brand), Louis Hanson, Emil J. Paidar, and finally Theo. A. Kochs, whose firm had sold more than 30,000 barber chairs prior to 1885.

Most Victorian barber chairs were constructed of oak, maple or black walnut. Porcelain enameled iron became a favored construction material after World War I. Between these two styles was a transitional period in which wood and iron were combined in a marriage of uncommon beauty.

Today there are only a half dozen people in the country who specialize in the restoration and sale of antique barber chairs. Very ornate wooden chairs from the 1880–1910 period are in demand by interior decorators and upscale styling salons. Prices for professionally restored examples range from $2,000 to $4,000 each.

Children's chairs featuring wooden or metal figureheads of horses, bears, and elephants sell for $1,500 to $2,500. Pedal cars, mounted as chairs, bring similar prices in pristine condition. Both varieties appear in catalogs of the 1920's and 1930's.

Cast iron, porcelain enameled, adult-size chairs, with nickel-plated filigree trim, can be purchased in a wide range of styles and conditions at prices ranging from $250 (with missing parts) to $1,800 for a replated and reupholstered beauty ready for den or office display.

The secret to getting a good buy on a vintage cast iron chair is to be in the right place at the right time with two husky men and a pickup truck. We once hauled away a "free" 1920s chair from an antique shop run by a pair of ladies who had grown tired of hiring men to move it every time they changed their floor display.

For similar reasons antique auctions are good places to pick up barber chairs, or even an entire shop interior, complete with back bar. Non-specialist dealers won't touch them with a ten-foot pole.

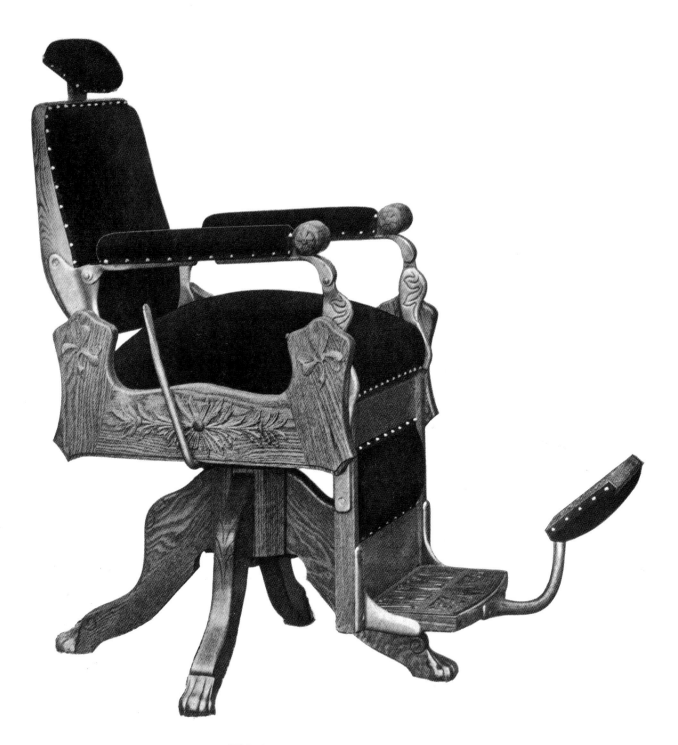

KOCHS' COLUMBIA CHAIR, No. 58.

REVOLVING AND RECLINING.

PATENTED DEC. 8, 1891, AND JAN. 11, 1898.

Made of Oak, antique finish. Upholstered with Mohair Plush, crimson, green or old gold, or with Maroon Leather; nickel-plated trimmings. The metal feet used upon this chair are made of solid brass.

PRICE, ... $33.00.

KOCHS' GOLD MEDAL
HYDRAULIC BARBERS' CHAIR, No. 325.

RAISING AND LOWERING.   REVOLVING AND RECLINING.

PATENTED DEC. 8, 1891; JAN. 11, 1898; FEB. 8, 1898.

Made of Quarter-sawed Oak, golden finish. Upholstered with best quality Mohair Plush,
crimson or green, or with Maroon Leather; nickel-plated trimmings.

PRICE, ... $50.00

The base of this chair is made of iron, nicely japanned to harmonize, and is fitted
with polished solid brass rim. This chair stands firmly alone. Can also be furnished
in antique finish on short notice, if desired.

Strauss Building Barber Shop, CHICAGO

The Barber Shop in the new Whitcomb Hotel, SAN FRANCISCO, CALIF.

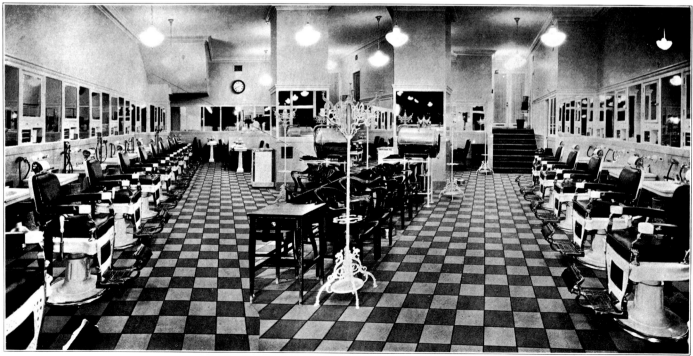

The Barber Shop of the Palace Hotel, SAN FRANCISCO, CALIFORNIA

PAIDAR Barber Chairs

can be equipped with

{ **Ring for Razor Strop**

{ **Rack for Hair Cloth**

or Towel

{ **Socket for Various Attachments**

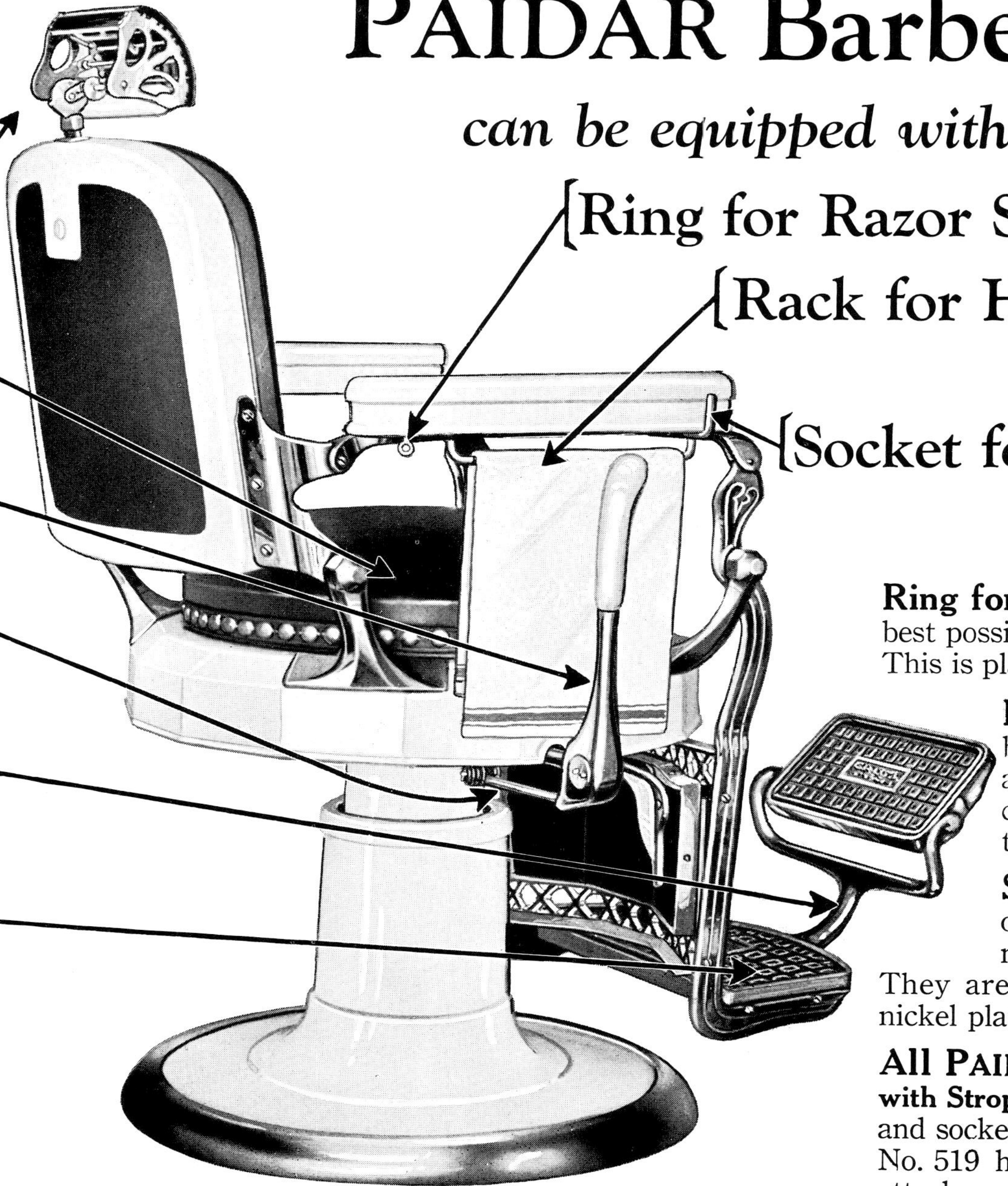

Ring for Razor Strop is placed in best possible position for barber's use. This is placed on every chair.

Rack for Hair Cloth is a brass bar, highly nickel plated, attached under the arm of the chair, provides a place to hang the hair cloth when not in use.

Sockets for manicure bowls or trays or other attachments now used on barbers' chairs. They are made of brass and highly nickel plated.

All PAIDAR Chairs are fitted with Strop Ring. No. 314 chair has ring and sockets, while No. 517, No. 518 and No. 519 have all the above mentioned attachments. A slight extra charge is made for these attachments when placed on chairs not mentioned above.

A Few Reasons Why PAIDAR Chairs Are Superior

PAIDAR Spring Cushion Headrest, both sides perfectly smooth, nothing to catch the barber's coat.

Upholstery is of the highest quality. All materials used are the best, and in the seat we use a special spring construction which makes our chair superior.

Hand Lever controls all operations. Mechanism most simple. No parts to wear out.

Shock Absorber-Spring Bumper. This bumper is on all PAIDAR Chairs and prevents noise and jar when the chair has been raised from a reclining position.

Single Arm Footrest, stronger than double arm footrest on account of its construction, and permits customer more space to get in and out of the chair.

Platform or Step, extra large, allowing customer more space. The manner in which the horn for footrest is attached leaves platform clear for the feet.

Extra Weight. PAIDAR Chairs weigh approximately 35 lbs. more than any other chair, this weight being distributed over the entire chair, making it the strongest.

Nickel Plating. Best known method; six operations; one coat of copper, two coats of nickel. Most lasting finish.

55

Kochs' Hydraulic Barbers' Chair, *No. 139*

Porcelain-Enameled Iron

Raising   Lowering   Revolving   Reclining

Patented May 10, 1910; Aug. 23, 1910 (two patents); May 21, 1912; Dec. 24, 1918

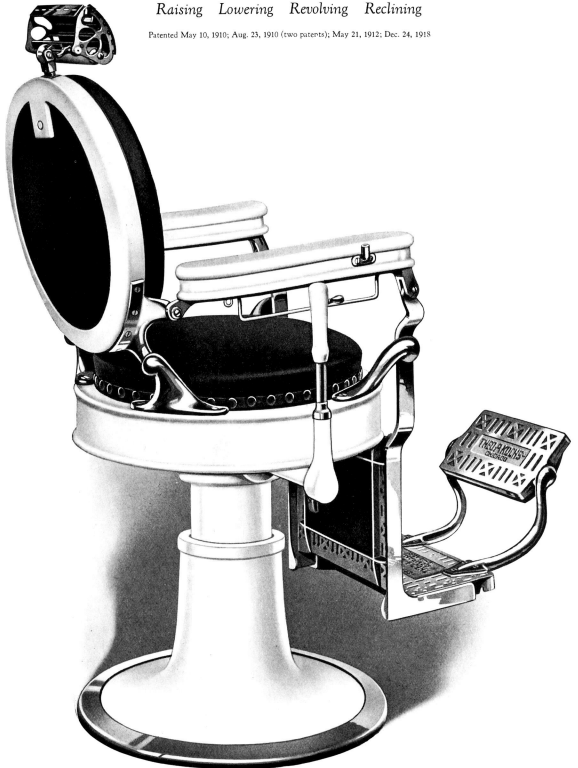

AN ATTRACTIVE model of the all-round style. Made entirely of iron, porcelain-enameled, including one-piece base, seat-frame, round back-frame and arms. Equipped with Kochs' patent telescoping porcelain-enameled housing, which covers the entire hydraulic mechanism. All other exposed metal parts are heavily nickel-plated, including floor-rim on base, step, footrest, seat and arm brackets, as well as the side bars to which the ornamental, nickel-plated apron is attached. Extension footrest to suit tall or short customers. Porcelain-enameled lever handle. Arms equipped with strop ring, haircloth bar and Ideal manicure sockets. Kochs' Patent Spring-cushion Headrest, mounted on a narrow, nickel-plated steel slat which runs in a steel casing. Best upholstery; double-stitched edges throughout. Covered with genuine leather, black or Spanish brown.

Kochs' Hydraulic Barbers' Chair, *No. 800*

Porcelain-Enameled Iron

Raising   Lowering   Revolving   Reclining

Patented May 10, 1910; Aug. 23, 1910 (two patents); May 21, 1912
Aug. 12, 1913; Dec. 24, 1918. Design Patented

MANY of the leading hotels throughout the United States and up-to-date metropolitan barber shops in the large cities of the country are equipped with this model. This chair embodies every late improvement known in barbers' chair construction. It is massive and roomy and yet of highly artistic and graceful design. Made entirely of iron, porcelain-enameled. One-piece fluted base, equipped with Kochs' patented telescoping housing, which completely envelopes the hydraulic mechanism and protects it from dust and hair clippings. Fluted seat-rail, to match base. Back-frame and arms are porcelain-enameled. Ideal manicure sockets, strop ring and haircloth bar attached to arms. Porcelain-enameled lever handle. The floor-rim, step and footrest are cast in solid German silver; all other metal trimmings heavily nickel-plated. Kochs' Patent adjustable Spring-cushion Headrest with paper roll and cutter. Upholstered in the best possible manner; seat and back cushions made with double-stitched edges and covered with finest quality leather of any color.

Kochs' Hydraulic Child's Chair, No. 44

With Hobby Horse Head

Patented May 10, 1910; Aug. 23, 1910; May 21, 1912; Dec. 24, 1918

Raising   *Lowering*   *Revolving*

MADE of iron, porcelain-enameled in snowy white, and fitted with a finely carved horse head. Equipped with hydraulic mechanism for raising, lowering and revolving. The hydraulic pump is encased in a cast-metal, porcelain-enameled telescoping housing, eliminating the exposure of the oily hydraulic stem and all danger from the children coming in contact with it. The chair top can be raised or lowered 9 inches, thus affording a wide range of elevation.

The pedestal is cast in one piece, finely porcelain-enameled and fitted with nickel-plated floor-rim. Seat-frame, arms, back-frame and handle also porcelain-enameled. Apron, foot-step and brackets connecting arms and back with seat are highly nickel-plated. The foot-step is adjustable to various heights by a mere pressure upon a lever conveniently located under the front edge of the step. Seat and back cushions are covered with best quality black or gray leather.

The horse head may be removed when desired and as readily attached ·to the seat-frame of the chair. An ingenious clamping device holds it in rigid position. The head is handsomely painted and is fitted with glass eyes and stout leather reins.

A chair of this kind will prove most valuable where children's work is made a specialty.

Kochs' Hydraulic Child's Chair, No. 43

With Automobile Top

Patented May 10, 1910; Aug. 23, 1910; May 21, 1912; Dec. 24, 1918

Raising   *Lowering*   *Revolving*

THIS combination of a high hydraulic base with an automobile top will prove a source of delight for the youngsters and a decidedly good fixture for the up-to-date shop. Little girls especially require no coaxing to be placed in the roomy and comfortable seat of the auto, which is of extra large proportions and equipped with all the modern accessories of a real automobile. Rubber-tired disc wheels, a windshield with mirror, horn on steering-wheel column, headlights and spot-light, self-starter which can be wound up, bumper in front, brake and trunk with hinged lid, upholstered leather seat, all combine to make the outfit decidedly realistic. The auto is handsomely painted in bright colors and should not be compared with the cheaper outfits generally used for the purpose.

The hydraulic base is the same as is used on our Nos. 44 and 45 chairs illustrated on this and the following page. It is porcelain-enameled in snowy white and is fitted with nickel-plated floor rim.

"First Haircut." Cleveland, Ohio, 1930.
—*Cleveland State University Library*

Kochs' Folding Barbers' Chair, No. 52

A Portable Chair for Hotel Room Service
The Standard Army Chair—Different and Better Than Any Other

THIS Folding Chair is the most practical and serviceable of any similar chair made.

It is made of choicest quarter-sawed oak, extra heavy stock, and specially finished in oil. The finish is absolutely water-proof and no varnish whatever is used.

It is the only chair of the kind which is equipped with a steel folding brace. This insures absolute rigidity and prevents the base from spreading, no matter how heavy the weight of the occupant may be.

It is the only Folding Chair which is equipped with full length solid wood arms, adding greatly to the comfort of the occupant.

It is the only Folding Chair upon which the back can be reclined by a simple lever device located at the right hand of the back and within easy reach of the barber. By means of this device, the occupant may be reclined in the chair instantly without the necessity of unbuckling straps.

Kochs' Folding Barbers' Chair is of somewhat larger dimensions than all other similar chairs. It is very roomy and exceptionally comfortable. The height of the seat from the ground is just right for both hair cutting and shaving. The distance of the footrest from the chair is just right to fit the average size man.

As a covering for the seat, back and footrest, extra heavy Army Khaki Duck is used, instead of the usual velour or white canvas, which easily soil.

All joints and hinges are made with extra heavy bolts and rivets so as to insure absolute durability.

The chair is fitted with leather covered head-rest, which is adjustable to any height.

This chair can be compactly folded up as shown in the picture. It has been especially designed as a portable chair for hotel room service and as an Army Barbers' Chair for service in the field or barracks.

Shoe-Shining Stand, No. 540

Shining stand. Made of steel, copper oxidized. Oak seat, polished. Foot rests adjustable to any angle. Handy shelf under seat for brushes and polish.

Child's Hair-Cutting Chair, No. 77

Made of heavy steel wire and tubing, oxidized copper finish. Polished oak seat, mounted on screw stem for raising and lowering. Adjustable foot-bar.

Child's Seat, No. 100

Made of steel, nickel-plated. Seat covered with imitation leather.

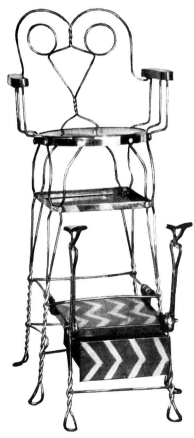

Shoe-Shining Stand

Double bootblack stand. Is made of solid selected oak, finished in golden, highly polished. Top is covered with extra heavy sheet brass. Foot rests are extra heavy. Large compartment for brushes, etc. Size, 3 feet 5 inches by 4 feet.

Shining Stand, No. 502

Single bootblack stand. Made of steel, copper oxidized finish. Polished oak seat and arms. Is made exceptionally strong.

STEAM STERILIZERS

Red Cross Sterilizer, No. 65

Made of heavy copper, highly nickel-plated on outside and tinned on inside. The horizontal sterilizing chamber is fitted with large drop-door and affords easy access to the towels. The vertical water tank has an indicating gauge and draw-off faucet. The sterilizer is mounted on a grooved iron stand, enameled in white and fitted with gas burner and connection attached ready for use. Ornamental top, with stained glass sign and red cross. Suitable for four to eight chair shops. An attractive and serviceable equipment for modern barber shops.

Cabinet Sterilizers

Made of heavy copper, nickel-plated. Two towel compartments, with removable porcelain perforated trays holding 20 to 25 Turkish towels each. Beveled plate-glass door. Equipped with water gauge, thermometer, brass faucet and dome with swinging sign of ruby glass. Nickel-plated brass legs.

No. 30—With gas burner and 18-inch legs.
No. 31—With gasoline burner and 18-inch legs.

Vulcan Sterilizers

These sterilizers meet all the requirements of the up-to-date barber shop. They are very attractive in appearance and are so constructed as to offer every convenience.

Made of 32-ounce planished copper, highly nickel-plated and tinned on the inside. The sterilizing chamber has a large drop-door; it can be turned in any direction so as to be accessible from all sides. Mounted on a nickel-plated copper stand, which conceals gas burner and pipe connections. Fitted with water gauge, draw-off faucet and gas connection with burner, complete.

No. 50—For four to six chair shops.
No. 51—For six to ten chair shops.

Buffalo Sanitary Sterilizers

Made of heavy copper, nickel-plated, with two hinged covers and mounted on white-enameled steel stand. Towel compartment holds 12 to 14 Turkish towels. Porcelain tray, water gauge, brass faucet and pet cock. Water capacity about four gallons.

No. 10—With gas burner and 30-inch stand.
No. 11—With gasoline tank and burner and 30-inch stand.
No. 21—Same as No. 11, with 3-inch brass legs.

No. 65

Nos. 30-31

Nos. 50-51

Nos. 10-11-21

—Deborah Cooney

One of the super-sanitary "Terminal Method" Barber Shops, started in New York City's Terminal Station in 1916.

Formalin Lamp, *No. 1820*

For use with Formalin Pastils, illustrated above. Produces 100 per cent pure active formaldehyde gas for sterilization purposes, without loss or waste. Absolutely safe. Vapor does not corrode instruments. Price includes one box of Formalin Pastils, illustrated above.

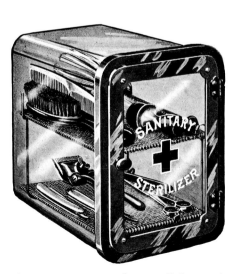

Sanitary Sterilizer, *No. 14*

Height, 9¾ inches. Width, 7¼ inches
Depth, 10½ inches

THE BARBERS' POLE

An 1890s Barber Pole still stands in front of this South Dakota shop. November, 1937. —*Library of Congress*

The Modern Barber Pole originated in the days when bloodletting was one of the principal duties of the barbering trade. The two spiral ribbons painted around the pole represent two long linen bandages, one twisted around the arm before bleeding (to make the veins stand out), and the other used to bind it afterwards.

The patient clutched the staff firmly during the entire operation. Originally, when not in use, the pole with bandage pre-wound (so that it might be ready when needed) was hung at the door as a sign. Later an imitation was painted and given a permanent place on the sidewalk outside." So states the *Barber's Manual*.

This verse from a book of fables printed in 1727, describes a typical 18th century barber's store front:

> *His pole with pewter basin hung*
> *Black rotten teeth in order strung.*
> *Rang cups that in the window stood*
> *Lined with red rags to look like blood*
> *Did well his threefold trade explain*
> *Who shaved, drew teeth and breathed a vein.*

Trade signs were widely utilized in the civilized world before the time of Christ. The earliest were simply large wooden cutouts of various figures; a goat for milk vendors, a bunch of grape leaves for a wine bar, a twisted loaf of bread for a bakery, etc. There were so many signs hanging over innkeepers' doorways in ancient Britain that streets became named after them.

In Europe, early barber-surgeons carried a staff or spear as a symbol of their authority, and the first European barber poles were iron spears with shiny brass basins hanging from them. German doctors often wrapped their bloodstained poles with white fur for an added attention-getting effect. British surgeons of the period were allowed to display a red flag and a druggist's glazed galley pot on their poles to differentiate them from the common barber's emblem.

Some historians credit the blue stripe on American poles as having been transported from the blue-and-white bands on English poles of the 1700's. Other authorities say that American barbers added a blue stripe to their red-and-white poles as a patriotic gesture. However, we do know that by the early 1800's English barber poles were routinely painted in three colors, and that pewter basins no longer hung from them as in former times.

The majority of early American barber poles were freestanding sidewalk pillars ranging from six to twelve feet in height. During the late 1890's municipal authorities began to outlaw barber poles and cigar store Indians as public safety hazards. The wooden Indians were taken inside for a while, but eventually more than 100,000 of these obsolete figures were thrown in rivers, buried in garbage dumps or fed to fireplaces. Only about 3,000 authentic cigar store Indians exist today in museums and private collections.

Early American barber poles were almost carbon copies of the tall, slender British type with gold acorn finials. Gradually these skinny cousins evolved into the fat, healthy barber emblems we know today.

Most wooden barber poles simply did not survive the outdoor elements of wind, rain and hungry termites. Although not as rare as tobacco figures, early poles with original paint intact are quite scarce. Recent auction prices have ranged from $1,000 to $12,000 each. Among the most valuable today are the flat-sided stained glass poles that often hung in hotel lobbies. Koch's offered a 12-inch-diameter leaded glass globe in their 1926 catalog. Few of these have survived.

The first revolving-cylinder poles were driven by key-wound clock movements and ran all day on a single winding. Lighted poles became popular in the early 1900's. Electric motors came later.

Modern barber poles, with revolving interior cylinders, cost from $300 to $750 each and are still available from the last remaining factory outlet, the William Marvy company of 1538 St,. Clair Avenue, St. Paul, Minnesota. The Marvy factory has produced more than 75,000 poles over the last half century. Today much of their activity centers around replacement parts and restoration work; but they still offer a selection of nine barber poles ranging from eighteen to forty-seven inches tall.

Cleveland, Ohio, 1888. Three generations of the Saxen family operated this Barber Shop at 612 and 712 Hancock Street. —Author's Collection

BARBERS' POLES—Continued.

TURNED POLES.
Nos. 3 and 4.

BATH SIGN.
Gilt Letters on black ground on
both sides.
Price..............$2 25

BOX POLE.
Nos. I and 2.

WALTER'S POLE,
WITH LANTERN.
Nos. 7 and 8.

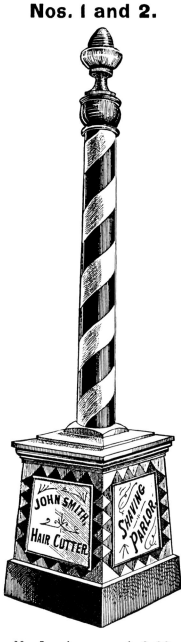

JOHN SMITH
HAIR CUTTER.

SHAVING
PARLOR.

No. 3A—8 in. diam., price, $ 9 00

No. 3 —10 in. " — " 13 00

No. 4 —12 in. " " 15 00

No. 1, price ......$ 9 00
No. 2, " 12 00

No. 7, 12-inch, price...$30 00
No. 8, 10 " " ... 25 00

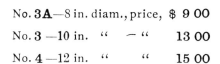

(From a circa 1900 Catalog)

BARBERS' POLES.

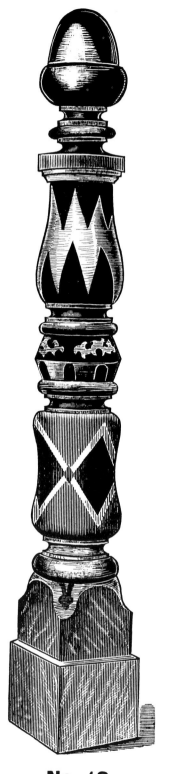

No. 12.   **No. 13.**   **No. 14.**

10 in. Pole...........$15 50	6 in. Pole...........$ 6 50	10 in. Pole...........$18 00
12 in. Pole........... 18 00	8 in. Pole............ 8 00	12 in. Pole........... 20 00
	10 in. Pole.......... 10 50	

These Poles have **3**-inch hole bored through the center.

Marion, Ohio, 1901. Roseberry Shaving Parlor employees pose for a photograph with their mascot. (From left) E.P. Bondley, Arthur Urschlitz, and Neal Anderson. —Hal Tilton

We have noticed more than one pit bull in vintage barber shop photographs. "Cocoaine" was a hair-care product. Lillian Russell poster dates this in 1890s. Portable barber pole was taken indoors at night. Michael Griffin

West Unity, Ohio, 1908. "Dear Myra, we each caught a fish today.   I am sore all over from rowing the boat.   It is hot here, but cooler in the pool room, next door to the barber shop."
—Author's Collection

BARBERS' POLES—Continued.

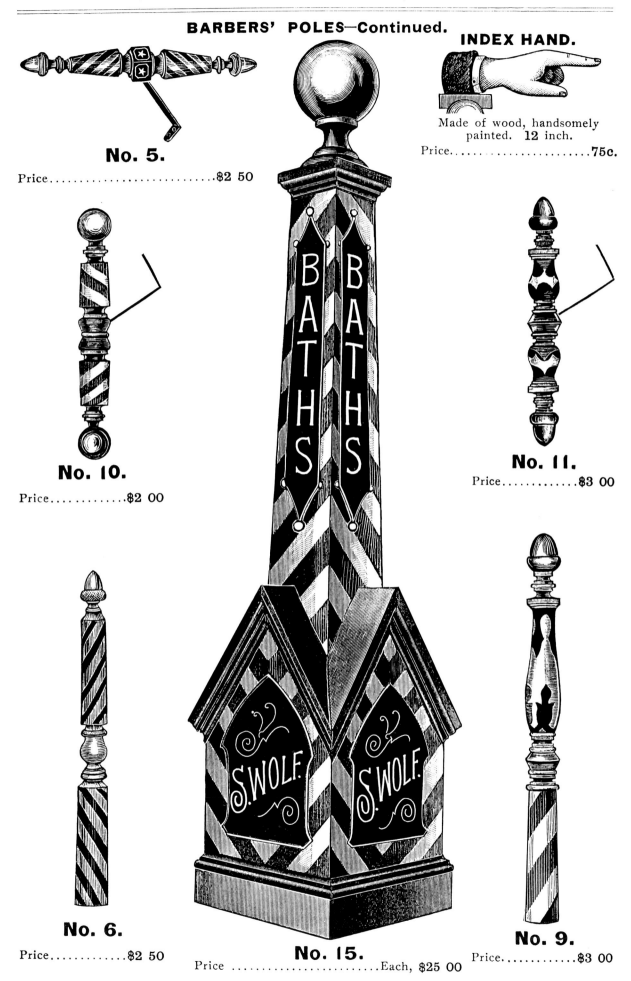

INDEX HAND.

Made of wood, handsomely painted. **12** inch.
Price..........................**75c.**

No. 5.

Price...........................$2 50

No. 10.

Price.............$2 00

No. 11.

Price.............$3 00

No. 6.

Price.............$2 50

No. 15.

Price ....Each, $25 00

No. 9.

Price..........$3 00

BATHS BATHS

S. WOLF. S. WOLF.

Belle Fourche, South Dakota. November, 1937.

No. 468.   Price....$2.00

No. 381.   Price......75c

No. 636.

Size, 12x24 inches. Wood sign,
furnished with iron, for hanging,
as shown.

Price....................$3.00

No. 608.
Price...$2.00

No. 607.
Price...$1.75

No. 2.

8-inch......$ 8.75
10-inch 10.75

No. 7.

6-inch..$5.75   10-inch..$ 9.75
8-inch.. 7.50   12-inch.. 12.50

(From a 1902 Catalog)

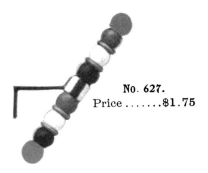

No. 627.
Price.......$1.75

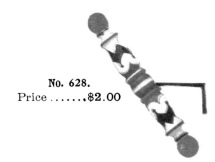

No. 628.
Price.......$2.00

No. 4.
12-inch.....$14.75
14-inch..... 18.00

No. 5, with 4-inch pole......$ 9.75
No. 6, with 6-inch pole....... 11.50

No. 3.
10-inch....$11.50
12-inch..... 13.50

Big Falls, Minnesota. August, 1937.

Minneapolis, Minnesota, May, 1937.   —*Library of Congress*

Kochs' Non-Revolving Poles

THESE poles have the appearance of revolving poles but are stationary. In place of the usual glass cylinder a striped porcelain-enameled steel cylinder is used. This cylinder, of course, cannot be lighted, but light is used in the glass globe. The globes on all of these poles are of 10-inch diameter, except No. 58, which is fitted with 8-inch globe. Each of the five different styles shown on this page, Nos. 56, 57, 58, 59 and 62, is furnished complete with brackets or bolts and wired, ready to attach to wall or sidewalk. These steel and iron poles are exceedingly attractive, and being much lower in price than revolving poles, are preferred by many purchasers.

No. 58

No. 58

Iron and steel. Entirely porcelain-enameled. 8-inch opal glass globe. Height, 35½ inches.

No. 56

Iron and steel. Entirely porcelain-enameled. 10-inch opal glass globe. Height, 41½ inches.

No. 56

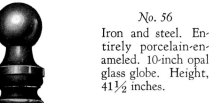

No. 62

Iron and steel. Entirely porcelain-enameled. 10-inch opal glass globe. Height, 7 feet 2 inches.

No. 57

Iron and steel. Pedestal painted in brilliant colors. Upper section entirely porcelain-enameled. 10-inch opal glass globe. Height, 6 feet 10½ inches.

Cedar Wood Column Poles

No. 20

Painted with finest colors. Red, white and blue stripes. Ball covered with pure gold leaf. Height, 7 feet, 6 inches. Made in two sizes: 6 or 8-inch diameter.

No. 59

Iron and steel. Entirely porcelain-enameled. 10-inch opal glass globe. Height, 6 feet 6½ inches.

Wall Bracket Pole

No. 45

Painted red, white and blue with gold-leaf stars and decorations. Length, 4 feet 8 inches. Fitted with 10-inch opal glass globe lettered on two sides. Furnished with brackets and wired for electric light.

Kochs' Revolving Barbers' Poles

MADE OF IRON, PORCELAIN-ENAMELED

An Attractive Barbers' Pole—Your Best Advertisement

A modern Revolving and Illuminated Barbers' Pole is as indispensable and important to every well-regulated barber shop as up-to-date interior equipment. Make the exterior of your shop inviting to the public. Nothing will accomplish this more effectively than a handsome barbers' pole.

Kochs' Revolving Poles

are economical for the barber. The striped cylinder is kept in motion by the clock-work mechanism and it costs you nothing to keep it going. You wind it in the morning, and the pole will run all day without further attention. Electricity is required only for lighting the globe and glass cylinder at night.

For Prices of
GLASS CYLINDERS
and
PAPER CYLINDERS
for
KOCHS' REVOLVING POLES

See Price List

Kochs' Revolving Poles

are the up-to-date poles. They are the most shapely and attractive in appearance. They can be seen a great distance both day or night. They are always moving and do not get out of order. They are a good investment because they are business getters and advertise your shop. They pay for themselves in a short time.

For Prices of
GLASS GLOBES
and
WINDING KEYS
for
KOCHS' REVOLVING POLES

See Price List

Column Revolving Pole No. 10

Height, 7 feet 10½ inches. 12-inch opal glass globe. Diameter at base, 16 inches. Diameter of glass cylinder, 8 inches. Entirely porcelain-enameled, including red and white striped steel tube section. Iron base porcelain-enameled in blue.

Pedestal Revolving Pole No. 7

Height, 6 feet 10½ inches. 10-inch opal glass globe. Diameter of pedestal, 3½ inches. Diameter at base, 12½ inches. Diameter of glass cylinder, 8 inches. Pedestal finished in dark green metallic color. A very desirable style.

For Lettering on Globes and Non-Freezing Lubricating Oil for Kochs' Revolving Poles See Price List

Column Revolving Pole No. 9

Height, 6 feet 7½ inches. 10-inch opal glass globe. Diameter at base, 16 inches. Diameter of glass cylinder, 8 inches. Entirely porcelain-enameled, including red and white striped steel tube section. Iron base porcelain-enameled in blue.

Barber and customer head for shelter in a Bronx subway during a December, 1951 Civil Defense A-Bomb drill. —*Author's Collection*

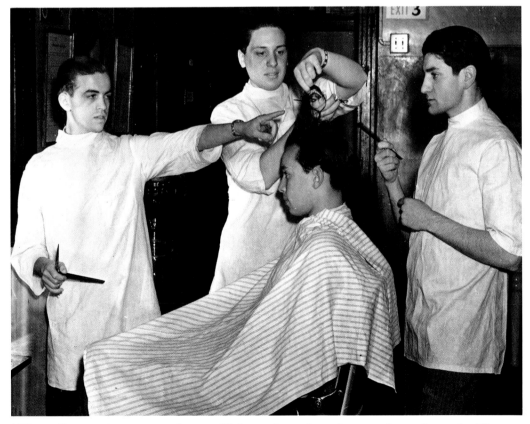

"These Depression-era students will be eating when they graduate from the Metropolitan Vocational High School in New York. All four have chosen Barbering as their career." —*I.N.P. 1940*

Kochs'
Revolving Barbers' Poles

THEY RENDER THE MOST SATISFACTORY SERVICE

Automatic Oiling Attachment

Kochs' Revolving Barbers' Poles are equipped with automatic oiling attachments. This means that the bearing which requires occasional lubrication can be reached without taking the housing apart; simply remove the globe, inject a few drops of oil into the oil cup, which is located in the top of the pole, and the oil is automatically fed through hollow wire to the bearing which should be reached. This is an original feature in Kochs' Revolving Poles.

The Mechanism

Kochs' Revolving Poles are equipped with Clockwork Mechanism which positively is the most reliable made. Kochs' Poles are always running because the clockwork mechanism is sturdy and scientifically constructed. All principal gears are made of hardened steel and the entire mechanism is made rust-proof by a secret process.

Economical in Operation

Kochs' Revolving Poles cost practically nothing to operate. Electricity is required only for lighting the globe and glass cylinder at night. The clockwork mechanism, wound up each morning, keeps the striped cylinder running all day without further attention.

Narrow or Wide Stripes

All styles of poles are regularly furnished with 2-inch striped revolving cylinders, red, white and blue. If specially mentioned when ordering, 2-inch red and white striped cylinders can be had. If preferred, we can furnish 4-inch red, white and blue striped revolving cylinders in all styles of poles except No. 18, which is equipped with narrow stripes only as shown.

Kochs' Poles are Furnished Complete

All poles are furnished with brackets or bolts, ready to attach to the wall or sidewalk. They are also completely wired in accordance with the requirements of the National Board of Fire Underwriters. All Poles are furnished with Winding Keys.

Accessories

Glass Cylinders for all of Kochs' Revolving Barbers' Poles can be furnished at any time when required, also Paper Cylinders to fit the different styles of poles illustrated on these pages, also plain and fancy glass globes of 10 or 12 inches diameter. All of these accessories will be found illustrated elsewhere in this catalog and are quoted in the price list.

Beware of Imitations

Kochs' Poles are imitated because they are the most popular. They are not merely assembled poles, but every part of them is made in the Kochs' factories by experienced mechanics. Kochs' Poles render the most satisfactory service.

Buy an Original Kochs' Revolving Pole Instead of an Imitation. Be sure that the Kochs Name Plate is on the Pole.

Bracket Revolving Pole
No. 18

Height, 36 inches. 8-inch opal glass globe. Diameter of glass cylinder, 6 inches. Especially suited for use "in pairs," one on each side of the shop entrance. Entirely porcelain-enameled.

Bracket Revolving Pole
No. 21

Painted in brilliant colors. Very attractive. Height, 51½ inches. 10-inch opal glass globe. Diameter of glass cylinder, 8 inches.

Bracket Revolving Pole
No. 6

Height, 42 inches. 10-inch opal glass globe. Diameter of glass cylinder, 8 inches. Entirely porcelain-enameled.

Bracket Revolving Pole
No. 2

Height, 51½ inches. 10-inch opal glass globe. Diameter of glass cylinder, 8 inches. Entirely porcelain-enameled.

Arm Pole
No. 537

24 inches long. Diameter 3 inches. Striped red, white and blue. Gold-leaf ball. Furnished with iron for hanging.

Kochs' Electric Street Sign, No. 471

Canteen style, heavy white glass globe, 16 inches diameter. Sand-blasted lettering and decoration on both sides of globe executed in burnt-in red coloring. The nature of decoration and bold lettering render this sign very conspicuous by day or night; when lighted, it is especially brilliant. Equipped with heavy steel tubing bracket and chains. Wired, ready to attach to wall.
Height over all, 26 inches.
Projection from wall over all, 35 inches.

Rotary Wind Sign
No. 174

Painted red, white and blue on sheet steel. Mounted with tempered steel bearings on cast metal brackets. The slightest air current will set it in motion. Height, 28 inches.

Wall Bracket Pole
No. 43

Painted red, white and blue. Length 4 feet. Diameter 6 inches. Gold-leaf ball. Furnished with iron brackets.

Kochs' Wrought Iron Sign, No. 907

A substantial and very attractive street sign which will fit on to narrow spaces. The wall bracket is handwrought from heavy iron and the sign is made of sheet steel, porcelain-enameled on both sides alike. Red and white stripes, blue border and white lettering on blue background.
Height of wall bracket, 29 inches.
Height over all, 39 inches.
Projection from wall over all, 30 inches.

Wall Bracket Pole
No. 49

Painted red, white and blue. Length 4 feet 5 inches. Furnished with 8-inch glass globe, rubber-covered electric feed-wire, electric-light socket and iron wall brackets.

Art Glass Globes
For Barbers' Poles

Made of colored glass which will not fade out. Red, white and blue spiral stripes and lettering in varicolored glass, securely leaded. 4-inch brass flange. These globes are unusually attractive.
No. 927—Diameter of globe, 10 inches.
No. 928—Diameter of globe, 12 inches.

Opal Glass Globes
For Barbers' Poles

Finest quality opal glass, producing a pure white light. All sizes have 4-inch opening.
No. 1008—Diameter of globe, 8 inches.
No. 1010—Diameter of globe, 10 inches.
No. 1012—Diameter of globe, 12 inches.
For lettering on these globes, see price list.

Canteen Style Opal Glass Globes—For Barbers' Poles

Made of extra heavy white glass. Sand-blasted sunk lettering and decoration in burnt-in red coloring on both sides. 4-inch opening.
No. 477—Diameter of globe, 12 inches.

Paper Cylinders for Kochs' Revolving Barbers' Poles

Carried in stock in the following colors: red, white and blue, red and white and blue and white. The red, white and blue cylinders may be had in narrow stripes as shown or wide stripes, 4 inches in width.

Index Hand
No. 381

Made of wood, 15 in. long, painted on both sides.

Translucent Window Signs

24 inches long   5 inches wide
Printed in transparent colors on transfer paper to be applied to window. Directions with each sign. Furnished with lettering as follows:

Barber	Manicuring	Baths
Facial Massage		Hair Cutting

Porcelain-Enameled Iron Sign, No. 447

Both sides alike. Striped red, white and blue. Size 12x24 inches, with 1½-inch flange.

Porcelain-Enameled Iron Corner Sign
No. 446

Striped red, white and blue. Size 18x24 inches. Furnished complete with hangers.

Porcelain-Enameled Iron Sign, No. 448

Size, 6x29 inches, to fit narrow spaces. Striped red, white and blue.

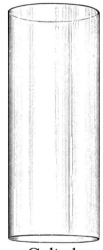

Glass Cylinders for Kochs' Revolving Barbers' Poles

When ordering specify style and number of pole, or give length and diameter of glass cylinder.

No. 446

No. 448

GLOBES FOR POLES

128.—Size 10 inches,
129.—Size 12 inches,

No. 126. ELECTRIC BARBER SIGN

The above cut is an illustration of our 19-inch Electric Sign. The outside frame on this sign is made of 22-gauge iron and has a convex glass on either side with the lettering and painting on the inside of the glass. This protects the paint from the weather. The sign has a cast iron cap or fitter, threaded to fit the standard half-inch pipe. Frame is enameled red, white and blue. The glass is lettered with a panel in center with the word "BARBER" in white letters

No. 127. ELECTRIC BEAUTY PARLOR SIGN

This sign measures 19 inches over all and is made with a metal frame, white enamel finish, and two glass sides, which are convex in shape and are painted on the inside, which tends to preserve the lettering.

This is a very attractive sign and shows up well both in the day and in the night. We recommend that the 100-watt lamp be used.

9 Signs in One

This sign has the electric Flasher of the most approved type, which can be controlled by a screw. Two-tone polychrome frame. Size over all, 11x14 ins. Size of plate, 9x12 ins. Each sign is fitted with two pieces of glass; inserts are placed between the glass. Make your own insert if desired. This sign has best quality cord, eight feet in length, with plug; connects to any light socket.

Flashlight Sign No. 125

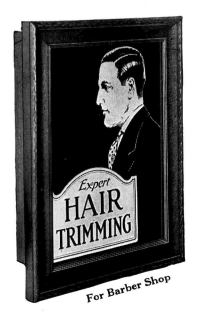

For Barber Shop

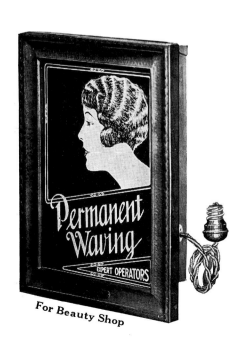

For Beauty Shop

WHEN PA BEGINS TO SHAVE

WHEN Sunday mornin' comes around
    My Pa hangs up his strop,
An' takes his razor out an' makes
    It go c'flop! c'flop!
An' then he gits his mug an' brush
    An' yells t' me, "Behave!"
I tell y'u, things is mighty still—
    When Pa begins t' shave.

Then Pa he stirs his brush around
    An' makes th' soapsuds fly;
An' sometimes, when he stirs too hard,
    He gits some in his eye.
I tell y'u, but it's funny then,
    To see Pa stamp and rave;
But y'u mus'n't git ketched laffin'—
    When Pa begins t' shave.

Th' hired hand he dassent talk,
    An' even Ma's afeard,
An' y'u can hear th' razor click
    A-cuttin' through Pa's beard!
An' then my Uncle Bill he laffs
    An' says: 'Gosh! John, you're brave;"
An' Pa he swears, an' Ma jest smiles—
    When Pa begins t' shave.

When Pa gits done a-shavin' of
    His face, he turns around,
And Uncle Bill says: "Why, John,
    Y'ur chin looks like ploughed ground!"
An' then he laffs—jest laffs an' laffs,
    But I got t' behave,
Cos thing's apt t' happen quick—
    When Pa begins t' shave!

Harry Douglas Robins.

Burma-Shave roadside advertising signs sprouted like daisies along rural highways for more than three decades, and then disappeared almost overnight when the Burma-Vita Company was sold to Philip Morris Inc.

The six hundred feet of rented pasture land required for each set of six signboards eventually became an overwhelming burden. Burma-Vita was paying farmers $200,000 a year when the campaign finally terminated in 1963.

Burma-Shave blossomed in 1927 when two Minnesota brothers, Allan and Leonard Odell, and their father, Clinton, sold nearly half the stock in their new brushless-shaving-cream company in order to finance a last-ditch roadside advertising gamble.

The fresh funds were invested in several hundred 12-inch by 40-inch white wooden signboards, mounted on stakes and planted three feet in the ground at 100-foot intervals along the right hand side of the highway. Allan Odell calculated that his red-lettered advertising verses could be read in about eighteen seconds by motorists traveling at thirty-five miles an hour—which was the average roadway speed in 1927.

The gamble paid off. Soon after the signs were in place, orders began coming in. It wasn't long, however, before the family exhausted their supply of original shaving rhymes. New jingles could have been purchased from Madison Avenue, but the Minnesota farm boys had a better idea. Why not run an annual contest for both amateur and professional writers? Maybe the ploy would expand their jingle file and customer base at the same time.

The rules were simple:

The best copy is that which effectively makes the selling point in the fewest number of words.

In no event should any one signboard contain over five words.

Each winning verse writer received $100, which was a substantial sum during the Great Depression. The contest was a huge success! Entries poured in at the rate of 50,000 annually for the next several decades.

Here are a few examples of winners from the 1940's:

The one-hoss shay
Has had its day
So has the brush
And lather way
Use
Burma-Shave

Buy a jar
Take it from me
There's so
Much in it
The last half's free
Burma-Shave

Half a pound
For half a buck
Come on shavers
You're
In luck
Burma-Shave

Does your husband
Misbehave
Grunt and grumble
Rant and rave
Shoot the brute some
Burma-Shave

Don't take
A curve
at 60 per
We hate to lose
A customer
Burma-Shave

It's best for
One who hits
The bottle
To let another
Use the throttle
Burma-Shave

A peach
Looks good
With lots of fuzz
But man's no peach
And never "wuz"
Burma-Shave

Soaps
That irritate
Their mugs
Turn jolly gents
To jitterbugs
Burma-Shave

It's a good old
Spanish custom
Take your mug
And brush
And bust 'em
Burma-Shave

Are your whiskers
When you wake
Tougher than
A two-bit steak!
Try
Burma-Shave

Substitutes and
Imitations
Send 'em to
Your wife's
Relations
Burma-Shave

The 50¢ jar
So large
By Heck
Even the Scotch
Now shave the neck

Torrey's Razor Strops.

Combination of German Belt and Hone.

No. 8 X.

		Per dozen.
No. **000,** 13½ in., Single Rod,	.	$5 00
No. **7,** 13½ " With Hone,	. .	5 00
No. **7X,** 13½ " Double Rod, with		
Hone,	. . . . .	6 00
No. **8X,** 13½ in., Pat. Combination,		5 50

German Belt Strops.

No. 8.

Double Rod.

Nos.			Per dozen.
1, 13½ Inch,	. . . .	.	$4 00
2, 13½ "	. . . .	.	5 00
8, 13½ "	Heavy Belt, .	.	6 00
9, 13½ "	Leather Finish,		7 00
11, 13½ "	Linen Canvas,	.	8 00

Wood Frame.

Nos.			Per dozen.
3, 13½ Inch,	. . . .	.	$3 25
4, 13½ "	Single Rod,	. .	4 00
5R, 12 "	Double Rod,	.	5 00
5S, 13 "	" "	.	6 00

No. 40.

Drawer Strop—Drawer for Razor.

No. **40,** Flannel Cushioned, per doz., $4 00

Cushion Belt Strops.

No. 230.

		Per dozen.
No. **200,** Imitation Morocco Case,		$5 75
No. **220,** Gold Embossed Mor. Case,		9 00
No. **230,** Imitation Mor. Case, with		
Hone,	. . .	6 00
No. **240,** Comb. of Elastic and Belt,		6 50
No. **270,** " " Cushion & Flat,		7 50

Cushion Belt Strops, Italian Rock Hones.

No. 730.

Nos.	700	720	730
Per dozen,	$18 75	20 00	15 00

Square Strops.

No. 70.

		Per dozen.
No. **0,** Red, White and Blue,	.	$1 00
No. **100,** Root Hog or Die,	. .	1 20
No. **105,** Bay State, Gilt Label,	.	1 25
No. **12,** The People's, with Hone,		1 65
No. **15,** The Medium, " "		2 00
No. **70,** Once Tried, Always Used,		2 00
No. **76,** Large, Practical, with Hone,		4 00
No. **60,** Lithograph Label, Oil Hone,		4 00

Genuine Emerson.

Emerson Strops.

		Per dozen.
90 E, 12 Inch, One Side Oval,	.	$6 25
96 C, 13½ " " " "	.	6 50
97 D, 12 " Both Sides Oval,		6 50
98 B, 13½ " " " "		7 00
Imitation Emerson, 13½ Inch,		2 00

J. R. Torrey Razor Co.'s Razors.

All with Black Handle.

Full Concave.				**Extra Hollow Ground.**				**Hollow Ground.**				**Plain Ground.**			
Nos.			Per dozen.	Nos.			Per dozen.	Nos.			Per dozen.	Nos.			Per dozen.
126,	¾ Inch, Round,		$17 00	**337,**	⅞ Inch, Round,		$10 00	**551,**	⅝ Inch, Round,		$8 00	**770,**	¾ Inch,	. . .	$5 00
136,	¾ " "		18 75	**340,**	½ " Square,		9 50	**555,**	¾ " "		8 00	**775,**	⅝ "	. . . .	5 00
144,	½ " Square,		15 00	**341,**	⅝ " Round,		9 50	**560,**	⅝ " Square,		8 00				
145,	⅝ " "		15 00	**342,**	⅝ " Square,		9 50	**563,**	¾ " "		8 50		**Swedish.**		
146,	¾ " "		15 00	**343,**	¾ " Round,		9 75	**583,**	⅞ " "		10 50	Nos.			Per dozen.
147,	⅞ " "		15 50	**348,**	¾ " Square,		9 75	**586,**	¾ " Round,		7 50	**10,**	⅝ Inch, Thin,	.	$25 00
185,	⅝ " Round,		14 00	**350,**	¾ " Round,		12 00		Corn Razor,		8 00	**15,**	¾ " "	.	25 00
186,	¾ " "		14 00	**390,**	¾ " Square,		12 00					**20,**	¾ " "	.	17 00

(From an 1884 Catalog)

ANTIQUE STRAIGHT RAZORS

Straight razors are an old invention. Men began making basic hunting tools about a million years ago, and by 100,000 B.C. tools for specialized functions such as shaving began to evolve. The first crude razors were sharpened clam or oyster shells, but glass-like obsidian and flint stone were also popular among Neolithic barbers. By 4,000 B.C. man had learned how to hammer copper into a much harder form which could be sharpened into razors or polished into functional hand mirrors. Other innovations in metalworking followed quickly.

The Hittites discovered how to convert iron into steel in 1,400 B.C., and by 500 B.C. the Bronze Age had ended. Razors made by the Greeks, Romans and Egyptians between 500 B.C. and 400 A.D., came in various shapes ranging from crescent, to axe head, to butcher knife and everything in between.

Europeans finally caught up with Middle Eastern iron-workers in the 14th century A.D.. By the early 15th century, the narrow-bladed folding straight razor as we know it today had developed.

British blades manufactured between 1750 and 1830 were often stamped "Cast Steel" and "Warranted" along with the maker's mark. Straight razors made before the early 1800s were usually plain, with no etching or engraving work. Hollow grinding was introduced in the 1820's and became a highly perfected machine process by the 1880's. (Hollow ground blades have concave sides.)

From the 1830s onward, etched blades with trademarks, ads and mottos came in vogue. In Civil War times patriotic themes were very popular and eagles, flags and "Save the Union" messages decorated many a blade. There are other technical points to look for in dating razors. "Silver Steel" is a mark found on razors containing one-fifth of one percent silver. These were widely distributed from 1824 to 1840. "Indiana Steel" appears on tools made shortly thereafter.

Razor handles were made of the same materials as pocket knife grips. Some examples are: metal, horn, shell, ivory, bone, mother-of-pearl, wood, gutta-percha, hard rubber and celluloid. Most handles of the Victorian period were black or clear horn. As can be observed from trade catalog illustrations, barbershop razors were the plainest type made.

"Day of the Week" sets of seven razors with blades marked "Sunday," "Monday," "Tuesday," etc. were popular from 1820 to 1930. The theory of "resting" blades to keep them sharp and pointing them in a north-south position during storage prompted the manufacture of such sets. Some barbers hung 7-day razor sets on their back-bar mirrors as status symbols. Today these sets are highly sought after by collectors. Prices range from $50 to $275 per set, depending upon age, maker, handle material, and condition. Pre-1830 sets with interchangeable blades are extremely rare.

The average utilitarian straight razor you might find in an antique dealer's showcase today will be priced between $8 and $15. It will be of German or American manufacture, usually produced within the last century.

Fancy British razors, marked "Sheffield," with flat-sided (rather than hollow ground) blades, were made before 1870-1880 and are more valuable than "Solingen" marked instruments, which are German made.

Decorative etching increases collector appeal, as do important makers names such as: American, Baker & Sons, Boker, Case, Holley, Greaves, Packard, Price, Wade & Butcher, Jos. Rodgers and Winchester, to name a few. Extra fancy razors by these makers sell for $50 to $250. An example of the high end of this price range would be Robert E. Lee etched in gold on the blade and an extremely decorative handle..

Floral scroll work is a common handle decoration. Advanced collectors covet masculine motifs such as fish and game, or embossed horses, cowboys, eagles, peacocks, automobiles and of course, voluptuous nudes. Celluloid examples with these motifs range from $50 to $200. Figural handles, actually shaped like an animal or object are among the rarest one might find.

How efficient were these dangerous, Victorian shaving tools? Well, a lot depended upon the skill of the operator. We offer this clipping from *The Strand Magazine* of January 1909:

> The quick-shaving champion of England and possibly the world is Mr. Robert Hardie, of Shepherd's Bush. Mr. Hardie's record of shaving five men in 1 minute and 15 seconds stood for some years, but not long ago the champion of the razor thought he would try for new and better times, so he managed to shave six men in 1 minute and 25 seconds. Mr. Hardie a little time back issued a challenge to the world for £500, and this money can be won by anybody who will take up the cudgels at either quick or blindfold shaving, and is able to beat the existing champion's times.
>
> Mr. Hardie can shave one man, no matter how harsh his beard, in 12 seconds, or he will allow himself to be blindfolded and then make a clean job of it in 27 seconds. Besides these times, which are accomplished by the aid of an ordinary razor, Mr. Hardie will give any man a perfectly satisfactory shave with the aid of a carving knife, in 45 seconds, and with a penknife in 28 seconds.

Mr. Hardie's American counterpart might have been George N. Rich, a Portland, Maine, barber who swore he had the figures to show that he shaved ninety men in one day in 1906. Luke Whalen of the same town was widely known as the only "official one-minute barber" in the city. Apprentices from far and wide sought his counsel.

Five to ten minutes was a quick shave in an average turn-of-the-century tonsorial parlor on this side of the Atlantic. Mr. Hardie must have been employed in a penal institution or a lunatic asylum where no one was counting ears and noses.

Millions of straight razors are still lingering out there, waiting to be discovered again as popular collectibles. Back in 1980, auctioneer Robert A. Doyle of Fishkill, New York, wrote the classic reference, *Straight Razor Collecting*; an illustrated history and price guide, based on his personal collection of more than 4,000 items. The book is currently out of print but well worth locating if one is serious about the hobby.

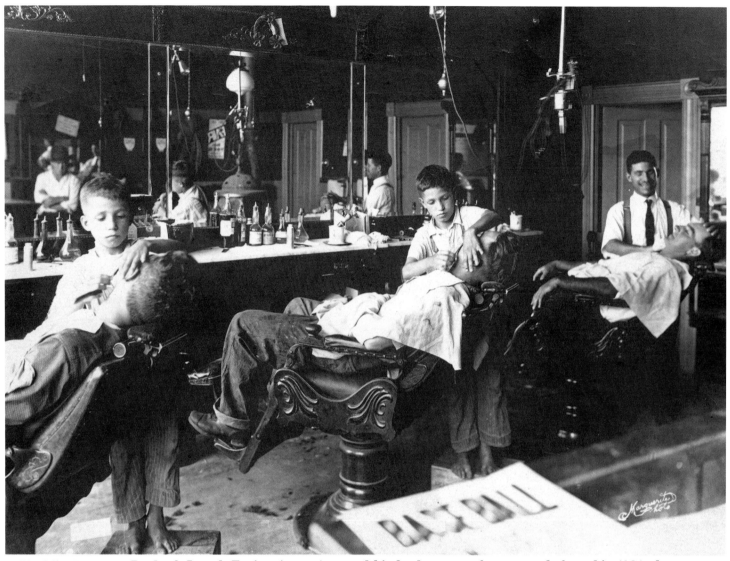

World's Youngest Barber? Joseph Farina (center) passed his barber exam four years before this 1921 photo was taken. He was seven years old when an inspector walked into his father's New Buffalo, Mich. shop and directed the boy to shave him. No blood was drawn and a certificate was issued. Brother, Russell, age 7½, works standing barefoot on a box (at left). Their father, Giovanni—who arrived in this country penniless and ended up owning an entire city block of rental property—smiles as he cleans up a client (at right). —Farina Brothers Plumbing

Two oil lamps at every station in this 1890s shop in Scio, Ohio. (From left to right) Claude McKinney, John Gibson, Frank Willett and H.B. Heckler.

A San Francisco Dandy of the Burnsides era.
—Author's Collection

RAZORS

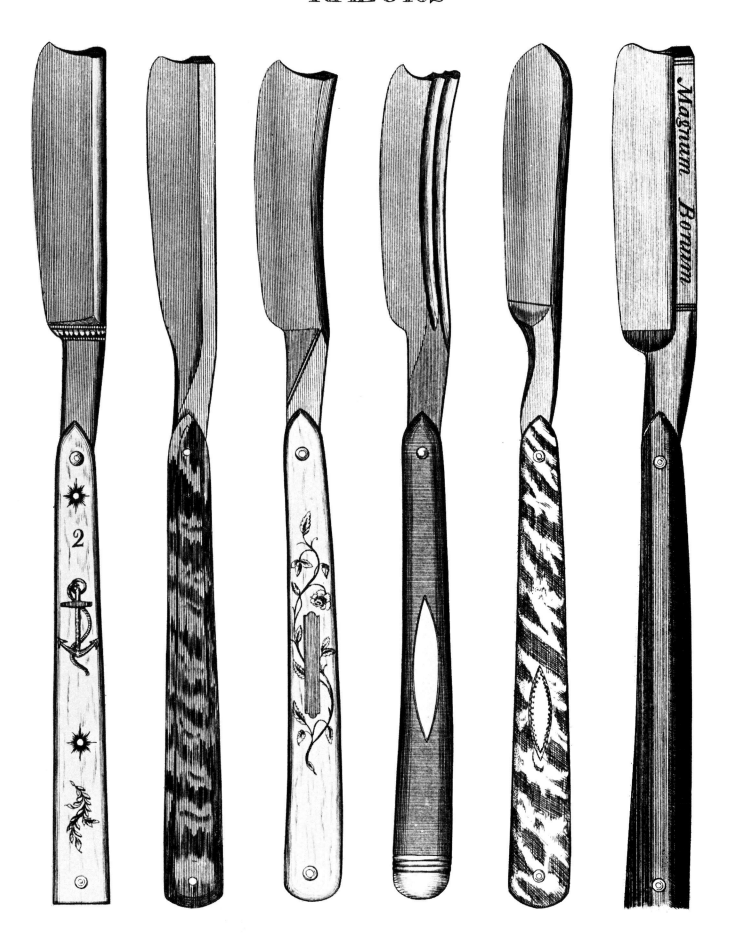

English Razors, circa 1800, from Joseph Smith's catalog "Key to Sheffield Manufactories."

QUEEN RAZORS.

HENRY SEARS & SON, 1865.

Full size cut of No. 770 I. M., ⅝-inch.—With rib and full concaved edge.

No. 770-I. M. Figured, mottled rubber handle, Hamburg ground, square point, etched Queen, ⅝ inch.....................per doz., $22 50
" 552-I. " black " " " " " " ⅝ " .... " 22 50
" 486-I. " " " " " " " round point, " " ⅝ " .... " 22 50
" 489-I. " " " " " " " " " " ⅝ " .... " 22 50
" 488. " " " " " " square point, " " ⅝ " .... " 22 50

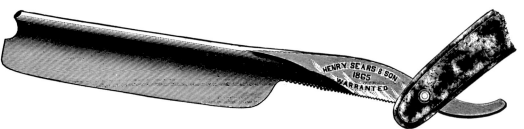

Full size cut of No. 40, ⅝-inch.

No. 40. Shell handle, heavy back. concave blade, full polished, ⅝ inch...per doz., $ 9 00

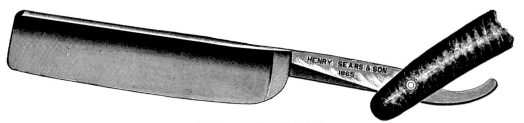

Full size cut of No. 492, ⅝-inch.

No. 492. Black rubber handle, hollow ground, "The Gold Dollar," ⅝ inch... ....per doz., $12 00

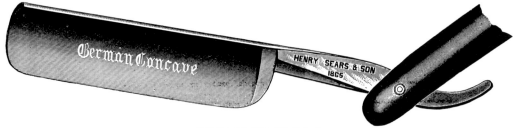

Full size cut of No 493, ⅝-inch.

No. 493. Black rubber handle, hollow ground, round point, etched in gilt, ⅝ inch...............................per doz., $15 00
" 494. " " " " " square " " ¾ inch... " 13 50

Full size cut of No. 700, ⅝-inch.

No. 670. Mottled rubber handle, extra hollow ground, Crow razor, ½ inch.....................................per doz., $15 75
" 700. Black " " " " " " ⅝ " .... " 15 00

(From an 1890 Catalog)

ATOMIZERS.

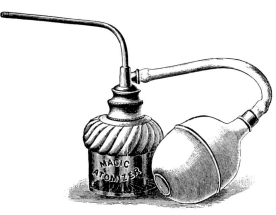

No. 30. Per doz., net.................$12 00   No. 1. Magic..................per doz., net, $9 00   —THE ORIENTAL. per doz., net, $ 11 50

No. 12. Per doz., net...................$3 75   No. 33. Per doz., net......$6 50   No. 6. Per doz., net..............................$8 00

Fine imported atomizer continuous spray
will never get out of order.
No. 5760. Plain crystal...... each, $1 10
No. 5761. Finished " .... "   2 25

It throws a perfect continuous spray,
and does not get out of order. **Price,
per doz. $11.00.**

No. 3. Hard rubber tubes, continuous
spray, patented, ¼ doz., in package...................per doz., $18 00

The Union Barber Shop sign is dated 1902. The mug rack has an owl on top and the back room has bathtubs for rent. Note kerosene lamp and marble top back bar. Cigar counter features a penny slot machine, "Win a Free Cigar." —Michael Griffin

RAZORS.—Full Hollow-Ground.

THE "PERFECTO" RAZOR.

Fancy carved handle—Old Ivory finish.

Price, each..................$ 1.75

Per dozen..................... 21.00

THE "LUCIFER" RAZOR.

Black handle—The Old Reliable brand.

Price, each..................$ 1.75

Per dozen..................... 21.00

THE "WIZARD" RAZOR.

Best quality shell handle.

Price, each..................$ 1.50

Per dozen..................... 18.00

THE "ADMIRAL" RAZOR.

Red Carnelian handle.

Price, each..................$ 1.50

Per dozen..................... 18.00

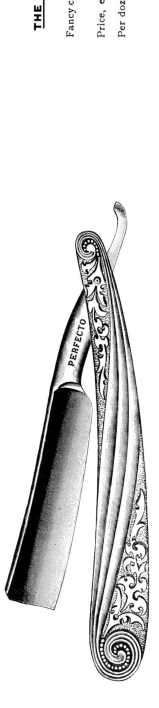

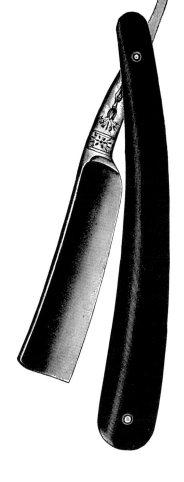

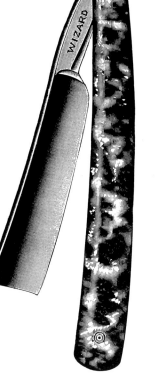

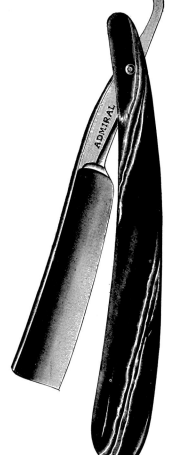

OUR SPECIAL BRANDS.

"PERFECTO."   "LUCIFER."

"WIZARD."   "ADMIRAL."

We guarantee every one of these razors, for they are made of specially selected material and are ground by the best concavers. In the grinding of *every* blade extreme care is taken to produce a perfect edge, and, in short, we offer in these razors the result of years of experience.

Our Special Brands are neat and attractive, the handles being novel and of pleasing design, and each razor is put up in a colored case stamped in gold. **Be sure you get the genuine.** Every one of these razors bears our Trade Mark, which we have adopted for the protection of our customers, and which is universally conceded to be a guarantee of excellence of quality.

93

THE vom CLEFF & CO. RAZORS.

HAND FORGED.

No. 180.—Celluloid Handle, Full Concaved,

$\frac{5}{8}$ $\frac{6}{8}$ inch.

per doz.

No. 194½.—Rubber Handle, Full Concaved,

"   194. —Celluloid Handle, Bamboo, Full Concaved,

$\frac{5}{8}$ $\frac{6}{8}$ inch.

per doz. "

No. 177.—Fancy Back, Celluloid Handle, Full Concaved,

"   177.—Plain   "   "   "   "

$\frac{5}{8}$ $\frac{6}{8}$ inch.

per doz. "

THE vom CLEFF & CO. RAZORS.

HAND FORGED.

No. 97.—Celluloid Handle, Bamboo, Full Concaved,

$\frac{5}{8}$ $\frac{6}{8}$ inch.

per doz.

No. 101.—Celluloid Handle, Full Concaved,

$\frac{5}{8}$ $\frac{6}{8}$ inch.

per doz.

No. 99.—Celluloid Handle, Antique, Full Concaved,

$\frac{5}{8}$ $\frac{6}{8}$ inch.

per doz.

The vom Cleff & Co.
"LION" POCKET CUTLERY.

(From a 1906 Catalog)

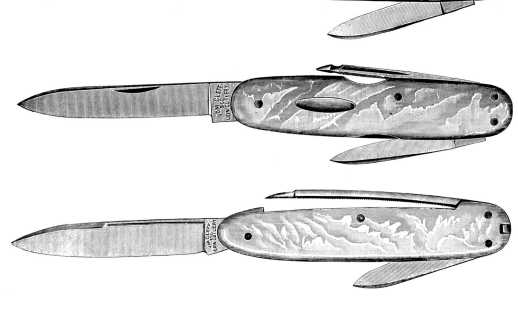

2306 Oxidized.

2534 Oxidized.

290 Pearl.

7816 Pearl.

THE vom CLEFF & CO. RAZORS.

HAND FORGED.

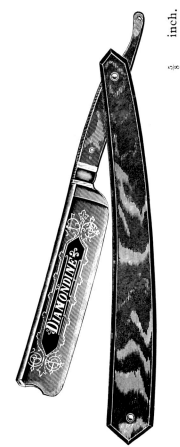

4 5/8 6/8 inch.
         per doz.
          "

No. 191.—Fancy Black Handle,
  "   191.—Plain Oval Black Handle,

4 5/8 6/8 inch.
         per doz.

No. 193.—Ivory Handle, Extra Concaved, Crocus Polished,

5/8 inch.
         per doz.
          "

No. 212.   —Genuine Shell Handle, Shell Tang,
  "   212½.—   "   "   "   Steel Tang,

Razors

Registered Trade Marks:

Blue Ribbon
Blue Steel
Crystal
    „   Jr.
Dandelion
Grand Royal
Gun Metal
Indigo
Lilly Blue
Perfecto
Solid Steel
Waleko

R 66 Imt. Shell Handle. — Tang oxydised. — Sizes ⁶/₈, ⁵/₈, ⁴/₈.

R 68 Oval white Handle. — Blade 2¹/₂ inches long.

R 72 Oval white Handle. — Sizes ⁶/₈, ⁵/₈, ⁴/₈.

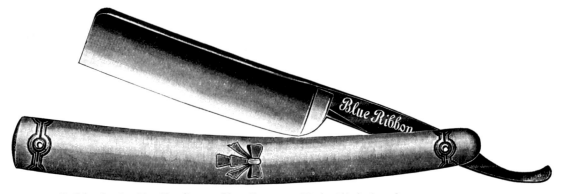

R 74 Oval white Handle. — Blue Tang. — Blade 2¹/₂ inches long.

(From a 1927 Catalog)

Razors

Registered
Trade Marks:

Blue Ribbon
Blue Steel
Crystal
  ,,   Jr.
Dandelion
Grand Royal
Gun Metal
Indigo
Lilly Blue
Perfecto
Solid Steel
Waleko

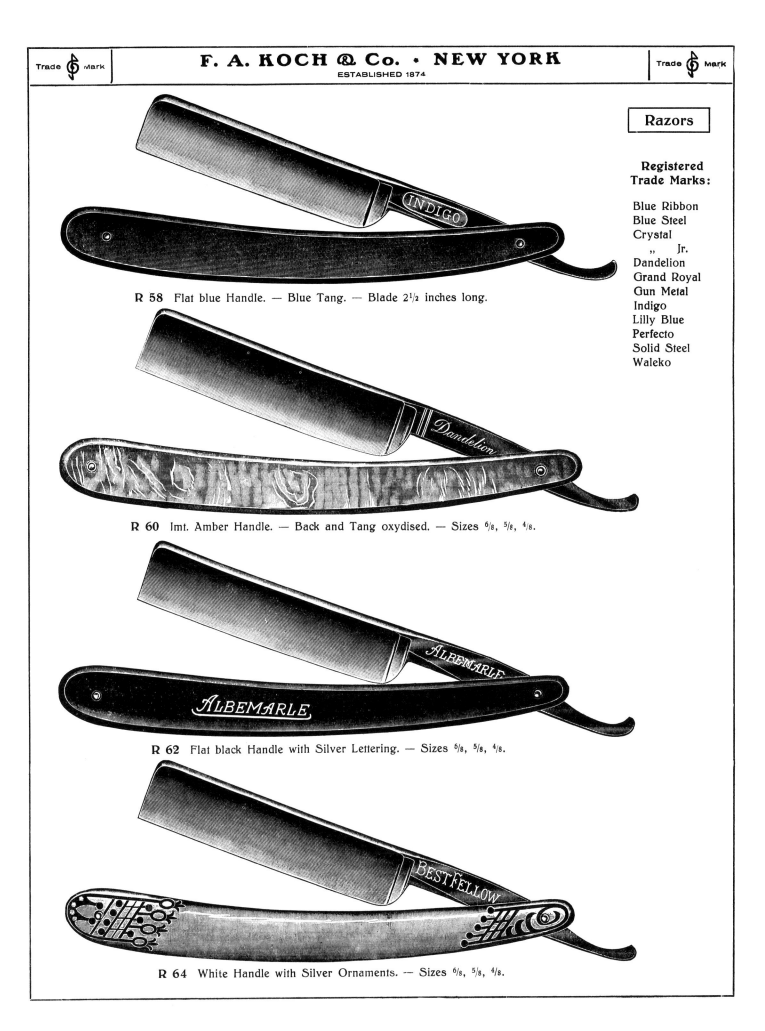

R 58   Flat blue Handle. — Blue Tang. — Blade 2½ inches long.

R 60   Imt. Amber Handle. — Back and Tang oxydised. — Sizes ⁶/₈, ⁵/₈, ⁴/₈.

R 62   Flat black Handle with Silver Lettering. — Sizes ⁶/₈, ⁵/₈, ⁴/₈.

R 64   White Handle with Silver Ornaments. — Sizes ⁶/₈, ⁵/₈, ⁴/₈.

The Arc Magnetic Razor.

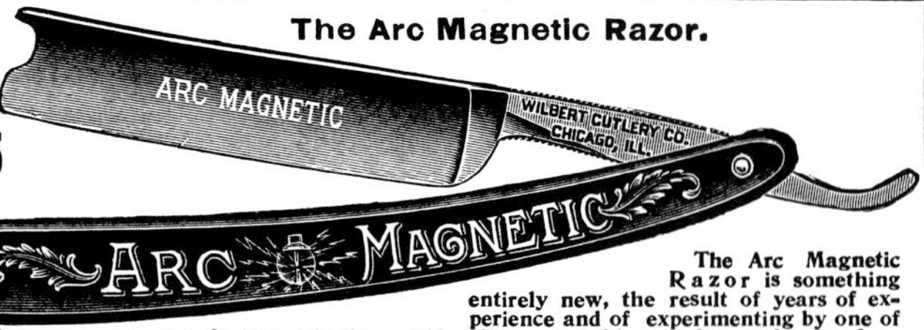

$1.75

The Arc Magnetic Razor is something entirely new, the result of years of experience and of experimenting by one of the most famous razor manufacturers in the world. For years this man has endeavored to bring forth a magnetized razor which would have just the right degree of temper, and which would shave equally well under all conditions. The blade of this razor is forged from the solid bar by hand. It is tempered by a secret electrical process which absolutely insures uniform temper from heel to point. The blades are ground by most experienced workmen according to the good, old fashioned Hamburg method, on a 1½-inch stone. The blades are highly magnetized, which is a valuable feature. By magnetizing the blade the minute grains of steel are more closely drawn together, insuring the greatest possible cutting power. This highly magnetized blade has particular merit as it prevents irritation and is particularly desirable for those people who experience a burning sensation after shaving with an ordinary razor. It has a curative effect on eruptions of the skin. The manner in which this blade is ground, tempered and magnetized, causes it to remain sharp longer than any other razor, and for private use if properly handled, would not have to be honed more than once a year. Blade beautifully polished, double shoulder and gimped tang. The polished flat black rubber handle is handsomely decorated as shown in the illustration. No detail in the construction of this razor has been overlooked, and it is without question one of the most serviceable and handsomest razors on the market today.

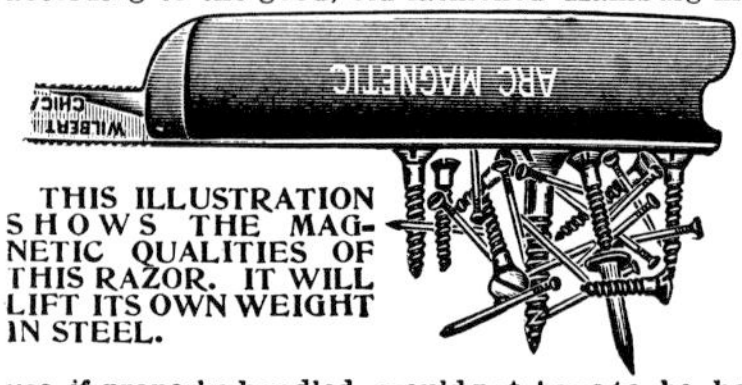

THIS ILLUSTRATION SHOWS THE MAGNETIC QUALITIES OF THIS RAZOR. IT WILL LIFT ITS OWN WEIGHT IN STEEL.

No. 6L17813 ⅝-inch hollow point. Price **$1.75**
No. 6L17814 ⅝-inch square point. Price **1.78**
No. 6L17815 ¾-inch square point. Price **1.80**
If by mail, postage extra, 5 cents.

WILBERT RAZORS ARE GUARANTEED TO GIVE SATISFACTION.
Sent on thirty-day trial. See our guarantee on preceding page.

Wilbert High Art Razor.

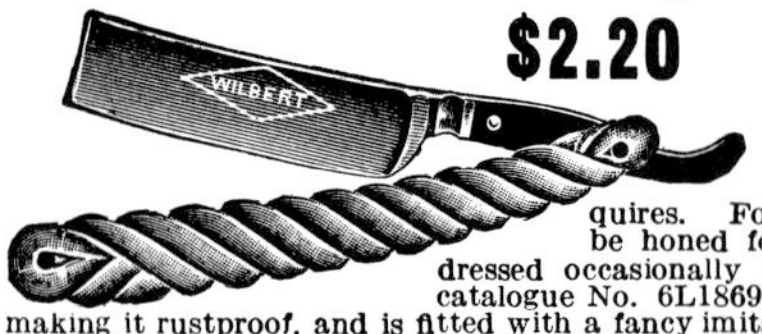

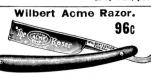

$2.20

Full tempered by electricity and guaranteed to be of uniform temper. Owing to the high grade of material used and to the secret process in tempering, this razor will hold an edge longer than any other razor on the market. A few strokes on the strop before shaving is all this razor requires. For private use, this razor will not have to be honed for several years, especially if the strop is dressed occasionally with KELSO STROP DRESSING (see catalogue No. 6L18697). This razor has a black rubber tang, making it rustproof, and is fitted with a fancy imitation onyx handle. A handsome, serviceable razor and guaranteed to shave any beard or you may return it after thirty days' trial and your money will be refunded or a new razor given instead.

No. 6L17905 Width of blade, ½ inch. Price **$2.20**
No. 6L17906 Width of blade, ⅝ inch. Price **2.25**
No. 6L17907 Width of blade, ¾ inch. Price **2.30**
If by mail, postage extra, 5 cents.

Wilbert Acme Razor.

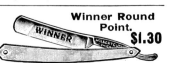

96c

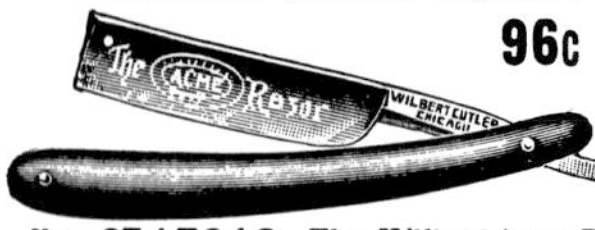

No. 6L17912 The Wilbert Acme Razor. Hollow ground, ⅝-inch blade, heavy gimped tang. This razor will probably "fit" more beards than any razor we sell. **It is ground by experts and is suitable for barbers' or private use.** A better razor than those usually sold for $1.50. Our price **96c**
If by mail, postage extra, 5 cents.

Winner Round Point.

$1.30

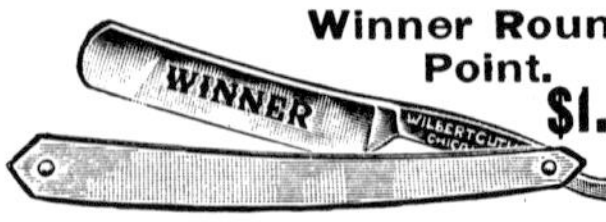

No. 6L17919 The Winner, fancy **pattern, polished white ivoroid handle,** hollow ground ⅝-inch round point, full polished blade, graceful double gimped tang, blade finely tempered and ground by experienced workmen. Guaranteed to give satisfaction. An excellent razor for barbers' and private use.
Price **$1.30**
If by mail, postage extra, 5 cents.

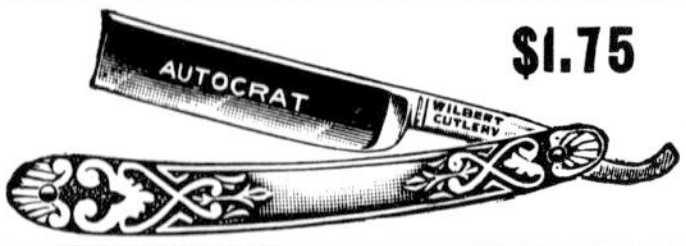

$1.75

No. 6L17932 The Wilbert Autocrat Razor, has fancy white ivoroid handle, ⅝-inch blade, full crocus polished, full hollow ground. Is suitable for barbers' or private use, and is best value ever offered in a high grade razor. Fully warranted.
Price **$1.75**
If by mail, postage extra, 5 cents.

$1.80 RAZORS MADE TO ORDER — HAVE A RAZOR MADE TO FIT YOUR BEARD $2.00

WITH YOUR NAME ENGRAVED ON THE BLADE IN GOLD LETTERS

IT IS IMPOSSIBLE for you to adapt your face to any razor, but it is possible for us to make a razor that will adapt itself to your face. It is generally known that no two men can get the same degree of satisfaction from the same razor. A razor that gives one man entire satisfaction will irritate another man's face. We have made thousands of razors, in all styles and patterns, and our peculiar position in manufacturing and selling direct to the consumer enables us to give the art of razor manufacture the study that no one else has ever been in a position to do. This knowledge born of years of experience in manufacturing and selling enormous quantities of razors enables us to make a razor that we will absolutely guarantee to give you perfect satisfaction, provided you answer the following questions:

How often do you shave?
Is your beard fine or coarse?
What is the color of your beard?
Is your beard stiff or soft?
Is your skin tender?
What shaving soap do you use?
Have you a good strop?

DO NOT FAIL WHEN WRITING YOUR ORDER to give catalogue number of the razor desired, also specify width of blade and plainly write the name you wish engraved on the blade of the razor. We will engrave your name in gold letters on the blade same as shown in the illustration, putting your name in place of the name George W. Brown or John G. Smith as shown in the illustrations.

THESE MADE TO ORDER RAZORS are hand forged out of the best Swedish steel, tempered by electricity, which insures a uniform temper. They are extra full concave, have a mirror polish, they combine the highest quality of material, the best workmanship and the finest value ever produced in a razor.

TIME REQUIRED TO MAKE. As every razor is tempered and ground in accordance with the requirements of the purchaser, it takes from 5 to 8 days to make shipment.

DON'T FAIL TO STATE NAME YOU WISH ENGRAVED ON BLADE.

Wilbert Made to Order Razor.

$1.81

Wilbert Made to Order Razor, with black rubber handle, square or hollow point; blades ½, ⅝ or ¾ inch wide. Full polished, with your name engraved on the blade in gold letters.

Don't fail to give width of blade wanted and name you wish engraved on blade.

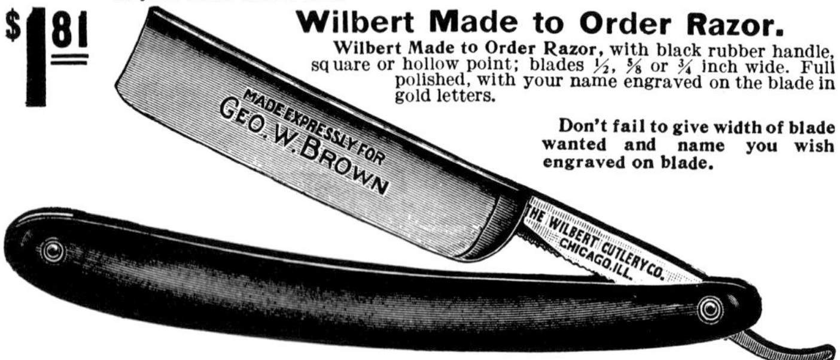

Width of Blade	No. 6L17950 Square Point	No. 6L17951 Hollow Point
½ inch	$1.81	$1.80
⅝ inch	1.86	1.85
¾ inch	1.90	1.89

Wilbert Made to Order Razor.

$2.00

The accompanying illustration, showing razor engraved "John Smith," is our semi-transparent wine color handle, which forms a handsome contrast with the highly polished blade with gold lettering. Furnished with either hollow or square point, as desired. Be sure to give catalogue number and state which point and width you prefer.

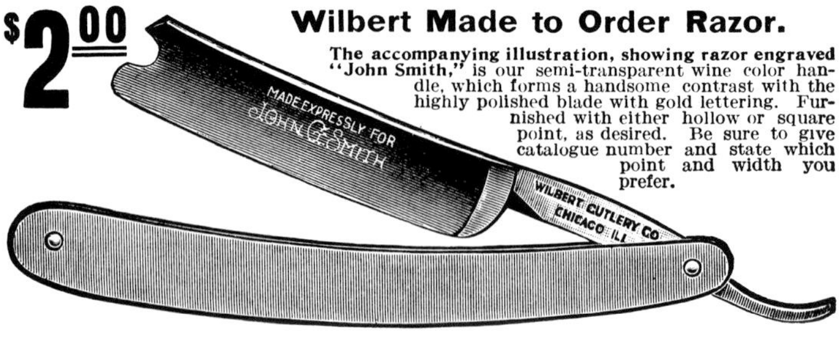

Width of Blade	No. 6L17952 Hollow Point	No. 6L17953 Square Point
½ inch	$2.00	$2.01
⅝ inch	2.02	2.03
¾ inch	2.05	2.06

The Surprise Razor, $1.95.

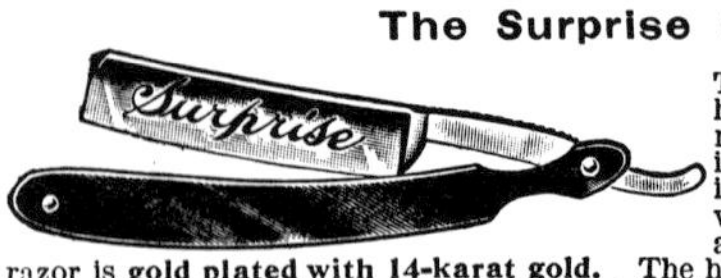

No. 6L17927 Something entirely new; The Surprise razor is well named, for no matter how carefully we might describe this razor, you would still be surprised at its beauty upon receiving it. This razor is full hollow ground by most experienced workmen, the blade double shouldered, and is full polished. The tang of this razor is **gold plated with 14-karat gold.** The handle is green celluloid, the green transparent celluloid harmonizing beautifully with the heavily gold plated tang and beautiful mirror polished blade. This razor is as good as it looks. The workmanship is the very best, and it is guaranteed to shave any beard. Price, ⅝-inch blade, special square point **$1.95**
If by mail, postage extra, 5 cents.

The Wilbert Regal Razor.

No. 6L17933 The Wilbert **Regal Razor** has ivory tang fancy imitation ivory handle, has ⅝-inch blade, is full crocus polished, full hollow ground, fancy diamond, back. One of the neatest looking razors made and makes an elegant present, while for shaving qualities and workmanship it cannot be excelled. Fully warranted.
Price **$2.00**

$2.00

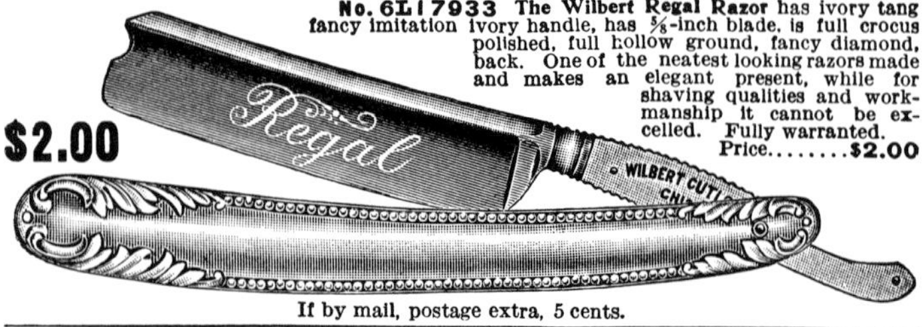

If by mail, postage extra, 5 cents.

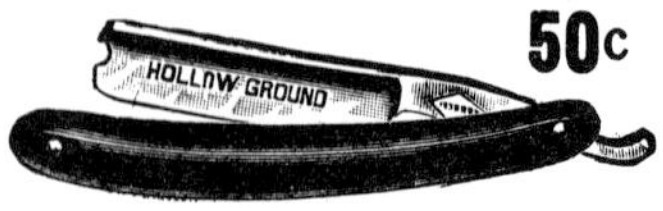

50c

No. 6L18019 Wilbert Medium Hollow Ground Razor. Hollow blade, black rubber handle. A good razor, equal to those sold by all dealers for $1.00. Price **50c**
If by mail, postage extra, 5 cents.

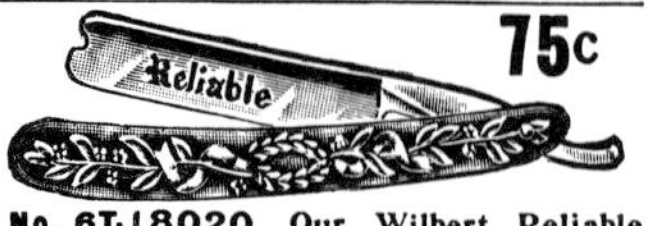

75c

No. 6L18020 Our Wilbert Reliable Razor, ⅝-inch blade, hollow ground, hollow point, fancy thumb hold, imitation tortoise shell handle. Guaranteed to give satisfaction. Price **75c**
If by mail, postage extra, 5 cents.

Antiseptic Felt Pad Razor.

$2.44

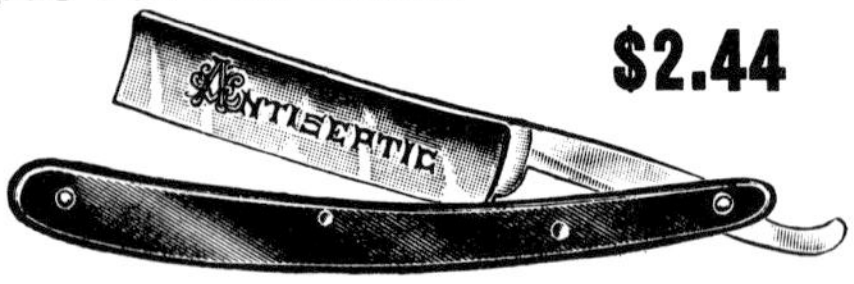

No. 6L17938 This razor, **as indicated by the name, is an antiseptic razor; in fact, the best antiseptic razor made.** The flat rubber handles are lined with felt pads which are saturated with an antiseptic oil (Parmoline), which protects the sensitive edge of the blade from rust and keeps it sanitary and sharp. The Antiseptic Razor keeps sharp longer than any other razor as the edge is kept free from rust. For private use this razor ought not require honing more than once a year. Every razor is thoroughly tested and inspected before being shipped. Guaranteed to give satisfaction. ⅝-inch full hollow ground blade, square point, double shoulder, broad comfortable tang, flat polished black rubber handle, well finished throughout. Price, each, including nickel plated oiler filled with Parmoline.. **$2.44**
If by mail, postage extra, 5 cents.

$8.00 Set of Ern Razors for $3.94.

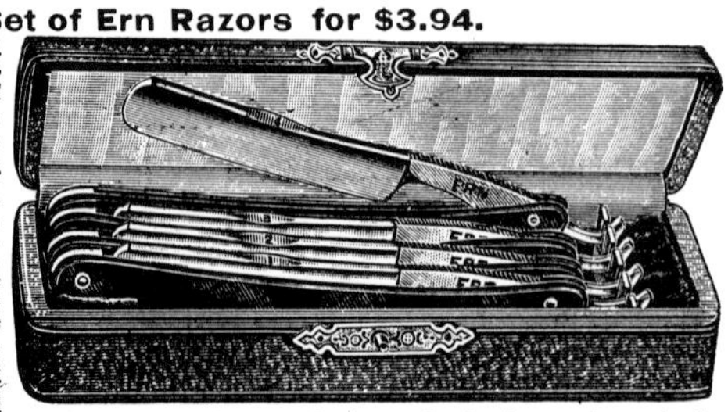

No. 6L18194 For $3.94 **we furnish this beautiful four-piece razor set,** consisting of four highest quality round point, full hollow ground razors, packed in a beautiful hinged, satin lined, partitioned, leather box, with heavy metal clasp. These razors, sold separately, would retail for $2.00 each. They are the famous Ern razors, made in Wald, Germany, one of the oldest and most famous razor factories in the world. The razors are full hollow ground, ⅝-inch round point, with double gimped finger fitting tang, fitted with flat, polished black rubber handle. These razors have small indentations on the back, as shown in the illustration, and are numbered 1, 2, 3 and 4, respectively. Buy this set of razors for $3.94 and you will have a set that will last for several generations. You will always have a sharp razor and a different razor every time you shave. Compare this set of razors, which will last you a lifetime, with any of the $5.00 safety razors on the market for which you are continually obliged to buy new blades, calling for a continuous additional expenditure.
Price of set of four razors, packed in a beautiful satin lined, partitioned, hinged, leather box........ **$3.94**
If by mail, postage extra, 13 cents.

GERMAN RAZORS.

THE BISMARCK RAZOR.
FULL HOLLOW GROUND. GUARANTEED.

NOTE
THE
RIDGE
OR
BACK-
BONE.

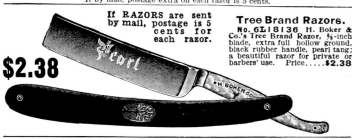

$1.34

The Bismarck Razor represents the best production of one of the most famous factories in Germany. This razor is made complete in Germany and imported by us. We offer it as the finest razor of its type on the market. It is extra full ground and, as shown in the illustration, has a ridge extending the full length of the blade, which serves as a backbone to the edge and gives the blade strength, life and cutting power not found in any of the other German razors on the market. The material, workmanship and finish of this razor are perfect, and we guarantee it to give absolute satisfaction or your money and transportation charges refunded. Fitted with a polished black rubber handle. Each razor branded BISMARCK, as shown in the illustration.

No. 6L18090 "Bismarck" Razor. Width of blade, ¾ inch. Price........$1.35
No. 6L18091 "Bismarck" Razor. Width of blade, ⅝ inch. Price......... 1.34
If by mail, postage extra on each razor is 5 cents.

If RAZORS are sent by mail, postage is 5 cents for each razor.

$2.38

Tree Brand Razors.
No. 6L18136 H. Boker & Co.'s Tree Brand Razor, ⅝-inch blade, extra full hollow ground, black rubber handle, pearl tang; a beautiful razor for private or barbers' use. Price.....$2.38

$1.50

No. 6L18135 H. Boker & Co.'s Tree Brand Razor, extra full hollow ground, black rubber handle. Width of blade, ⅝ inch. Price.......................$1.50

THE SURPRISINGLY LOW REDUCED PRICES prevailing in this catalogue mean greater savings to our customers than ever before.

$1.29

No. 6L18137 H. Boker & Co.'s Tree Brand Razor, extra stiff for the man with the heavy beard who shaves but once or twice a week. ⅝-inch blade, square point, beautifully polished, fully hollow ground, file tang, double shoulder and fitted with oval black rubber handles. This razor is made especially for us, and we guarantee it to be equal to any $2.00 razor on the market. Price...............$1.29

30c

No. 6L18165 A Fair Grade German Razor, ⅝-inch blade, medium hollow ground, engraved. It is a razor that is usually sold at from 50 cents to $1.00.
Price............................30c

Our 65-Cent Magnetic German Razor.
65c

No. 6L18166 A Good Quality German Razor, ⅝-inch blade. Finely ground, made of best steel, polished and gimped tang, magnetized, warranted. Price........65c

Genuine German Razors for Barbers' Use.
The Figaro Razor. Our Own Importation.

$1.50

No. 6L18192 The Figaro Barbers' Razor, made in Solingen, Germany, by the most skilled workmen. Has the new Galalith non-shrinkable handle (color of old ivory). Blade is ⅝-inch, full concaved, finely finished and the best value ever offered in a German make razor. Fully warranted. Price........$1.50

ENGLISH RAZORS.
Jos. Allen & Sons' Celebrated NON-XLL Razors.

No. 6L18199 NON-XLL medium hollow ground ⅝-inch square point razor with oval black rubber handle. Blade is nicely etched and finished. This is a good, stiff, heavy razor and will give satisfaction. Price 60c

60c

All Razors illustrated and described on this page, if by mail, postage extra, each, 5 cents.

No. 6L18200 NON-XLL Razor, grained celluloid handle, imitation ivory; full hollow ground, square point, ⅝-inch blade, finely polished and etched; is made by Jos. Allen & Sons, one of the leading cutlery manufacturers of Sheffield, England, and is fully warranted. Price ..$1.20

$1.20

No. 6L18202 NON-XLL Razor, fancy carved celluloid handle, ⅝-inch blade with round point, full hollow ground, polished and etched. A razor which is warranted and which cannot fail to give satisfaction. Price...........$1.25

$1.25

Pearl Handled, German Silver Lined Razor.

$2.87

No. 6L18203 Joseph Allen & Sons' NON-XLL Pearl Handled Razor. The handle of this razor is genuine pearl, reinforced with fine German silver lining. The blade is full polished, making this one of the finest appearing razors on the market. ⅝-inch hollow point blade, heavy round back, file tang, ground so as to fit any beard. Guaranteed to give satisfaction This is one of the finest razors ever turned out by the old firm of Jos. Allen & Sons, whose name alone signifies quality. Price.......................................$2.87

GEORGE WOSTENHOLM IMPORTED ENGLISH RAZORS. REDUCED PRICES.

We offer a line of razors made by George Wostenholm & Sons, of Sheffield, England, manufacturers of the genuine IXL cutlery and Pipe Brand Razors, which are so widely known all over the world.

70c

No. 6L18255 George Wostenholm & Sons' Genuine, Original and True Pipe Razor, medium hollow ground, black rubber handle. Width of blade, ⅝ inch. This razor is known all over the world and has established a most enviable reputation. Price............ ....70c

$1.25

No. 6L18261 George Wostenholm & Sons' Celebrated IXL Razor, all hollow ground, black rubber handle. Width of blade, ⅝ inch. Price....................$1.25

89c

No. 6L18257 George Wostenholm & Sons' Original Pipe Razor, hollow ground, Width of blade, ⅝ inch, square point. A first class razor for general use. Price........................89c

$1.50

No. 6L18265 George Wostenholm & Sons' Celebrated IXL Razor, ⅝-inch blade, hollow ground, round point, imitation ivory handle; an excellent razor for private use. Price......................$1.50

98c

No. 6L18258 George Wostenholm & Sons' Original and True Pipe Razor, medium hollow ground. Width of blade, ½ inch. A fine razor for the beginner; also used for shaving a second time over; has black rubber handle, file cut tang. Price..............98c

$2.00

No. 6L18266 George Wostenholm & Sons' Original and True Pipe Razor, ⅝-inch blade, the best razor Wostenholm makes. Black rubber handle, file cut, gimped back tang. A razor that if properly cared for will give the very best satisfaction. Price........................$2.00
If by mail, postage extra, 5 cents.

WADE & BUTCHER'S RAZORS.

No. 6L18315 Wade & Butcher's Hollow Point, Medium Hollow Ground Razor, rubber handle.

74c

Fully warranted and a superior cutter, ⅝ inch blade. Price........................74c

SOCKS GUARANTEED SIX MONTHS. See Hosiery Section of this Catalogue.

No. 6L18321 Wade & Butcher's Special Razor. Full hollow ground. A super-

$1.35

fine barbers' razor. Black rubber handle. Width of blade, ⅝ inch. Price ...$1.35
No. 6L18322 Wade & Butcher's Special Razor. Same as above, except blade is ¾ inch wide. Price..............$1.40

SWEDISH RAZORS.

These razors are genuine Swedish razors imported by us direct from Sweden. They are not to be compared with the many cheap imitations that are offered in competition with these high grade razors.

Joh. Engstrom, Eskilstuna, Sweden, Garanti.

98c

No. 6L18334 Genuine Imported Swedish Razor. The blade of this razor is forged separately from the back. The blade is straight ground, finely tempered steel, firmly set in the round quill back. While this blade is comparatively thin, it is very stiff and will shave any beard. ⅝-inch square point. Fully guaranteed. Price...............98c
If by mail, postage extra, 6 cents.

$1.75

No. 6L18335 Our Special Hand Forged Swedish Razor, manufactured by Klaas Tornblom, Eskilstuna, Sweden. This is one of the finest razors manufactured in this large and famous factory. The blade is straight ground, full round quill back, beautifully polished and etched. This razor is guaranteed to shave any beard. Made of high carbon Swedish steel and ground by the most experienced workmen. With ordinary care this razor will last a lifetime. ⅝-inch square point blade; fitted with flat, polished, black rubber handles. Price...........................$1.75
If by mail, postage extra, 6 cents.

Adjustable Razor Guard.

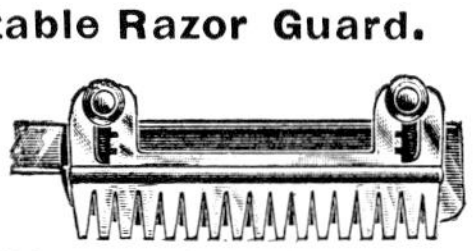

No. 6L18339 The "Shavezy" Razor Guard, reversible and adjustable to any razor. Makes a perfect safety razor of your own favorite blade. Full directions accompany each guard. It is finely finished and heavily nickel plated.
Price........................15c
If by mail, postage extra, 2 cents.

Razor Handles.

No. 6L18345 Black rubber oval razor handles. Price, complete with rivets. 11c

No. 6L18346 Fancy white celluloid razor handles. Price, complete with rivets........24c
If by mail, postage extra, 1 cent.

The Genuine Star Safety Razor.

$1.50

No. 6L18449 Genuine Star Safety Razor, made by Kampfe Bros., New York. Improved frame, hand forged, full concave blade, finely finished, guaranteed to give satisfaction. Packed one in a neat box, with extra handle for stropping and one blade.
Price, postpaid. **$1.50**

No. 6L18451 Extra Blades for Star Safety Razor. Price, each, postpaid **85c**

Our $2.00 Star Safety Razor Set.

No. 6L18465 Star Safety Razor Set. Put up in elegant satin lined morocco case and contains one safety frame and one blade.
Price, postpaid. **$2.00**

No. 6L18467 Star Safety Razor Set. Elegantly finished in morocco. Contains one safety frame with two blades, and is a gem in the full sense of the word.

Price, per set, postpaid, **$3.10**

Star Safety Razor Set.

No. 6L18469 Star Safety Razor Set. Put up in an elegant satin lined morocco case, and contains one safety frame with two perfectly adjusted **blades of fine silver steel; box of** finely perfumed shaving soap; holder for stropping and honing blades; shaving brush, comb and cosmetique; in fact, everything requisite for an easy, quick and luxurious shave.
Price, per set, postage paid........ **$5.00**

Gillette Safety Razor Set.

Gillette Safety Razors are quoted for the accommodation of some of our customers who want this particular razor. We don't claim that this razor will give better satisfaction than the lower priced safety razors quoted on previous page. This razor is manufactured and sold under a licensed price of $5.00; and we are, therefore, prevented from offering it at a price consistent with the prices and values we quote on other makes and styles of safety razors.

No. 6L18475 The well known Gillette Safety Razor, three-piece silver plated frame with 12 double edge steel blades, all packed in a leather box with snap button fastener. **$5.00**

Price, postpaid..... **$5.00**

No. 6L18476 Blades for the Gillette Safety Razor, 10 for 50c

We do not exchange old blades.

Wafer Blade Stropper.

No. 6L18477

Don't throw away your Gillette blades. Buy a stropper and make your blades last ten times as long. This stropper does the work. The blade is firmly secured, no parts to get lost. With the aid of this stropper you can strop the Gillette blade on any strop, the same as you can strop an ordinary razor. Nicely nickel plated, fitted with hardwood handle. Length over all, 7½ inches; weight, 2 ounces.
Price.............................. **45c**
If by mail, postage extra, 4 cents.

Aluminum Shaving Soap Box.

No. 6L18500 Aluminum Shaving Soap Box, with screw top cover, 2 inches high, 2½ inches in diameter, will hold several cakes of shaving soap or can be used as a traveling shaving mug. A cake of Williams' Soap just fits in the bottom of this box. The box is sufficiently deep to permit the working up of sufficient lather. Finely finished and embossed. Price **12c**
If by mail, postage extra, 3 cents.

SHAVING BRUSHES AND SOAP

Reliable Aluminum Shaving Brushes, Sold Only by Us.

They are made by a special process. The bristles are put together under a heavy pressure and cemented with a special waterproof cement, and the heavy aluminum ferrule is further clinched over the bristles in such a manner as to absolutely guarantee these brushes against shedding. There is no ferrule to crack, no twine to rot. They are the most durable and most sanitary brushes made. Reliable Aluminum Shaving Brushes are sold only by us.

No. 6L18544 Reliable Aluminum Ferrule Shaving Brush, with best selected white French bristles, 1⅞ inches long, polished aluminum ferrule, black ebony handle. Guaranteed not to shed bristles. Price..... **14c**
If by mail, postage extra, 5 cents.

No. 6L18548 Reliable Aluminum Ferrule Shaving Brush with selected white French Bristles, 2¼ inches long, buffed aluminum ferrule, finely finished black ebony handle, an extra full sized brush intended especially for barbers' use. Price...... **22c**
If by mail, postage extra, 5 cents.

No. 6L18551 Our Kant Kum Out Brush. Solid brass ferrule, heavily nickel plated. Flat end ebonized handle. A feature much desired by private users. Genuine French bristles, non-shed, are 2 inches long. Diameter at ferrule, 15-16 inch. Entire length, 3½ inches. For utility and finish this brush cannot be excelled. Price.. **21c**
If by mail, postage extra, 5 cents.

No. 6L18552 Shaving Brush. Genuine horn ferrule boxwood handle. Genuine French bristles, guaranteed not to split or lose bristles. Length of bristles, 2¼ inches. Diameter at ferrule, ¾ inch.
Price....(Postage extra, 5 cents.).... **20c**

No. 6L18554 Our Wire Ferrule Shaving Brush, with brown enameled handle, selected white French bristles. The ferrule is enameled wire, making this brush far superior to the wood ferrule brushes, which swell and crack. A good, serviceable brush. Length of bristles, 1⅞ inches. Diameter of brush at ferrule, ¾ inch. Price **9c**
If by mail, postage extra, 3 cents.

No. 6L18559 Non-Shed Barbers' Brush, twine bound, walnut handle. Fine boiled French bristles, reinforced with patent metal plate under twine, which prevents corrosion or fouling. Will wear to ferrule and not lose a bristle. A favorite with barbers. Length of bristles, 2½ inches. Diameter of ferrule, 1 inch.
Price.............................. **34c**
If by mail, postage extra, 4 cents.

No. 6L18572 Our Fancy Handle Lily White French Bristle Shaving Brush, with fine white bone handle, ferrule of pure, natural black horn. This is a very neat, handsome brush, guaranteed not to spread, swell or crack, and will give satisfaction. Length of bristles, 2¼ inches. Length of entire brush, 5 inches. Diameter of ferrule, ⅞ inch.
Price............................ **24c**
If by mail, postage extra, 3 cents.

No. 6L18574 Midget Badger Shaving Brush. For the man who prefers a small brush, we recommend the Midget Badger. It is sufficiently large to work properly, and at the same time has not that bulk that most people object to. This is a very neat brush, made of pure badger bristle, fine horn ferrule, cocobolo handle; length over all, 3½ inches; diameter of ferrule, ⅞ inch. Price..... **47c**
If by mail, postage extra, 3 cents.

China Shaving Mugs.

No. 6L18490 Carlsbad China Shaving Mug. Floral decorations. Gold trimmed. Price, **12c**
If by mail, postage extra, 15 cents.

No. 6L18492 Genuine Austrian China Shaving Mug. Beautiful floral decorations. Heavily gold decorated.
Price **24c**
If by mail, postage extra, 16 cents.

No. 6L18578 Pure Badger Hair Brush. Our latest design. Double octagon white bone handle, with black horn ferrule. The bristles in this brush are guaranteed genuine badger hair and are 2 inches long. Diameter of ferrule, ¾ inch. This brush is guaranteed to give satisfaction. Price.... **72c**
If by mail, postage extra, 5 cents.

Rubberset Brush.

No. 6L18579 The celebrated Rubberset Pure Badger Hair Shaving Brush. The bristles are vulcanized together with rubber cement under heavy pressure, and the brush is absolutely guaranteed not to shed. Made with fancy hard rubber ferrule and cut bone handle. Entire length 4½ inches; length of bristles, 1¾ inches.
Price............................ **77c**
If by mail, postage extra, 5 cents.

No. 6L18582 Genuine Badger Hair Folding Handle Travelers' or Tourists' Shaving Brush. As shown in the illustration, this brush can be folded and the bristles placed in the hollow nickel plated handle. There are cheaper shaving brushes of this kind on the market, but we know the traveler has great need for a perfect brush, and we offer this brush as being the best folding brush on the market, or your money refunded. The bristles of this brush are guaranteed genuine badger hair, the handle and ferrule made of brass, heavily nickel plated. Length of brush complete, 4½ inches; length when folded, 2½ inches. Price... **34c**
If by mail, postage extra, 3 cents.

Shavade.

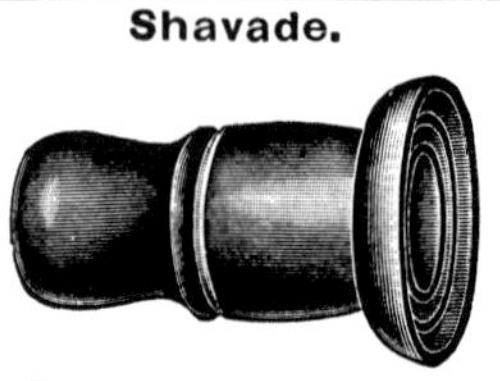

No. 6L18583 A valuable assistant to **the barber, or for private use,** to rub in lather and soften the beard. Made of pure red rubber, with black ebonoid handle. Apply lather with brush in the usual manner, then use Shavade. Has three deep, circular edges in cup, or bulb, which serve to rub in the lather and soften the beard. With the use of this little article, shaving is greatly facilitated. A smooth, velvet shave is guaranteed, and you will be surprised how well your razor cuts after your beard is thoroughly softened. Length over all, 2¼ inches; weight, 1 ounce.
Price **14c**
If by mail, postage extra, 2 cents.

Williams' Shaving Soap.

The Genuine World Renowned Standard Shaving Soap.

Williams' Shaving Soap, finest made, 6 cakes to pound.

No. 6L18595 Williams' Shaving Soap. Price, per pound....... **35c**
If by mail, postage extra, 20 cents.

No. 6L18596 Williams' Shaving Soap, per 10-pound box **$3.25**

Williams' Shaving Sticks

Genuine Williams' Shaving Sticks. In leatherette box; handy when traveling; also for home use. No waste; always clean and ready for use.

No. 6L18597 Williams' Shaving Sticks. Price, per box....... **18c**
If by mail, postage extra, 5 cents.

Armour's Shaving Soap.

Manufactured by Armour & Co. Very popular with barbers throughout the United States. Guaranteed not to dry on the face; will work up into a rich, smooth, creamy lather.

No. 6L18598 Armour's Supercream, six cakes to the pound, price per pound, **27c**
If by mail, postage extra, 20 cents.

Aluminum Shaving Mugs.

Engraving initials on aluminum shaving mugs, extra, per letter, 5 cents.

No. 6L18496 Pure Aluminum Shaving Mugs. Size, 3¼ x 3¼ inches. Cast aluminum handles strongly riveted to cup. Satin finish body neatly engraved. Bead and band polished bright. Very strong and serviceable. Price....... **40c**
If by mail, postage extra, 8 cents.

No. 6L18498 Pure Aluminum Shaving Mugs, ebony finished body, neatly engraved. Rim and bead polished bright. A very neat design. Price..... **44c**
If by mail, postage extra, 9 cents.

RAZOR STROPS.

The best razor is no good without a first class strop.

No. 6L18653 Belt Two-Side Extension Razor Strop. A fair grade strop. Full length, 13 inches. Price **23c**
If by mail, postage extra, 10 cents.

No. 6L18655 The Twentieth Century Cushion Razor Strop, one of the finest cushion strops made. It has a stropping surface of 8½ inches, length over all 13 inches. One side fine heavy red leather for honing, the other side white buff for finishing. Heavy wire handle, wire bound, giving this strop protection and strength, a feature not found in ordinary cushion strops. Weight, 7¼ ounces. Price **49c**
If by mail, postage extra, 10 cents.

No. 6L18656 Combination Four-Side Extension Razor Strop with cushion buff. A fine strop. Full length, 13 inches. Price, **35c**
If by mail, postage extra, 12 cents.

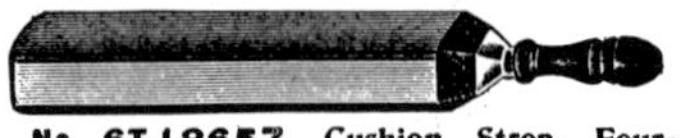

No. 6L18657 Cushion Strop, Four-Side. This is a very superior strop of this old favorite style, solid enameled wood handle. Full length, 14 inches. Price **52c**
If by mail, postage extra, 14 cents.

Freeman's Celebrated Metallic Strop, 64 Cents.

No. 6L18660 Patent Metallic Strop, for razors and surgical instruments, will quickly put a razor in condition to split a hair and shave easy, sharp as the best hone without its harshness. You cannot spoil your razor with this strop. Full length, 13 inches.
Price.............................. **64c**
If by mail, postage extra, 7 cents.

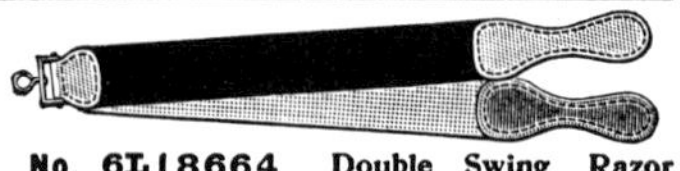

No. 6L18664 Double Swing Razor Strop, black leather on one side, tubular cotton hose on the other; has swivel and stitched fashioned handle. Width, 2 inches; entire length, 22½ inches. Price **23c**
If by mail, postage extra, 6 cents.

No. 6L18665 Double Swing Razor Strop. Porpoise hide oil finished leather on one side and prepared tubular cotton hose on the other; has a swivel and fashioned handle. Width, 2 inches; entire length, 23 inches.
Price.............................. **34c**
If by mail, postage extra, 6 cents.

No. 6L18667 Our 50-Cent Leader. This is the greatest value for the money ever offered in a razor strop. This is a double swing strop. Special porpoise hide, oil finished leather on one side and extra prepared webbing on the other. Has swivel and padded leather handle. Width, 2⅜ inches; entire length, 24 inches. Price.............. **50c**
If by mail, postage extra, 7 cents.

No. 6L18672 Double Swing Strop. Porpoise hide, oil finished leather on one side and pure Irish linen hose, prepared and polished, on the other. **Nickel plated removable swivel, fashioned handle.** A fine strop for professional barbers. Width, 2⅜ inches; entire length, 25 inches. Price **75c**
If by mail, postage extra, 9 cents.

Double Swing Horsehide, $1.00

No. 6L18676 Double Swing Strop, very extra quality, satin finished **genuine horsehide leather** on one side and pure Irish linen hose, prepared and polished, on the other. **Removable nickel plated swivel, fashioned handle.** A superior strop, good and durable, for any use. Width, 2⅜ inches; entire length, 25 inches.
Price....(Postage extra, 8c.).... **$1.00**

No. 6L18680 Single Swing Barbers' Strop, porpoise hide, oil finished prepared leather. The strop that barbers buy. **Fashioned handle and eyelet.** Width, 2⅜ inches; entire length, 24 inches. Price **26c**
If by mail, postage extra, 4 cents.

SHAVING OUTFITS.

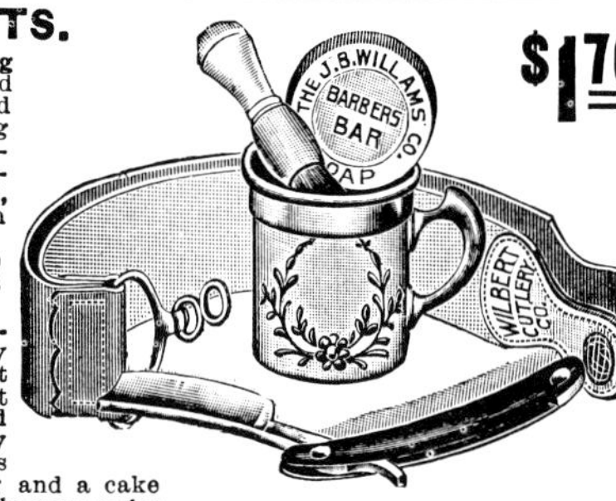

$1.70

No. 6L18372 Our Acme Shaving Set consists of a high grade hollow ground razor, a good double swing horsehide and prepared web razor strop, a good shaving brush, a seamless hand engraved aluminum shaving mug, and a cake of Williams' Yankee shaving soap. **Remember, the razor is fully warranted.** Put up in neat paper box.
Price, complete set..............**$1.70**
We cannot furnish made to order razors with shaving outfits.

No. 6L18378 Our Bon Ton Shaving Set consists of your choice of any razor quoted by us, at $2.00 or less, except the made to order razor, which we do not furnish with outfits, a good leather and prepared web double swing strop, a fancy celluloid handle shaving brush, a seamless hand engraved aluminum shaving mug and a cake of Williams' Yankee shaving soap. Make your order for the above shaving set thus: "No. 6L18378, 1 shaving set with No.......... razor, filling in the blank with the catalogue number of the razor you select. Put up in neat black pasteboard box.
Price for complete set..............**$2.69**

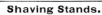

Shaving Sets.

$1.75

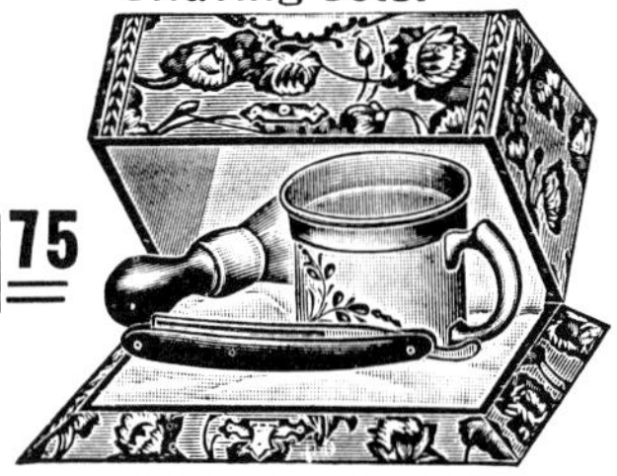

No. 6L18386 Our Celluloid Shaving Set. Fancy shaped shaving case with handsome celluloid decoration on top; sides, back and bottom of case handsomely embossed in fancy design. Full satin lined, with large mirror inside of cover. This set contains one satin finished, nicely decorated aluminum shaving mug, one aluminum ferrule shaving brush with best French white bristles, one good grade hollow ground German razor. A very handsome, serviceable set. Size of case, 4¾ inches high, 8½ inches long, 6½ inches wide. Shipping weight, 32 ounces.
Price, per set..............**$1.75**
If by mail, postage extra, 37 cents.

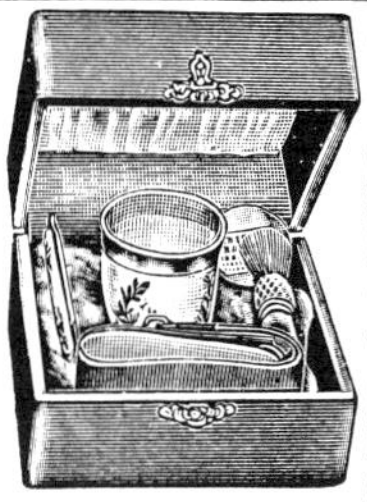

No. 6L18395 Our Figaro Shaving Set consists of one Figaro genuine Solingen razor, a double swing strop, an engraved pure aluminum shaving mug, a Raven razor hone, a good quality lather brush and a cake of Williams' Yankee shaving soap. All in neat imitation leather case. The best assortment ever offered in a shaving set. Dimensions of case, 9x9x5 inches.
Price for complete set..............**$4.20**
If by mail, postage extra, 60 cents.

Oak Case Travelers' Set, $3.27.

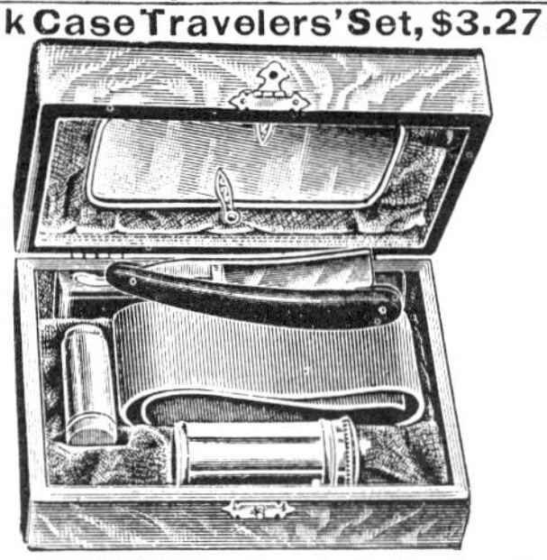

No. 6L18396 Travelers' Shaving Set, put up in a compact, finely finished oak case, 7¼ inches long, 5¼ inches wide and 2½ inches high. The case contains one famous BISMARCK Razor, one genuine badger hair folding shaving brush with brass ferrule and handle finely nickel plated, one highest quality single swing shell horsehide strop, one stick of best shaving soap in nickel plated screw top box, and one 5¾-inch shaving mirror with imitation tortoise shell back, which can be either hung or stood up. This is a high grade shaving set; every article in this set is of highest quality. We guarantee this set to give satisfaction or money refunded. Price, per set......**$3.27**
If by mail, postage extra, 40 cents.

Shaving Mirror.

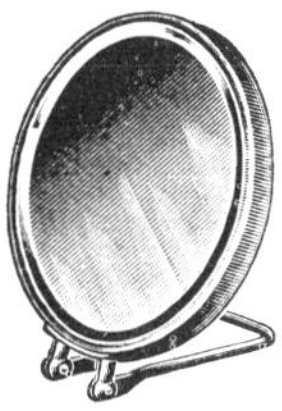

No. 6L18400 Shaving Mirror. Can be hung up or stood on table with glass tilted at various angles. This mirror is of imported French plate with heavy bevel, 6 inches in diameter, mounted in brass frame, heavily nickel plated. A high class mirror.
Price..............**$1.35**
If by mail, postage extra, 18 cents.

Shaving Stands.

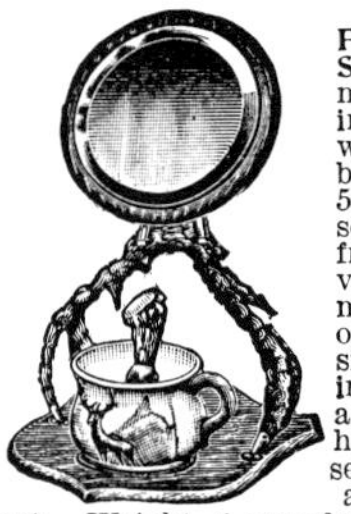

No. 6L18402 French Stag Shaving Stand. The mirror is mounted on handsome imitation stag antlers with hardwood base board. The mirror is 5 inches in diameter, set in a fine hardwood frame, adjustable to various angles. The mug is handsomely decorated with stag design. Badger brush with imitation stag handle and fine gilt ferrule. A handsome, ornamental, serviceable set. Weight, 4 pounds.
Price..............**$1.90**

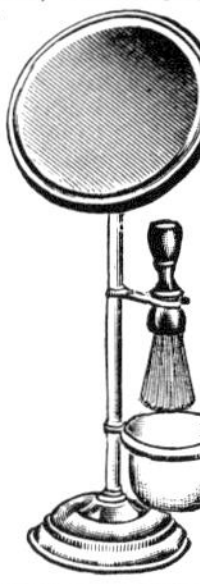

No. 6L18404 Our Nickel Frame Shaving Stand. Fine French 6-inch glass, nicely beveled, mounted on nickel plated brass frame, adjustable to any height from 10½ to 17 inches and at various angles. As illustrated, this stand has brackets which hold a fine white bristle, ebony handle shaving brush and an opaque removable shaving mug. Strong, durable and handsome. Weight, 5¼ pounds.
Price..............**$2.05**

Ever Ready Safety Razor Outfit.
TWELVE BLADES.

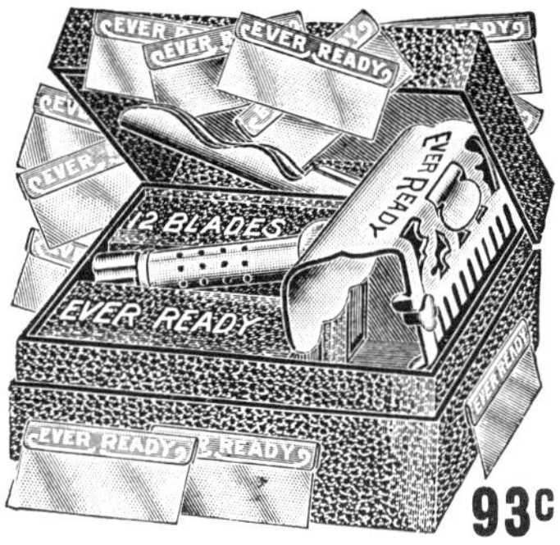

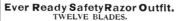

93c

No. 6L18421 The Improved Ever Ready Safety Razor Outfit with twelve blades at 93 cents. We furnish the safety razor frame with handle and holder for stropping the blades and twelve blades complete in a neat imitation leather case, as illustrated. The blades may be stropped and honed same as any blade, if desired.
Price, complete outfit, as described......**93c**
If by mail, postage extra, 6 cents.

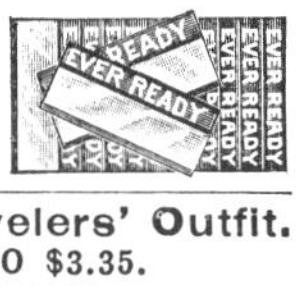

No. 6L18422 Extra blades for the Ever Ready Safety Razor.
Price, per dozen..**58c**
If by mail, postage extra, 2 cents.

Ever Ready Travelers' Outfit.
REDUCED TO $3.35.
TWELVE BLADES.

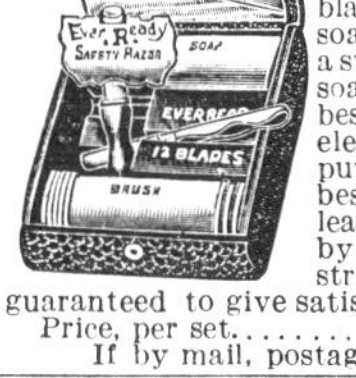

No. 6L18424 The Ever Ready Travelers' Outfit. One ebony handle safety razor with twelve blades, one nickel plated soap holder, containing a stick of the best shaving soap, one nickel plated best quality folding travelers' shaving brush, put up in a silk lined, best quality black grain leather case, 5 inches long by 3 inches wide. This is strictly a high grade set guaranteed to give satisfaction.
Price, per set..............**$3.35**
If by mail, postage extra, 15 cents

WE DO NOT EXCHANGE NEW SAFETY RAZOR BLADES FOR OLD ONES

Superior Safety Razor.

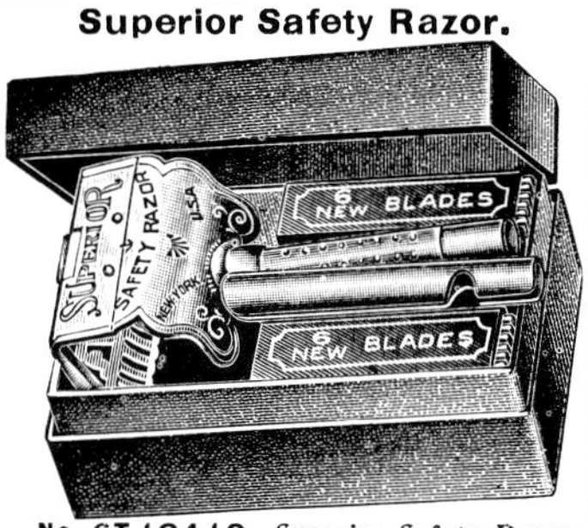

No. 6L18412 Superior Safety Razor, 75 cents. This is the first time a high quality safety razor with 12 flexible steel blades, which can be stropped and honed, has ever been offered at any such price. This razor is made specially for us of the best of material. The frame is of improved construction, rigid and strong, no hinges to break, no parts to get lost, easily cleaned, made of brass, highly nickel plated, complete with extra stropping handle. The price of 75 cents includes 12 keen, finely tempered and ground blades, which can be honed and stropped, the same as the blade on a regular razor. Each blade is guaranteed to give from 12 to 20 shaves without requiring honing or stropping. This razor is sent on 30 days' trial, and if found unsatisfactory for any reason it may be returned and money and transportation charges will be cheerfully refunded. Each razor is put up complete with 12 blades and an extra stropping handle in a neat box. Price..**75c**
If by mail, postage extra, 6 cents.

No. 6L18413 Extra blades for Superior Razor. Price, per dozen..............**45c**

Superior Travelers' Case, Price, $3.00.
TWELVE BLADES.

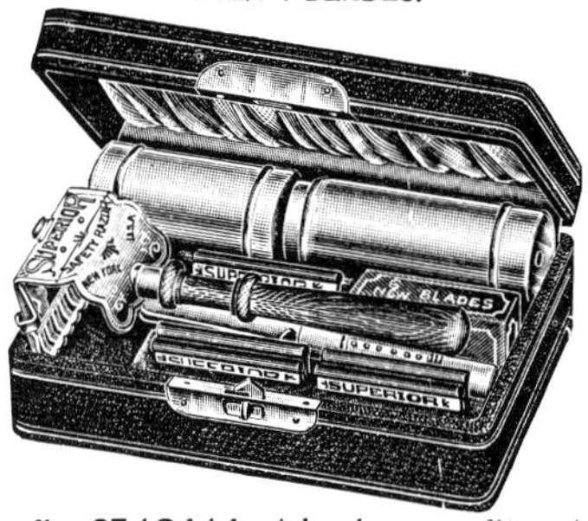

No. 6L18414 A handsome outfit, put up in a fine leather covered box, 5 inches long, 3½ inches wide, 1½ inches high, lined with blue satin and velvet, containing one Superior Razor with specially finished hardwood handle, one extra stropping handle, one fine badger folding shaving brush, one stick of shaving soap and 12 blades. This is a high quality set and, at our price of $3.00, most extraordinary value. An excellent set for home use and for the traveler, and makes a beautiful present. Price..........**$3.00**
If by mail, postage extra, 13 cents.

The New Wilbert Safety Razor
IMPROVED MODEL.

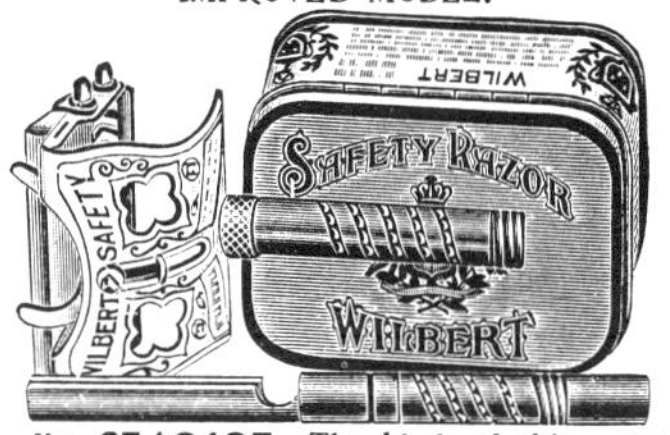

No. 6L18437 The blade of this razor is the same thickness as a blade of a regular razor, it is a hand forged, ground on a small stone, tempered and finished in the same manner as the highest priced razor on the market. **This blade can be stropped and honed the same as the regular blade.** The solid one-piece frame of the Wilbert Razor is strong and rigid. Two-jointed nickel plated handle with additional joint to hold blade for stropping. Each razor is put up in a neat metal case with complete instructions. We guarantee every Wilbert Razor to be perfect in material, finish and workmanship, and to give the user a clean, comfortable shave, or the razor can be returned to us and your money and transportation charges will be cheerfully refunded. It is impossible to cut yourself with a Wilbert Razor. Price..**94c**
If by mail, postage extra, 6 cents.

No. 6L18438 Extra blades for the Wilbert Razor. Price, each..............**50c**
If by mail, postage extra, 3 cents.

The Wilbert Stropping Machine Reduced to 80 Cents.

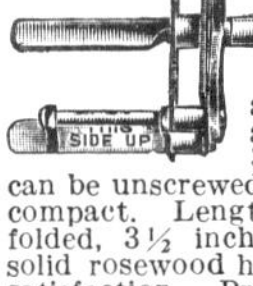

No. 6L18439 No better stropping machine made. Will strop blades for the Wilbert, Winner, Yankee and Star; in fact, will strop any razor blades from 1-16 to 3-16 inch thick. The handle can be unscrewed, making this machine very compact. Length, 6 inches. Length, when folded, 3½ inches. Fine nickel plated with solid rosewood handle. Guaranteed to give satisfaction. Price..............**80c**
If by mail, postage extra, 7 cents.

Wilbert Safety Razor Set.

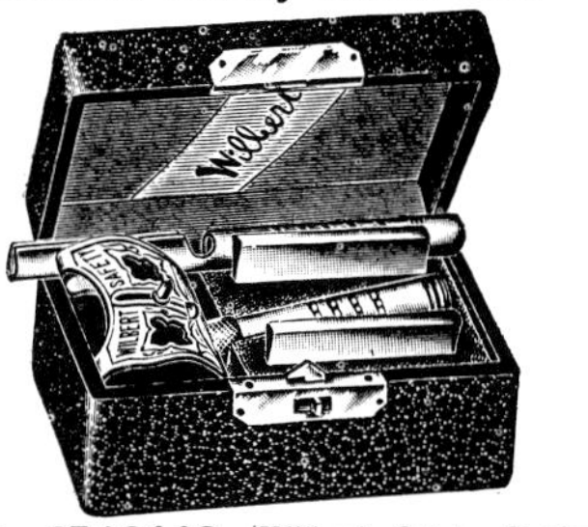

No. 6L18442 Wilbert Safety Razor Set, consisting of Wilbert Safety Razor and two blades. Put up in fine hinge cover imitation morocco leather case, lined with satin and chamois skin. An excellent set for the traveler. It also makes a handsome present.
Price..............**$2.00**
If by mail, postage extra, 6 cents.

Wilbert Combination Set.

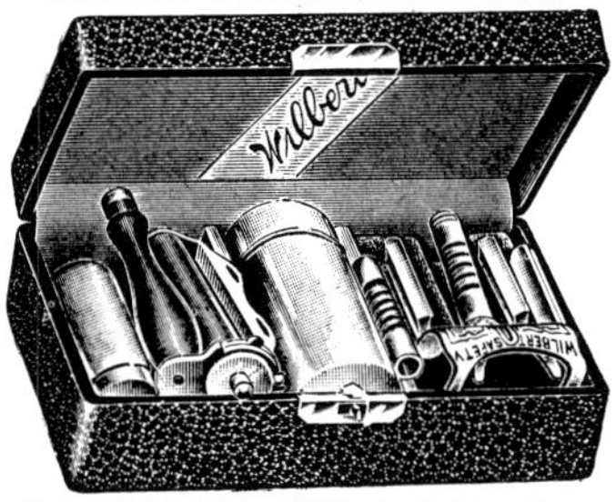

No. 6L18444 Wilbert Safety Razor Combination Set, consisting of high grade Wilbert Safety Razor, two blades, stropping machine, one best quality genuine badger hair folding handle shaving brush and one stick of best shaving soap in fine nickel plated tube. This set is put up in a fine satin lined imitation morocco case, hinge cover, patent clasp. A handsome and serviceable set.
Price..............**$3.65**
If by mail, postage extra, 14 cents.

Safety Razor Double Swing Strop, 40 Cents.

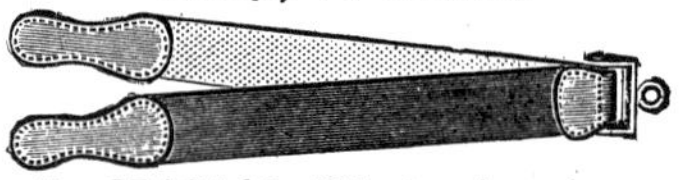

No. 6L18440 This strop is made specially for safety razors, such as the Star, Wilbert, Ever Ready, and any of the forged blade safety razors. It has just the right width and length to properly strop a safety razor blade. Double swing. One side finest quality Irish linen, specially prepared to put a keen edge on a razor; the other side of selected shell horsehide for finishing. Fitted with sewed leather handle, sewed leather end and nickel-plated swivel. Length of stropping surface, 12 inches; length over all, 18 inches.
Price..............**40c**
If by mail, postage extra, 5 cents.

Autostrop Safety Razor, $5.00.

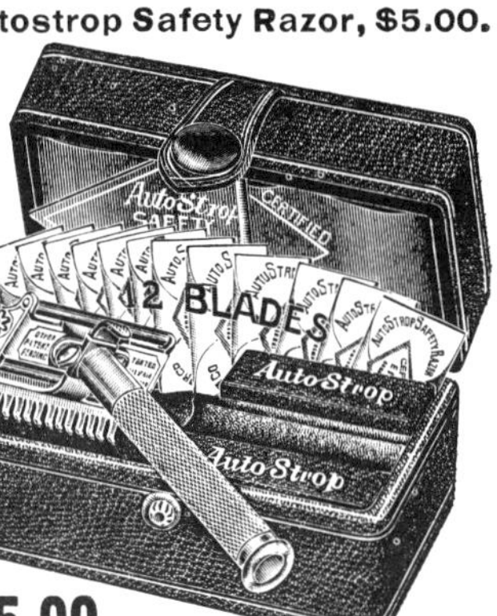

$5.00

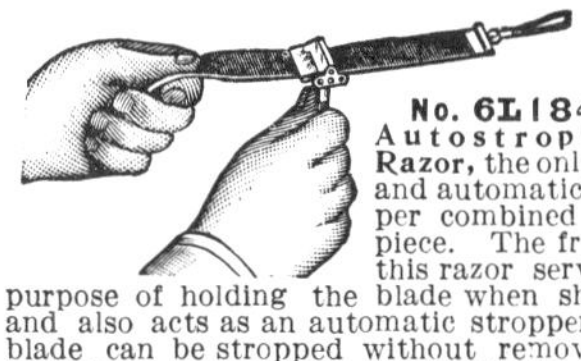

No. 6L18473 Autostrop Safety Razor, the only razor and automatic stropper combined in one piece. The frame of this razor serves the purpose of holding the blade when shaving, and also acts as an automatic stropper. The blade can be stropped without removing it from the frame by inserting the flexible horsehide strop which accompanies each razor, between the two rollers at the back end of the blade. This set consists of one finely silver plated frame, twelve blades, and one first quality horsehide strop, all packed complete in a handsome leather case.
Price, postpaid..............**$5.00**

No. 6L18474 Extra blades for Autostrop Razor.
Price, per dozen blades..........**50c**
If by mail, postage extra, per doz., 4 cents.

You see here a remnant of steel ribbon, from which "GILLETTE" blades have been stamped.

Over four and a half miles in length of this ribbon passes through my presses each day in order to supply the demand for the Gillette Razor. This makes more than one hundred and fifty thousand (150,000) blades, each having two sharp edges, which represent nearly seven miles of razor edge turned out by my factories daily.

To accomplish this requires six acres of floor space, upwards of twelve hundred people and more than five hundred special machines.

These little blades have solved the problem of sanitary self-shaving—saving time, money and labor. That is why every man should shave himself with the "GILLETTE."

The Gillette Safety Razor consists of triple silver plated holder — 12 double-edged blades, packed in velvet lined leather case. Price $5.00.

SOLD EVERYWHERE

Write for our Illustrated Booklet

GILLETTE SALES COMPANY

201 Times Building

NEW YORK CITY

Gillette Safety Razor
NO STROPPING NO HONING

KING CAMP GILLETTE

Safety Razors are not a modern concept. A "Hunting Razor" was advertised in the year 1800 as "Useful for the sea service, for young and timid shavers, for gentlemen with nervous complaints, or for hunters who wish to shave without leaving the saddle. Comes complete with six blades, being secured with a guard similar to a woodworking plane."

According to Phillip Krumholz, author of *A History of Shaving and Razors*, the first hoe-shaped safety razor patented in the United States was developed before 1880 by the brothers Otto and Frederick Kampfe. Oliver Wendell Holmes endorsed their "Star" safety razor and launched the Kampfe brothers on the road to a fortune.

The first customers for these new hoe-shaped safety razors were traveling salesmen who often had to shave while riding in rocking railroad cars, not knowing when they might find the next barbershop.

Imitators followed, trying to duplicate Otto and Fred's success. Dr. Scott's "Magnetic Safety Razor" was widely advertised in the early 1890's for $3.00 postpaid to any address. It consisted of an electrically charged safety razor with a wedge-shaped single-edged blade. The good doctor also marketed "electric" hair brushes, corsets, belts and tooth brushes; all imprinted with lightning bolts and the motto "The germ of all life is electricity."

King Camp Gillette claimed to have suddenly conceived the idea of a *disposable-bladed* safety razor while shaving (with a dull straight razor) one morning in 1895. More than likely, however, is the probability that he was very well acquainted with the safety razor patents of previous inventors and went on to develop his own concept of an extra thin throw-away blade with two edges instead of one.

Gillette was the son of a hardware supply store owner, who was also the town's postmaster. From early childhood King Camp loved to take things apart. As a young man he drifted from job to job, a dreamer of utopian ideals and also an industrial inventor of sorts. Gillette traveled through England selling Sapolio scouring powder, just before coming home to marry the daughter of a rich oil man. Always the dreamer, Gillette was torn between promoting his utopian concept of a giant "World Corporation" (whose stock would be held by all mankind) and a strong desire to get rich quick by inventing something disposable.

To identify a potentially profitable product with worldwide appeal, King leafed through a dictionary until he hit "R" for razor. Later he carved a wooden model and began an eight-year search for a cheap, long lasting, disposable blade.

He began experimenting with coils of a sheet-steel-ribbon used for clock springs; but several years passed and he still had not found an inexpensive metal that would retain a fine cutting edge. King persisted, as he said later, "Blessed by an ignorance of metallurgy."

Finally he humbly enlisted the help of an inventor, and engineering professor, named William Nickerson. Mr. Nickerson widened Gillette's narrow blade design and made the handle of heavier stock, which permitted the fine blade adjustment necessary for successful shaving.

Nickerson worked for months to develop a machine to harden and sharpen the clock-spring steel to a razor edge, only six thousandths of an inch thick. A grateful Gillette gave Nickerson a piece of the action and they quickly lined up financial backers.

The partners opened for business above a Boston fish market in 1903. Their first year's production was 51 razors and 168 blades. The next year production rose to an astonishing 90,000 razors and 2.4 million blades. Within a few years the Gillette Safety Razor Company had grown to cover five acres of land and to employ 2,000 workers.

The messianic message of King Camp Gillette was that "Every man should shave himself." A 1906 magazine ad by Gillette decried the customary men's social hour as a huge waste of our national resources, saying: "If all the time, money, energy and brainpower which are wasted in the barbershops of America were applied in one direct effort, the Panama Canal could be dug in four hours."

During World War I, over three million safety razor kits were issued to our troops. The Golden Age of the barbershop in America was rapidly drawing to a close.

Before the war, a survey of barbers revealed that scraping whiskers accounted for more than half of their gross sales. By the year 1930, razor skills accounted for only ten percent of the take.

In a 1925 editorial printed in *Square Deal Magazine*, a barber trade journal, Fred Fitch summed up Gillette's invention as a lost sales opportunity. He said:

> If the profession had only realized its great opportunity and welcomed the coming of the safety razor by giving it a place in its showcases—every barbershop would now be a thriving retail store.

Safety Razors are hot collectibles. In a recent mail order auction conducted by barberiana specialist Sigmund Wohl (P. O. Box 429, Bronxville, NY), a gold-plated Gem safety razor with blade holders and celluloid handle, in its original circa 1912 box, sold for $160. At the same event a "Roberts" safety razor with pivoting head, in a fitted metal-lined case, dated 1/12/12 brought a winning bid of $122.

Other brands that could have been picked up at flea markets for fifty cents each, two or three years ago, *now sell in the $15 to $150 range*. Keep your eyes peeled for these trademarks: Dr. Scott's, Fox, Torrey, Gem wedge-blade, Arnold, G. Gillette's Eureka, Griffon, Home, Sestra, Never Fail, Bismark, Collins wind-up, Roberts, and Witte's Pride.

In addition to Phillip Krumholz's *Value Guide for Barberiana & Shaving Collectibles* (available from the author at Box 4050, Bartonville, IL), serious collectors will want to order his newest title, *The Complete Gillette Collector's Handbook* from the same address. (Phil also plans to update his 1987 encyclopedic work, *A History of Shaving and Razors*, which currently is out of print.)

Another book worth owning is the *Safety Razor Reference Guide*, published in 1990 by the Tanroe Company and available from the author, Robert K. Waits, 594 Endicott Drive, Sunnyvale, CA.

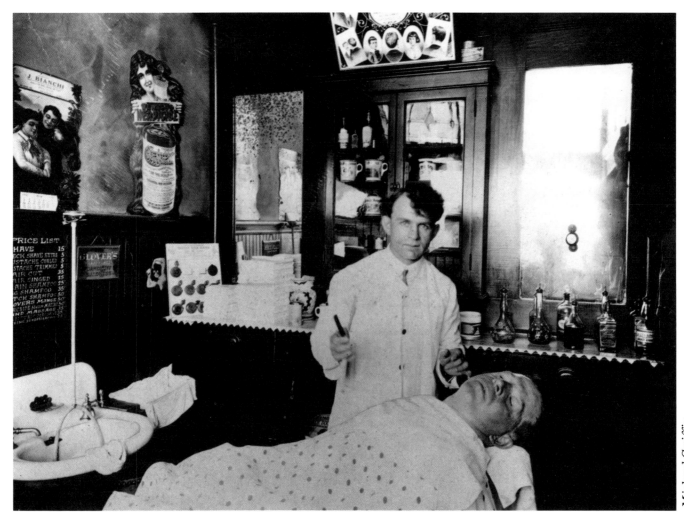

This San Francisco customer is "out like a light." The sign reads: Shave 15¢, Neck Shave (extra) 5¢, Mustache Curled 5¢, Mustache Trimmed 5¢, Hair Cut 35¢, Hair Singed 25¢, Plain Shampoo 25¢, Egg Shampoo 35¢, Fitch Shampoo 50¢, Hand Massage 35¢, Shaving on Sundays 25¢. The year is 1915, Johnnie Wilhelm, owner/barber.

The Brooklyn Eagle, July 4, 1908

Why a Good Many Men Take the Trouble To Shave Themselves.

Highly amusing that the first attack made upon candidate Taft charges him with declining to give a tip to the barber who cut his hair!

The fact is disclosed, also, that Mr. Taft always shaves himself. That is a mark of greatness not heretofore attributed to him. He is not the first man of great distinction who has refused to permit a barber to apply a razor to his face. Napoleon always shaved himself. His critics asserted that he was afraid conspirators would hire a barber to cut his throat. Perhaps there was foundation for the story. But several men are known to the writer who cannot stretch themselves in chairs, under barbers' razors, without suffering nervous attacks. One of them has told me that his disquiet is intense. He conjures up all manner of accidents that might occur to the workman while shaving his neck (like being bumped by a lather boy).

Another acquaintance retains a vivid memory of having been shaved by a barber not fully recovered from an attack of mania a potu. This fellow confidentially informed his customer that as soon as he finished with him he would cut the throat of an enemy who was awaiting his turn and always brought into the shop a volcano concealed in his coat pocket. The customer was asked to wait in the place until the barber enjoyed his long-contemplated revenge upon an enemy who constantly followed him about.

But there isn't any indication that lack of confidence in tonsorial artists causes Mr. Taft to shave himself. He prefers to do so. There are many reasons, including cleanliness and quickness, that justify him. If the barbers are to turn against the Republican candidate because he does not allow them to shave him, we may expect the keepers of public bathing establishments to join in the revolt, because, forsooth, Mr. Taft washes his body in his own tub!

Today, this 90-year-old morocco-covered shaving set might fetch $150 to $225 from a serious collector. It sold for $5 in 1905.

A "Lady Barber" takes a midday photo break in her neat and tidy Pennsylvania shop. The year is 1906. Over the door are photos of Presidents McKinley and Roosevelt. Decorating the walls are period advertising pieces that today's collectors would give a month's wages for.

Leslie's Weekly, Chicago, 1895: "I stopped to-day to get shaved at a tidy-looking barbershop with flowers in the window, and was struck in a heap when I found the barbers were all women—eight of them. I hadn't been barbered by a woman since my mother cut my hair. But it was all right. She didn't talk a bit. If I get sick we've got a woman doctor, and if I die, why, the sexton of our church—my wife's church, I should say—is a woman, so I suppose I'll be laid to rest, as I was first rocked to sleep, by a woman. Maybe it will be a woman, too, regularly, or-dained, who will say the last prayer at my grave."

The woman barber is, of course, a feature of special interest in this development of woman's activity in Chicago. If there ever was a prejudice against the applications of woman's taste and skill in this sphere of labor—and with old-fashioned folk that prejudice has undoubtedly been very pronounced—it has been effectively overcome with the lapse of time. As nothing succeeds like success, the time is probably not far distant when in our cities generally women will come into favor in this busi-ness, heretofore monopolized by the sterner sex.

And why not?

JOHN T. BRAMHALL.

Lipstick Container, circa 1890.

105

November 15, 1896

The San Francisco Examiner

WOMEN TAKE UP THE RAZOR.

More of the Fair Sex Who Are Entering the Business of Shaving Men's Grizzly Faces.

People have stopped wondering what woman will do next, for keeping up with what she is doing now takes all the public energies. Her latest audacity has been to lay hands on man's most sacred implements—the razor and strop—and to shave him right to his very face. And the strange part of it is that the man himself, now that he has caught his breath, rather likes the change, and sets out for the barber shop with a new expression of bland satisfaction and a startling expanse of clean collar. The very first time a man puts himself voluntarily under a woman's razor he generally does it out of curiousity, or for a bet, or to give a practical illustration of feminine incapability. He seats himself in the red velvet chair very much as though it were arranged for electrocution, and fixes a nonchalant eye on the ceiling to show that he is not nervous. He glances sharply at the tonsorial artist to see if she is laughing at him. But she is as grave and impersonal as though she were running a lawn mower, and as his self-respect begins to ooze back he suddenly realizes that he is being handled as he never was before. Light and firm and quick—no man ever had a touch like that, or ever will have. He closes his eyes with a long sigh of satisfaction, and this modern Delilah has added a new Samson to her list.

Of these lady barbers the most prominent may be found over on Howard street, not far from Fourth, in a modest little place, with the usual peppermint stick out in front and no sign to indicate the unexpected gender within.

Opening the door, I found myself in a narrow shop, exquisitely neat and quite unadorned. I had half feared that the decorative instinct, ever strong in women, would crop out in hand-painted pomade jars and red plush razor stands, but all was business-like, simplicity, unribboned and unfrilled. Four red velvet chairs attitudinized down the middle of the room, flanked by the necessary shelves and instruments, and facing a couple of long mirrors, and a modest price-list announced the different gradations from the ten-cent necessity of a shave to the twenty-five-cent luxury of a dyed moustache. Over the four chairs presided two young women in dark woolen dresses, big white aprons and turn-over white collars, looking as neat and business-like as their surroundings. One, a remarkably pretty brunette, was busy with a patient, or subject, or whatever the proper term is, but the other, a tall blonde, talked readily and pleasingly about the business.

"I don't know quite how I did come to go into it," she said. "I didn't like clerking and I couldn't cook and I wouldn't sew, and there didn't seem anything I could take hold of with any interest till a friend suggested this. I liked the idea, so about eight months ago I took the course at the barber's college, and then I worked some in a shop to get the experience, and then a couple of months ago my partner and I set up for ourselves. Of course, down here we can only charge 10 cents a shave, but in a 15-cent neighborhood we'd have to pay a 15-cent rent, and have things to correspond. We've built up a good business, and may have to take in a lady assistant before long."

"Weren't you nervous the first time you tried it?"

"I should say I was. I don't know which was trembling hardest, the man or I. It was my first day at the college, and I'd never had a razor in my hand before. Why, I'd always been afraid of them. You know at the college men get shaved for nothing by the students, and so they are ready to take the risk. If I could have chloroformed the man so that he wouldn't have looked so scared, I think I'd have been steadier, but I got through it all right, with the teacher to help out on the hard parts. It's all plain sailing

ant, for the Teuton closed his eyes with a beatific expression, as though he had at last found that ministering angel one reads about.

"Let me take your strop a moment. It is better than mine," said the blonde, and then they worked a few minutes in silence, while I watched and wondered. The brunette's razor gave an infintesimal slip.

"Oh!" she exclaimed remorsefully, lifting both hands and screwing up her face in an anguish of contrition. The man in the chair smiled.

Samson's words ran through my head: "If I be shaven I shall become weak and be like any other man." Delilah patted soothing things out of bottles onto the place where the wound might have appeared if it had been visible, and the blonde kept on shaving.

"Of course, your customers can't swear at you if you hurt them," I said, following a train of thought. "That must stand in the way of your business a little."

"They never do, certainly," said the blonde. "We never get anything but courtesy and kindness. Now and then, Saturday nights, a man comes in who has been drinking, but even those don't give us any trouble. You'd be surprised to see how hard they try to hide it. Lots of men come in just for the novelty of the thing, but they never bother us, and they most always come again. They're nervous the first time, but not the second, and they often settle down into regular patrons. We don't have much to contend with. We are the only lady barbers in the city who have our own establishment. There's one who works in a shop around on Fourth street. Then there was a woman studying at the college who dressed exactly like a man. You really couldn't tell the difference. You could hardly count her as a lady barber, though."

"I don't see why she did it," said the brunette. "Why, she wouldn't get any more custom than if she were a man. Next!"

The shop around the corner of Fourth street was still in the hands of the old-fashioned denomination of barber, though one plump, reserved little woman stood, razor in hand, within the entrenchments, a skirmisher from the great body of women who scan the horizon day and night for signs of a new career. In her case the magnetic attraction of the barber pole was easily understood, for it had stood for the profession of her husband and her father. It ran in the family, she said, and her deftness was a matter of inheritance. She had played in the shop as a little girl, she had shampooed her unappreciative kitten, and shaved her dolls, irrespective of sex. Razors had no terrors for her, and the brightest scissors round her crown could not make her wince. She needed no college education to teach her the geography of the human chin, for her childhood had been one long object lesson in its ways and peculiarities.

"Customers are just as ready to come to me as they are to the men in the shop," she said. "Some begin out of curiosity, just to see how it feels to be shaved by a woman; but after trying it once or twice they don't find it queer any more. They are always very kind and nice, but I don't talk while I work. If they ask anything of course I answer, but I don't see the need of carrying on a conversation. A woman has to be careful. I've never had any disagreeable experiences in my business, and I don't think any one need who knows how to behave. It all depends on yourself. No; I don't believe there are any other lady barbers besides the two on Howard street. There were two others, but they have just gone up to Eureka to start a shop. They will make a good thing of it, for you never get less than 15 cents a shave up there, and they have friends to help them. You may find some one studying up at the college."

The Barbers' College at present boasts just one feminine student, and I was fortunate enough to find her—a tall, bright-faced woman with a nimbus of little frizzes and an irresistable sense of humor. She had gone into the career in all seriousness, but the droll side of it was always present to her.

"I'd never touched a razor before I came to the college," she said. "I've got ten brothers, but they all shave out—all but two—who have not got anything to shave yet. The students generally spend the first day learning to hone and strop and getting their tools in order, but mine were all right by 11 o'clock, and I started in as cool as you please. Well, out of the nine men I shaved that day I cut eight. The first one I got along beautifully with, but the second had a sort of an unexpected cheekbone which I wasn't looking out for, and I pretty nearly removed it for life. Was I scared! I just held him down and shouted for the professor, who came and finished up the man. I wouldn't touch him again, and he didn't seem anxious to have me. He couldn't say much, for, you see, we shave the unemployed up there, and when you don't pay you can't swear. I was pretty nervous after that, and so I cut the other seven, one right after the other. The next day I only cut four or five, and the next even less, but for a while I had to holler "Next!" a good many times before I could get a customer.

The report had spread around that I was a pretty good butcher I suppose."

Yes, they have come to stay and beard the lion, these petticoated barbers, and perhaps man, when he realizes their light touch and gentle handling, will rise up and call them blessed. It is a perfectly justifiable way of earning an honest living, and we could give it a hearty sanction if we were not just a little bit afraid of encouraging woman in her present rampant condition. She really must stop somewhere.

JULIET WILBOR TOMPKINS.

when you come down the cheek, like this, but when you go up on the other side it's backhand, and that's a different matter. The very hardest place is across the chin. They don't trust you with that right at first. I'm never a bit nervous any more, and nearly every man we shave says something how much lighter our touch is than the men barbers. Really, some do go at it as if they were sawing wood. It's a shame."

A large man, tall and Teutonic, entered just then, and planting himself in the nearest chair, turned up a quivering expanse of chin with an air of childlike confidence that was in itself a tribute to the enterprise. A shave of such dimensions might have daunted anyone, since it is not allowable to charge by the square foot, but the blonde lady barber fell to work with quiet unconcern, manipulating with light, sympathetic fingers, whose touch must have been very pleas-

THE FEMALE BARBER OF GALVESTON, TEXAS.

Frank Leslies Illustrated News, November 23, 1867

Madam Gardoni is doing a good business in Galveston, Texas, having taken up the razor for a living. She is the first woman who has successfully invaded this particular masculine business, and her customers praise the style in which she harvests the stubble from the face of men. She is a thirty-year-old immigrant employing two men to assist in her shop. A female barber would probably do well in New York City, if as good-looking. Fancy the sensation of being asked, in dulcet, flute-like tones, 'Does the razor pull, sir?''

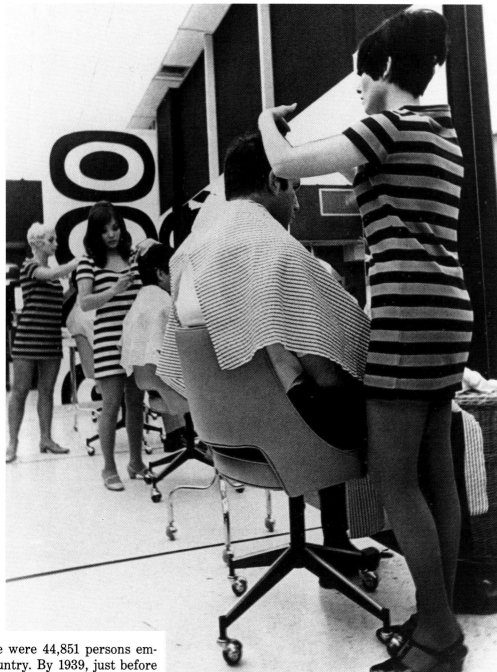

Beverly Hills, California Styling Salon, 1967.
—*Cleveland State University*

Postscript: In 1880, there were 44,851 persons employed as barbers in this country. By 1939, just before our entry into World War II, barber shops numbered about 122,000 nationwide. At the end of the war, only 92,000 remained in business.

Today's telephone book Yellow Pages list 62,034 barbershops and 288 barber schools in the United States. They are far outnumbered by beauty salons at 202,000, and beauty schools which total 2,729 nationwide. The state of New Jersey finally did away with its barber's apprenticeship program in 1984; it was the last state to do so. Since then, all new licensees have practiced a combination of both the barbers' and beauticians' trades as *cosmetologists/hairstylists*. No longer does the skill of haircutting alone suffice for a tonsorial certificate—sixty percent of today's graduates are of the fairer sex.

Yes, folks, old-time barbers are fast going the way of saloon keepers, livery stable owners, sideshow operators, coach painters, barrel makers, umbrella repairmen, tinsmiths, wheelwrights, handbill posters and barn painters. Grab your souvenirs now, tomorrow may be too late!

ANTIQUE SHAVING MUGS

Phil and John Eisemann's 1902 tonsorial parlor served as a showcase for their custom mug decorating and barber supply business. By 1920 the colorful shaving mugs had disappeared from barber shops. —*Dan Rader*

The hand basin and soap ball were used in England until the late 1600s and in primitive societies for the next 300 years. Early street barbers used their fingers to apply a lather which was probably more germ-free than that produced later by mug and brush. The chief advantage of a mug was that most of the soap stayed in the bottom for use on the next customer.

In the 1840's American barber-supply houses began to import fancy scented "shaving compounds" (soap) from France and England. These shaving creams were packaged in 3-inch-diameter porcelain containers embellished with elaborate advertising messages. By 1870, most of these lidded "boxes" had disappeared from the market, being replaced by paper-wrapped soap, made for use in shaving mugs.

Before individual shaving mugs were first introduced in the 1870s, most patrons shared a common cup and brush. The practice of decorating "private" mugs with occupational or fraternal designs, in addition to the owner's name, may have evolved from the few personalized porcelain soap boxes and barber basins which had been imported to America from Europe in the 1860s. In any event, millions of these custom painted mugs were sold before the widespread use of safety razors finally put most barbers out of the shaving business.

In 1938, Katherine Morrison Kahle wrote an article on old-time shaving mugs which was published in *The Magazine Antiques* and they have been popular collectibles every since. By 1949, writer/collector Porter Ware had accumulated more than 500 different mugs and wrote the first book about them.

Occupational shaving mugs are the crown jewels of all barbershop collectibles. Prices range from $75 to $7,500. The rarer the trade depicted, the higher the price.

Hand-painted occupational mugs are excellent examples of American folk art. Although seldom one of a kind, each bears the individual sign-painter style of a workman who obviously did not attend a formal art school. Decals, touched up and embellished a bit, were used on cheaper grade mugs. Basic stock designs were applied using a paper stencil or a metal plate, and then painted with ceramic glazes and trimmed in liquid gold leaf. Two or three firing sessions in a gas kiln were followed by the burnishing of all gold leaf surfaces.

A photograph applied to a mug, or a mediocre design developed from a customer's sketch, would of course be unique, but not necessarily of great importance to a seasoned collector. *The overall decorative impact*, the rarity of the occupation depicted, and significant detail touches are the overriding value determining factors. Collectors simply call it "Eye Appeal."

As with all antiques that reach stratospheric prices, occupational shaving mugs have been widely reproduced.

One obvious clue that a mug is a reproduction is the telltale rectangular dot pattern of a silk screen transfer. A lack of wear marks or a uniformly bright gold rim should also invite careful scrutiny. Subtle pastels that *simulate faded colors* are clear clues to modern origin; genuine old occupational mugs were brightly colored, and their ceramic glazes rarely fade unless worn away or frequently washed in strong detergent. The owner's name should be well executed, not sloppy, but not too precise, either. (Examine an authentic collection.)

Shaving mugs came in three sizes: small, medium and large. Collectors seem to prefer heavy cups of the large size made in France or Germany. Scuttle-shaped mugs, with separate brush compartments, are among the most commonly seen and reproduced. The dainty, thin porcelain variety with two openings, can be found in antique shops for $25 to $150 each; but we have seen them sell for $12 each in box lots at barber shop memorabilia auctions. Silver-plated shaving mugs appear in giftware cataalogs of the 1880 to 1920 period. Very ornate Victorian examples are still available at $25 to $55 each. Common floral-decorated china mugs, with owners names intact, can be picked up at flea markets and collector conventions for $25 to $50. "Limoges, France" is the mark that puts them at the high end of this range.

Advertising-embellished mugs often sell for $50 to $150. Fraternal mugs also command $50 to $150 each.

Only two books on the subject are currently available: *Antique Shaving Mugs of the United States*, and *Occupational & Fraternal Shaving Mugs of the United States*. Both were written and published in the late 1970s by a leading expert in the field, Robert Blake Powell. They can still be ordered from Mr. Powell at Box 833, Hurst, TX.

The National Association of Shaving Mug Collectors has grown from its founding membership of fourteen collectors in 1980 to more than 400 barbershop memorabilia buffs today, according to the club's newsletter editor, Michael J. Griffin of White Plains, NY. The group's librarian, Maxine E. Cook, of Park Ridge, IL, provides photocopies of the club's extensive bibliographic archive to members for a nominal fee. To join NASMC, contact Penny Nader, treasurer, at 320 S. Glenwood St., Allentown, PA 18104.

Philip Eisemann epitomzied the barber supply trade at the turn of the century. He was a tall, confident, meticulously groomed salesman with twenty years of experience behind the chair. Philip and his brother John expanded their Lancaster, PA tonsorial parlor and mug decorating business to include all the tools (and tonics) of the trade, and began their new wholesale venture in 1902.

Every major city of that time supported at least half a dozen independent barber supply houses, servicing hundreds of retail shaving salons. It was very important that their salesmen look good, smell good, and be of sterling character. John and Philip filled the bill and their business prospered.

Philip Eisemann was born in 1864 in Lancaster, and began his barbering apprenticeship at the age of fifteen. His artistic bent led him into custom decorating shaving mugs for other barbers, and he also started a successful razor-grinding business.

Mr. Eisemann passed away in 1958 at the age of ninety-four, and is fondly remembered by those in the trade he so faithfully served.

Nº 533

Nº 534

Nº 535

Nº 536

Nº 537

Nº 538

Nº 539

Nº 540

Nº 541

Nº 542

Nº 543

Nº 544

Nº 545

Nº 546

Nº 547

Nº 548

Nº 549

Nº 550

No 551

No 552

No 553

No 554

No 555

No 556

No 557

No 558

No 559

No 560

No 561

No 562

Shaving Mugs were status symbols for barbers and customers alike. The number of mugs on display mirrored the size and quality of a barber's business.

The giant Koken Barber Supply Company of St. Louis was founded in 1874 by a young free-lance shaving mug decorator named Ernest E. Koken.

As you can see from the wholesale catalog pages reproduced here, barbers paid from fifty cents to two dollars for custom painted mugs. A four-hundred percent markup was plenty of incentive for them to badger their chair-bound customers into buying a private mug. The following story illustrates our point.

August 8, 1884

The New York Times

HE CONQUERED THE BARBER
THE STORY OF A GILT LETTERED MUG.

"The smile that I wear," said the youth, "is one of demoniac exultation. It signifies that I have just got the best of a barber, who long held me a victim. Would'st hear the tale of my thralldom? Then listen!

"Four years ago, when I first came to live in New York, I was so very fresh and ignorant of the ways of the world that I allowed barbers to converse with me as they operated upon my countenance. It seemed to me then to be a very discourteous thing when a barber shoved the end of a towel down under my collar, gave me a thump in the chin to indicate that he would like me to put my head further back, and said it was a nice day, not to respond that it was quite pleasant, very pleasant indeed; in fact, about as

pleasant a day as we had had for a week. Then, if he continued talking about the weather, as he stuck his brush in my mouth, that I ought to buy a bottle of his hair preparation, I always felt obliged to stammer some excuse, while the lather ran down my throat, for not buying it, and the barber, realizing his power over me, talked and talked away, interspersing his thrilling tales of love and war with offers to sell me various toilet articles, all of which I refused in detail and felt that I was doing a very mean and small thing in so refusing.

"After I began to go to this barber shop," the young man continued, "the barber who claimed me there had but one object in life, one motive for existence, and that was to sell me a shaving mug for $2.50, and have my name put on it in gilt letters. I had no use for the mug, and did not have $2.50 that I wanted to throw away or I should have made the purchase only for peace with the artist. But every time I went into the shop, and that was about twice a week, that barber

insisted upon the necessity for my having a shaving mug, and begged, implored, and besought me to purchase it until I really felt that life was not worth living any longer. Finally, in desperation, I confided to my tormentor that I did not have the money then to buy the mug, and hoped that that plea would silence him. But it didn't. It had the reverse effect.

" 'You take de cup,' he said, 'and you pay for it when you get ready. I have your name put on; here it is! Vhen you get ready, den you pay for it.'

"I saw an opportunity for a slight reprieve from his importunities, and in a weak moment I agreed. Ah, how happy was my barber! To witness his hallowed joy was worth three times the price of the china vessel— particularly as I didn't pay for it—upon which my name soon shone resplendent in great gilt letters. Then how cheerfully he lathered my countenance therefrom, and how tenderly he shaved me for many weeks. But soon he began to desire to sell me some

117

hair invigorator dyes, shaving soaps, razors, and various other utensils on credit, and every time I was shaved he handed me a check for the mug as well as the shave. I would hand the check to the cashier and say 'I will pay the 15 cents only to-day. Just keep the other,' and he never objected for many a moon. At last the barber began to politely suggest that I pay for the mug, but I couldn't, of course, when I didn't have the money, and I began to think as I began to increase in worldly wisdom that it would serve that barber just about right if I never paid him, and as he had insisted, to begin with, that I needn't pay him until I was ready, it would be just as well for me never to get ready.

"Then there began a contest of politeness between the barber and myself. Every time I went into the shop he courteously hinted at the obligation under which I rested to the establishment, and I would gracefully put it off for some future time, and he would retire within himself with a smile on his face but venom in his soul, I well knew. Never did he use a discourteous word when he spoke of the amount due for the cup, and never did I speak harshly when I put off the payment into dim futurity.

"Thus matters went on for a year after I had assented to the purchase of the china vessel, and then I left the city. I have been gone three years, and in that time have been around the world, and have had myself shaved in every known language. I got back yesterday, and to-day I went into the old shop to be shaved. I had entirely forgotten the episode of the cup in the thrilling experiences I had been through since, and when the barber who shaved me remarked that it was a fine day, I closed him up with a sarcastic 'Who told you so?' and was shaved in silence. But when I received my check, lo! it was as of old for $2.65. In a moment the recollection flashed upon me, and I said calmly as of old: 'Just take 15 cents out of that. I'm not ready to pay the other yet.' Then I carelessly glanced around as I turned to go, and saw the barber who had sold me the cup four years ago before shaving a gentleman at the other end of the room. He scowled as he glanced at me, and I began to hope that I had accomplished my fond object and wearied out his patience. It seemed too good to be true, but I waited in the corridor until the gentleman whom he was shaving came forth. To him I explained the story, and, trembling with expectancy, I asked: 'Did he betray any emotion when I declined to pay the check?' 'Yes,' said my new acquaintance, 'he did.' He went on to inform me that the barber had sent the brush boy over to have the $2.50 added to my check. When the boy came back the barber had inquired eagerly:

" 'Bezahlt?'

" 'Nein,' replied the boy, 'Nicht bezahlt.'

" 'Dammerlungen!' the barber said in tones of bitter sorrow and heartrending despair.''

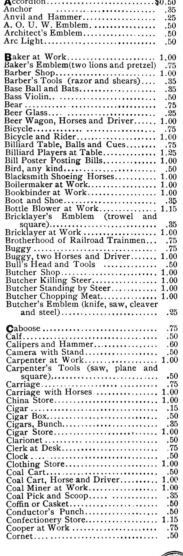

We can place upon a Shaving Mug and from our large selection of sketches c but if we should not have the especial de mug, reduced in size or enlarged, if a d Mug, large size, is the best style to use fo of our trade designs, and *these prices are to design is placed.*

Accordion	$0.50
Anchor	.35
Anvil and Hammer	.25
A. O. U. W. Emblem	.50
Architect's Emblem	.50
Arc Light	.50
Baker at Work	1.00
Baker's Emblem(two lions and pretzel)	.75
Barber Shop	1.00
Barber's Tools (razor and shears)	.35
Base Ball and Bats	.35
Bass Violin	.50
Bear	.75
Beer Glass	.25
Beer Wagon, Horses and Driver	1.00
Bicycle	.75
Bicycle and Rider	1.00
Billiard Table, Balls and Cues	.75
Billiard Players at Table	1.25
Bill Poster Posting Bills	1.00
Bird, any kind	.50
Blacksmith Shoeing Horses	1.00
Boilermaker at Work	1.00
Bookbinder at Work	1.00
Boot and Shoe	.35
Bottle Blower at Work	1.15
Bricklayer's Emblem (trowel and square)	.35
Bricklayer at Work	1.00
Brotherhood of Railroad Trainmen	.75
Buggy	.75
Buggy, two Horses and Driver	1.00
Bull's Head and Tools	.50
Butcher Shop	1.00
Butcher Killing Steer	1.00
Butcher Standing by Steer	1.00
Butcher Chopping Meat	1.00
Butcher's Emblem (knife, saw, cleaver and steel)	.25
Caboose	.75
Calf	.50
Calipers and Hammer	.60
Camera with Stand	.50
Carpenter at Work	1.00
Carpenter's Tools (saw, plane and square)	.50
Carriage	.75
Carriage with Horses	1.00
China Store	1.00
Cigar	.15
Cigar Box	.50
Cigars, Bunch	.35
Cigar Store	1.00
Clarionet	.50
Clerk at Desk	.75
Clock	.50
Clothing Store	1.00
Coal Cart	.50
Coal Cart, Horse and Driver	1.00
Coal Miner at Work	1.00
Coal Pick and Scoop	.35
Coffin or Casket	.50
Conductor's Punch	.50
Confectionery Store	1.15
Cooper at Work	.75
Cornet	.50

Cow	$0.75
Cowboy Lassoing Steer	2.00
Cyclinder Press	1.00
Deer	.50
Deer Head	.50
Dentist Drawing Teeth	1.00
Dentist's Emblem (set of teeth)	.50
Dog	.75
Dray	.75
Dray, Two Horses and Driver	1.00
Drove of Cattle	1.15
Drug Store	1.00
Druggist's Mortar and Pestle	.35
Druid Emblem	.50
Drum	.75
Dry Goods Store and Clerk	1.00
Eagle	.50
Eagle, Shield and Flags	1.25
Eagle with Two Flags	1.00
Epworth League Emblem	.50
Express Wagon	1.00
Express Wagon, Horses and Driver	1.00
Eye and Three Links	.35
Farmer Plowing, with Two Horses	1.00
Fire Engine (steam)	1.00
Fire Engine with Two Horses	1.00
Fireman's Hat	.35
Fish	.50
Flag of any Nation	.50
Flags, Two of any Nation (crossed)	1.00
Flag, Sword and Cannon	1.00
Flour and Feed Store	1.00
Flute	.50
Forester's Emblem (Independent Order)	.50
Forester's Emblem (Ancient Order)	1.00
Freight Car	.75
Freight Elevator	1.00
Furniture Emblem (sofa and chairs)	.75
Furniture Store	1.00
Fruit Stand	1.00
Gambrinus and Keg	1.00
Gas Fitter's Emblem	.75
Grain Elevator	1.00
Grand Army Republic Emblem	1.00
Grocery Store	1.00
Guitar	.50
Hand Car	.75
Hand and Pen	.25
Hands Clasped	.50
Hand Holding Card	.50
Hardware Store	1.00
Hare or Rabbit	.50
Hat and Cap	.30
Harnessmaker at Work	1.00
Harp and Shamrock	.60
Harp	.50
Hearse, Horses and Driver,	1.00
Hod	.35
Hod Carrier at Work	1.00
Hog	.50
Hog's Head, Knife and Steel	.50

WE CAN MAKE A

OTHER CATAL

SHEETS AT

QUOTED

FOR MUGS.

any design, drawing or lettering desired,
~~a~~n usually fill an order for anything desired;
~~s~~ign wanted, we can copy it on a shaving
~~d~~rawing or sketch be furnished. The No. 1
~~o~~r designs. We quote below prices for some
be added to the price of the mug on which the

Horn	$0.50	Patriotic Order Sons America Emblem	$0.75
Horse	.75	Photographer at Camera	1.00
Horse's Head	.50	Piano or Organ	1.00
Horse Shoe	.25	Pistol or Revolver	.75
Hook and Ladder Truck, Horses and		Plasterer's Trowel and Hock	.35
Driver	1.00	Plow	.50
Hose Cart, Horses and Driver	1.00	Plumber's Emblem	.35
		Policeman in Uniform	1.00
Ice Wagon, Horses and Driver	1.25	Portable Engine	1.00
Incandescent Electric Lamp	.50	Printer at Case	1.00
Iron Moulder at Work	1.25	Printer's Stick	.50
Jockey Emblem (cap and whip)	.40	Red Men's Emblem	.50
Jockey Driving Horse	1.00	Restaurant	1.00
Jockey Riding Horse	1.00	Roller Skate	.50
Jug	.35	Royal League Emblem	.75
Keystone (Masonic)	.25	Saddle	50c. to 1.00
Keg of Beer	.50	Safety Bicycle	.75
Knights of Golden Eagle Emblem	.75	Satchel	.50
Knights of Honor Emblem	.50	Saloon (bartender and customers)	1.00
Knights of Labor Emblem	.50	Saw Mill	1.00
Knights of Pythias Emblem	.50	Schooner Sailing	1.00
Knights of Pythias Emblem (uniform		Scotch Thistle	.35
rank)	.75	Sewing Machine	.75
		Sheaf of Wheat	.50
Lantern	.50	Sheep or Sheep's Head	.50
League of American Wheelman Em-		Shingles, Bunch	.35
blem	.75	Shirt and Collar	.60
Ledger	.50	Shoemaker at Work	1.25
Leopard	.75	Sign Painter at Work	1.25
Letter Carrier in Uniform	1.00	Skull and Cross Bones	.25
Livery Stable	1.00	Sportsman and Dog	1.25
Locomotive and Tender	1.00	Stage Coach, Four or Six Horses	1.50
Locomotive and Cars	1.50	Star and Crescent	.50
Lumberman's Rule	.35	Stationary Engine	.75
Lumber Yard	1.00	Steamboat	1.00
Lyre	.50	Stonecutter at Work	1.00
		Stove	.50
Machinist at Work	1.25	Street Car, Horses, Driver and Con-	
Mail Pouch	.50	ductor	1.50
Maltese Cross	.50	Surveyor's Transit	1.00
Man on Horseback	1.00	Switchman's Emblem	.75
Man Shearing Sheep	1.50		
Marble Cutter at Work	1.25	Tailor at Work	1.00
Masonic Emblem (square and compass)	.25	Tailor's Shears	.35
Mechanic's Emblem (hand and ham-		Tanner's Emblem	.75
mer)	.35	Telegraph Key	.40
Milk Can	.35	Telegraph Key and Hand	.75
Mill Stone	.35	Telegraph Operator	1.00
Miller Dressing Burr	1.00	Telephone	.75
Miller's Roller	1.00	Ten Pin Alley	.75
Miner's Design (two picks crossed)	.35	Three Links	.10
Moulder's Emblem	.50	Tinsmith at Work	1.25
Moulder at Work	1.00	Tinsmith's Furnace, Iron and Shears	.50
Mule	.50	Trunk	.50
		Tug Boat	1.00
Ocean Steamer	1.00		
Oil Derrick	1.00	Umbrella (open)	.65
Omnibus, Horses and Driver	1.00	U. S. Flags (crossed)	.50
Organ, Parlor	1.00		
Owl	.50	Violin and Bow	.50
Ox	.50		
Oyster	.50	Wagon, one or two Horses and Driver	1.00
		Watch	.70
Painter's Pallete	.35	Whisky Barrel	.50
Paint Pot and Brush	.35	Wind Mill	1.00
Paper Hanger at Work	1.00	Wood Turner at Work	1.25
Passenger Coach	.75		
Passenger Elevator	1.00	Yacht Sailing	1.00

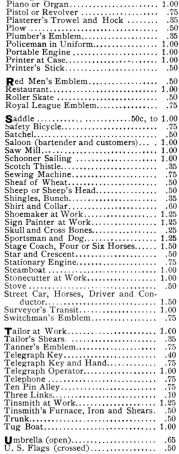

~~A~~NY MUG SHOWN IN

~~LO~~GUES OR MUG

~~IN~~ THE PRICES

~~STATED~~ THEREIN.

August 30, 1879

The New York Times

BARBERS TERRORIZE PUBLIC

There are evidences that the barber is gradually losing the influence which his system of terrorism once gave him over the timid public. There was a time when Court barbers so completely subjugated their royal patrons that through these they virtually ruled the States. We can readily imagine how this influence was attained and maintained. Let us suppose, for example, that Oliver, the famous barber of Louis XL, of France, desired to have a friend appointed to some vacant office. When shaving his Royal Majesty in the morning, Oliver would thoughtfully run his hands through the royal hair and remark, "Sire, your hair is getting pretty gray and thin;' to which the royal victim would feebly reply, "Is it?" After a brief pause, the barber would say, "By the bye, your Majesty, I notice that the position of third assistant groom of the royal canary-bird cage is vacant;" whereat the King would reply, "Ha!" and sometimes, "Hum!" Then the barber, returning to the subject of gray hair, would say, "I would recommend your Majesty to try a bottle of our hair tonic. It is only a dollar a bottle, and ——'' Here the monarch would exclaim, "Name of a dog! Tell me the fellow whom you want me to appoint, and I'll appoint him, if you'll dry up about that infamous tonic." Thus the cunning barber would attain his wish, and another of his friends would enter the civil service of France.

During the present century, the barber has certainly tyrannized to an almost intolerable extent over private citizens. He has cultivated conversational powers of the most appalling description, from which his victims have suffered the most terrible agonies. The records of our insane asylums show the fearful effects wrought by the conversation of barbers. No less than seventy-eight percent of the insane patients in public institutions in this State were in the habit of being shaved by barbers before they became insane. If this does not mean that to be shaved by a barber is to incur the risk of being talked into madness, statistics have no meaning.

Many persons have believed that the barber uses tonic solely with a view to torture his fellow-men. This is an error. Of course, the barber does not care how much his victim may suffer, but his purpose in keeping tonic perpetually before the public mind is simply to sell it. His plan has always been to talk to that extent that any man would gladly buy a bottle of hair tonic in order to purchase a few moments' peace. For many years this unholy practice met with great apparent prosperity. The sale of tonic in this City alone during the period from 1864 to 1875 was so great that no man who wishes to maintain a reputation for veracity dare mention the number of bottles.

89

91

93

94

95

96

97

98

99

101

102

103

109

114

119

123

124

125

129

130

139

154

155

156

120

121

122

126

127

128

140

141

147

158

159

160

Are these barbers twins? This circa 1890 photo was purchased at an estate sale.

—*Author's Collection*

124

Take a bath, rent a buggy, or buy a fine imported cigar after your tonsorial operation at L.B. Roseberry's barber shop on North Main Street in Marion, Ohio. November, 1901. —Hal Tilton

Los Angeles, California, circa 1890. Suburban shop featured indoor and outdoor chairs. —Author's Collection

Quadruple Plated Shaving Sets.

Cuts Shown One-half Size.

PRICES AS GIVEN.

Shaving Set.
VB 981 Burnished, fluted, gold lined $7 50

Shaving Set.
F 435 Satin, engraved...... ....$5 00

Shaving Set.
VB 984 Bright cut, gold lined................$3 95

Shaving Set.
VB 986 Bright cut or burnished, gold lined..$6 58

Shaving Set.
F 437 Burnished $5 33

Shaving Set.
R 903 Satin, engraved, ½ size $4 85

No. 37—SHAVING MUG.
Bright Silver, $10 25

No. 43—SHAVING MUG.
Embossed, Gold-Lined...... 6 25
No. 2817 Shaving Brush...... 3 75

No. 3503—SHAVING CUP.
Embossed $5 25

Fine Quadruple Plated Shaving Sets.

PRICES AS
GIVEN.

Shaving Mug and Brush.

M 268 Mug, gold lined............................$3 55
Brush, satin............................ 2 70

Shaving Stick Box.

M 156 Including soap..$3 67

Shaving Mug and Brush.

M 287 Mug, gold lined.............................$7 43
Brush, satin.................................. 3 43

Shaving Mug and Brush.

W 122 Satin, bright cut, gold lined, height 3 inches.........................$5 63
Mug...........$4 08 Brush........ ...$1 58

Shaving Mug and Brush.

D 3445 Mug, bright cut....................................... .. $6 05
Brush 3 03

Shaving Mug and Brush.

W 117 Repousse, burnished, gold lined, height 3¼ inches..................$6 58
Mug...........$5 00 Brush...........$1 58

Shaving Mug and Brush.

W 113 Colonial pattern, burnished, gold lined, height 3¼ inches..........$8 75
Mug...........$6 25 Brush...........$2 50

Goods Guaranteed to be True to Illustration and Description and to Give Satisfaction.

(From a 1902 Catalog)

BARBER BOTTLES

Barber Bottles stood in an impressive array of vibrant colors on the back bar of even the most humble turn-of-the-century tonsorial parlor. Next to a haircut, the sale of hair tonic was the most profitable business transaction a barber could make. He bought the alcohol-based brew by the gallon, for pennies on the dollar, or made up his own concoction from formulas appearing in early druggist manuals and barber school textbooks.

After adding a few drops of food coloring to the freshly mixed potion, the barber funneled this all-purpose "tonic" into a set of shaker-top display bottles and was ready to start selling the stuff for ten cents per teaspoonful, which was the price of a three-minute scalp massage commonly known as an "Osage Rub." Commercially manufactured colognes, lotions, tonics and cures were also packaged in fancy bottles, but more emphasis was placed on elaborate labels than on expensive glassware.

Fancy barber bottles were a simple merchandising ploy giving the appearance of real value to the mostly worthless preparations they contained. Bay Rum, Sea Foam, Tiger Rub, Bengaline, Mandroline, Brilliantine, Florida Water, and Russian Pine Tar Soap are but a few of the exotic labels these containers bore.

Regular patrons were often encouraged to purchase a custom-imprinted, personalized tonic bottle along with their occupational or fraternal shaving mug. Matching porcelain bowls were also available. Over the years barbers bore the increasing wrath of once-shorn journalists for their relentless sales pitches to a chair-bound clientele (We have included a few examples from newspapers of the period.).

The Pure Food and Drug Act of 1906 was supposed to put an end to the Snake Oil game, but even Sears Roebuck was still selling "Seven Sisters Hair Grower" from its mail order catalog in 1911. Eventually the barbers themselves discouraged the use of all but laboratory-tested hair preparations.

Shampoo magnate F. W. Fitch (1870–1951) was a leader in the battle to upgrade hair care products. His amazing story of an eleven-year-old runaway farmhand (who grew up to be a multimillionaire) is told in *The Shampoo King* by Denny Rehder, published in 1981 by the Waukon & Mississippi Press of Des Moines, IA. In a nutshell, Fred Fitch discovered that the wood alcohol-based tonics of the 1890's actually contributed to most cases of hair loss. He cured his own chronic scalp condition with a coconut-oil-based shampoo and then toured the country selling his product directly to barbers. By 1945, F. W. Fitch & Co. was grossing 12 million dollars a year.

Fancy barber bottles remained on back bar shelves until the early 1930's, long after most people had begun buying their hair care products at Rexall drugstores. The variety and beauty of these containers is indeed impressive; from hand painted porcelain to Bohemian art glass, from Mary Gregory's cranberry red to Louis Comfort Tiffany's irridescent blue. Collectors did not need any media campaign to get them interested in these jewels, the value was intrinsic.

An opalized robin's-egg blue bottle with its lower half in quatrefoil, white herringbone pattern, about seven inches tall, sold for $522 at a recent glass auction. A hand-painted milk glass example from France, with a barber supply imprint on its base, went for $165 at the same event where more than fifty percent of the offerings sold for between ninety and two hundred dollars. (Please see price guide section for more examples.)

Richard Holiner's 1986 book, *Collecting Barber Bottles, a Pictorial Price Guide*, published by Collector Books of Paducah, KY, is still the most authoritative text on the subject and, with few exceptions, prices haven't changed appreciably over the last few years. Currently in great demand are bottles with glass-encased labels, and also glass or porcelain examples with photographs of women fired under the glaze. These can be worth up to $500 to serious collectors.

Reproductions of old barber bottles have been on the market since 1937 when skilled Mexican glass blowers began supplying American antique dealers with new bottles for their window displays.

(Photos above are courtesy Glass-Works Auction, East Greenville, PA.)

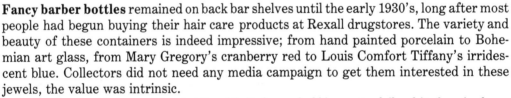

Schenectady, N.Y., 1918. Mr. DeLorenzo has painted everything in his shop a sanitary shade of white. Note the huge jars of tonic. Barbershop suppliers often gave away a free bohemian glass "stand bottle" with each gallon purchased.

November 8, 1876

The New York Times

NEEDED REFORMS

The worst features of tonsorial depravity are, however, exhibited in connection with the inevitable "tonic" which every barber offers for sale. No matter what may be the condition of the customer's hair—whether it is soft or coarse, black or gray, thick or thin—the barber informs him that he must use the "tonic" or he is lost. To sell to every customer a bottle of tonic is the unswerving purpose of every barber, and it is only the exceptionally obstinate and courageous man who escapes. In every barber's shop there are rows upon rows of bottles filled with "tonic" and bearing the names of victims who have been forced to purchase them. The story of their weakness and defeat is thus constantly kept before their eyes, and so depressing is its effect that the man who has once bought a bottle of "tonic" is thenceforth the barber's

slave. He may never use that bottle, but when, after an interval of two weeks, the barber tells him that the bottle is empty and that he needs a new bottle, he buys it without a word of protest.

BARBERS, BEER & CIGARS

The fight between the two rival factions into which the barbers of our country are now unhappily divided, grows fiercer every day; and the noise and dust of the conflict threaten to totally blind the eyes of the most intelligent barbers—as with misapplied bay rum—to the true interests of their profession. Those who style themselves the only legitimate and artistic practitioners of the tonsorial art denounce with vast energy the conduct of certain interlopers who have lowered the dignity of the profession by bribing the public with free cigars and gratuitous beer, to come and be shaved at half the regular rate. Barbers who have hitherto found no lack of customers who were anxious to be shaved at the rate of ten cents per head, forsee that when a rival offers to shave for five cents, and to

throw in a glass of beer or a cigar, the dignity and interests of legitimate practitioners must suffer.

The New York Times

1878 – A BLESSED BARBER

A simple but beautiful story comes to us from Capron, Ill. In that town there was a barber, one of the confirmed and hardened class who call themselves tonsorial artists. The other day this barber advertised that he would deliver a lecture in the Town Hall, at the end of which he would publicly kill himself. The price of admission to this entertainment was one dollar, and the hall was filled on the appointed night. The barber delivered, according to the local paper, an "eloquent lecture"—probably upon the uses of hair tonic, and then blew out his brains with a pistol, amid the uncontrollable enthusiasm of the audience. How cold and hard must be the heart that does not warm and quicken in reading of such a noble and beautiful deed!

An 1846 Hair Oil label. (Rub a little on your bald spot and go to Heaven with a full head of hair.)

A 100-year-old cartoon.

ILLUSTRATED CATALOGUE

For the Year 1894

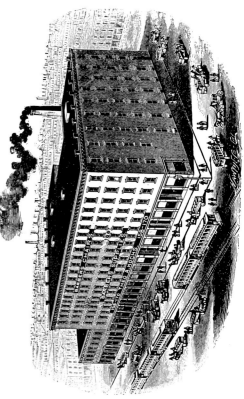

WE present our Catalogue for 1894 to our friends and patrons with the consciousness that we are fully abreast of the foremost in the march of improvement, and the Barbers' Chairs, Furniture and Supplies that we offer in the following pages will fully demonstrate this. Our Columbia Chairs are undoubtedly the most perfect of their kind upon the market to-day; our Lifting Treadle Machinery which we use upon our other chairs is the result of most careful thought and long experience; our Mirror Cases and Furniture are modern in every sense of the word, and our line of Supplies is complete and strictly "up to the times."

The World's Columbian Exposition brought to our city a number of our customers whom we had not the pleasure of meeting before, and afforded us the opportunity of demonstrating to them, by a trip through our factory, that we have the best possible facilities for the manufacture of the goods we offer. We are exclusively in the business of Barbers' Supplies, and every inch of our two acres of floor space is devoted to this. We receive the lumber in our basement and turn it out in our shipping room in the form of Barbers' Chairs and Furniture, carved, finished and upholstered, and as every department is in our own building and under our immediate supervision, we KNOW that what we ship is the best that it is possible to obtain. We have a machinists' department, where expert workmen put together the machinery used upon our chairs, and as the lathes, drills and tools that they have are used only for this purpose, we undoubtedly produce a chair machinery that is as near perfection as possible. In the same building we have our grind-shop, where we grind nothing but barbers' tools; our decorating department, where we decorate only shaving mugs and barbers' bottles, and our perfumery department, where we make our soaps, cosmetics and perfumery. In short, our vast establishment, from bottom to top and from one end to the other, is devoted to the manufacture of Supplies for Barbers. Our every thought and effort is for the advancement of that business, and everything we ship is of a quality that we know will add to the reputation that we now have.

The award of the First Medal that we received at the World's Columbian Exposition was very gratifying to us, but still more gratifying is the endorsement of our goods by the profession throughout the country, which is evidenced by our constantly increasing business. We appreciate this thoroughly, and can assure our patrons that we shall endeavor to show it by the most careful attention to the quality of the goods we ship.

We thank you for favors extended to us in the past, and, hoping that we shall continue to receive a fair share of your patronage, we remain,

Truly yours,

THEO. A. KOCHS.

THEO. A. KOCHS, CHICAGO.

GLASSWARE.

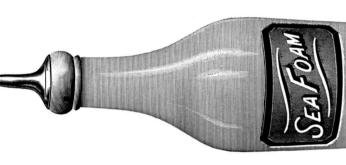

Octagon Recess Bottle.
With nickel-plated tube. Holds 11 oz.
Kept in white opaque.

Price, each..................40c.

Crystal Powder Box, with Cover.
Price, each..................50c.

Square Recess Bottle.
With nickel-plated tube. Holds 10 oz.
Kept in white opaque.

Price, each..................35c.

Metal Powder or Pomade Box.
Price, each..................35c.

Flint Water Bottle.
With nickel-plated tube. Holds 8 oz.
Kept in flint only.

Price, each..................35c.

Fancy Pomade Stand.
Flint, blue and amber.

Price, each..................10c.

American Powder Stand.
Canary, blue and amber.

Price, each..................20c.

THEO. A. KOCHS, CHICAGO.

HAIR PREPARATIONS AND TOILET WATERS.

Imported Bay Rum.

Put up in 12-oz. bottles, per doz. **$4.50**

Per bottle............................**.40**

KOCHS'

Lavender Water.

Double distilled, per dozen.......**$4.00**

Ambree, per dozen.................**5.50**

KOCHS'

Athenian Tonic.

Per dozen..........................**$3.50**

KOCHS'

Florida Water.

Per dozen..........................**$4.50**

KOCHS'

Hungarian Essence.

Per dozen..........................**$3.50**

THEO. A. KOCHS, CHICAGO.

GLASSWARE.

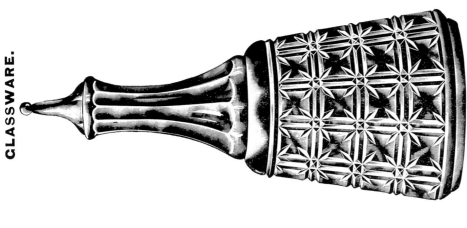

Marbled Bottle. Nickel-plated tube. Kept in rose, ruby-wine, blue and amber.

Holds 18 oz.

Price, each..........**75c.**

Marbled Bowl.

Kept in rose, ruby-wine, blue and amber.

Price, each..........**50c.**

Sparkling Bottle. Improved valve tube.

Kept in flint, blue or amber. Holds 12 oz.

Price, each..........**50c.**

Sparkling Bowl.

Kept in flint only.

Price, each..........**25c.**

Venetian Bottle. Nickel-plated tube. Kept in blue, canary and rose.

Large size, holding 25 oz., each..........**55c.**
Small size, holding 15 oz., each..........**45c.**

Venetian Bowl.

Kept in rose, blue and canary.

Price, each..........**40c.**

134

THEO. A. KOCHS, CHICAGO.

HAIR PREPARATIONS AND TOILET WATERS.

KOCHS'

Turkish Tonic.

Per dozen...............$7.00

KOCHS'

West India Bay Rum.

Per dozen...............$3.00

KOCHS'

Witch Hazel Rum.

Per dozen...............$3.50

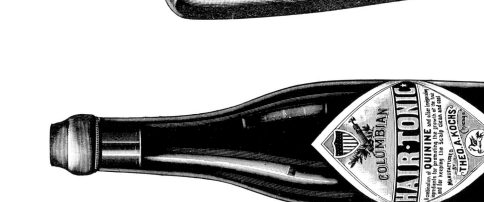

KOCHS'

Columbian Tonic.

Per dozen...............$3.50

KOCHS'

Dandruff Lotion.

Per dozen...............$4.00

BARBERS' TRAVELING CASE.

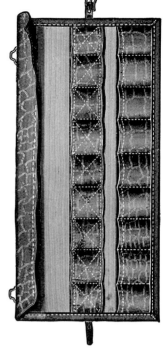

OPEN.

CLOSED.

This handy article, which has been found to fill a long-felt want, is entirely original with us, and everything has been done to make it strictly first-class in every particular. Inferior imitations have been placed upon the market and illustrated by identically the same illustrations which we use, and which we originated, but the genuine article is made in the best possible manner. Our traveling case is covered with leather and lined with velvet throughout, is furnished with a good nickel-plated lock and key, and is put together substantially. The arrangement is very compact, and the case measures upon the outside only 11¾ inches long, 6¾ inches wide, and 9 inches high.

Price, case only, with three empty bottles..................................$7.50

BARBERS' EMBLEM PINS.—Solid Gold.

No. 612.

Price, each..................75c.

No. 623.

Price, each..................$1.00

No. 667.

Price, each..................$2.00

Rotary hair brush. Rosewood handles.

Price..................$4.00

RAZOR POCKETS.

No. 723. Sheep Skin.

Stamped alligator pattern.

6 loops....................$0.75
9 loops.................... 1.00
12 loops.................... 1.25

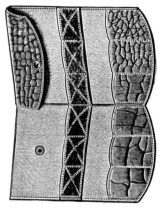

No. 722. Sheep Skin.

To carry in the pocket.

Each..................$1.00

No. 721. Genuine Calf Skin.

6 loops....................$1.00
9 loops.................... 1.25
12 loops.................... 1.50

THEO. A. KOCHS, CHICAGO.

ELECTROTYPES.—For Advertising Purposes.

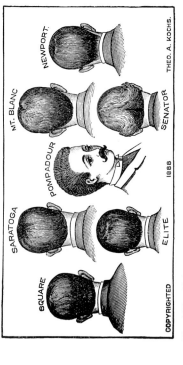

COPYRIGHTED 1888 THEO. A. KOCHS.

No. 181. Price, each......75c.

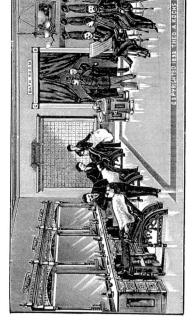

COPYRIGHTED 1892 THEO. A. KOCHS.

No. 182. Price, each......75c.

THE ELECTRIC BARBER SHOP.

COPYRIGHTED 1892 THEO. A. KOCHS.

No. 183. Price, each......$1.25

Copyrighted 1892, Theo. A. Kochs.

No. 178. Price, each......50c.

KOCHS GOLD MEDAL HYDRAULIC CHAIRS.

Price of the electrotype..$1.00

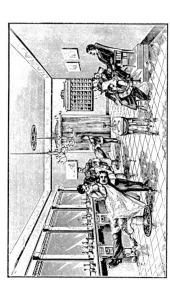

No. 927. Electrotype. For use upon envelopes or business cards.

Price of the electrotype......60c

TONSORIAL PARLOR
Shaving and Hair Cutting

THIS SPACE FOR NAME.

THIS SPACE FOR ADDRESS.

No. 925. Electrotype. For use upon letter-heads or business cards.

Price of the electrotype......75c

Black-owned Barbershop. Sign says "On and after Sept. 11, 1911, All Shaves 15 cents, Seafoam 15 cents, Trimming full beard 15 cents, Vandyke 25 cents."

—*Michael Griffin*

TWO-BOWL CENTER WASHSTAND, No. 62.

WITH OVAL BOWLS.

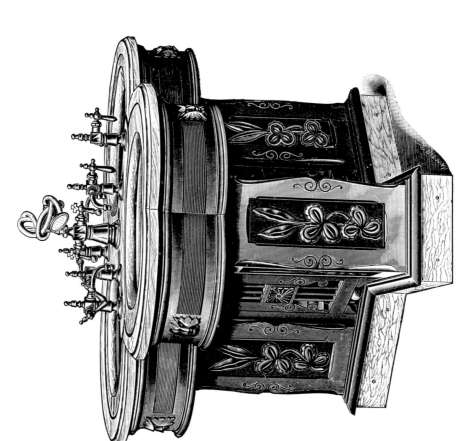

Made of OAK (antique finish), or of WALNUT. Fitted with oval bowls, 14x17 in. Italian marble base is used and Italian marble slab, 1¼ in. thick and countersunk, and nickel-plated Fuller basin cocks and shampoo cock, with rubber hose, and nickel-plated shampoo sprinkler, basin plugs and chains.

Price..$100.00

THREE-BOWL CENTER WASHSTAND, No. 63.

WITH OVAL BOWLS.

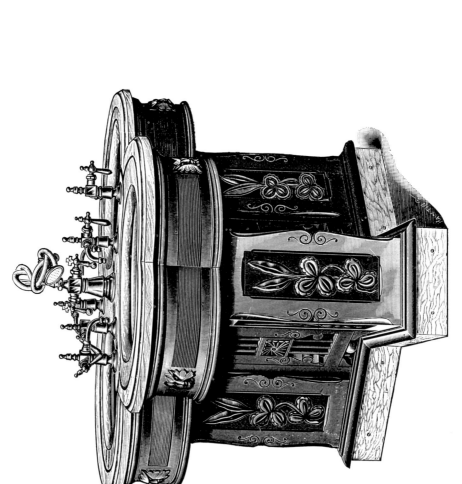

Made of OAK (antique finish), or of WALNUT. Fitted with oval bowls, 14x17 in. Italian marble base is used and Italian marble slab, 1¼ in. thick and countersunk, and nickel-plated Fuller basin cocks and shampoo cock, with rubber hose, and nickel-plated shampoo sprinkler, basin plugs and chains.

Price..$140.00

140

THEO. A. KOCHS, CHICAGO.

KOCHS' SALERNO BARBERS' CHAIR.

WITH LIFTING TREADLE.

Patented Sept. 30, 1890.

Design Patented.

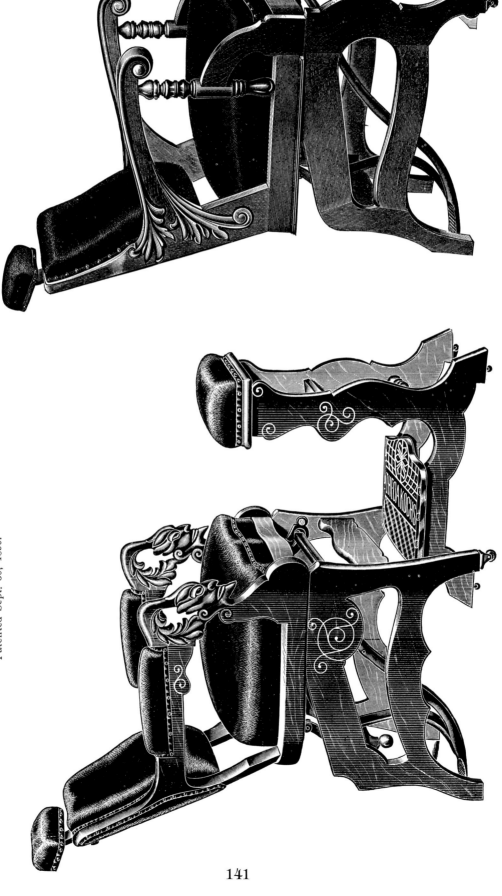

Made of OAK (antique finish), or of WALNUT.

PRICE :

Covered with Mohair Plush, Crimson, Maroon, Green or Old Gold............$32.00

KOCHS' HERRMANN BARBERS' CHAIR.

WITH LIFTING TREADLE.

Patented Sept. 30, 1890.

Made of OAK (antique finish), or of WALNUT.

PRICE:

Covered with Mohair Plush, Crimson, Maroon, Green or Old Gold............$38.00

CHAIRS ARE FITTED WITH THE LIFTING TREADLE MACHINERY DESCRIBED

THEO. A. KOCHS, CHICAGO.

KOCHS' BARBERS' CHAIR, No. 28.

WITH LIFTING TREADLE.

Design Patented July 7, 1891.

Patented Sept. 30, 1890.

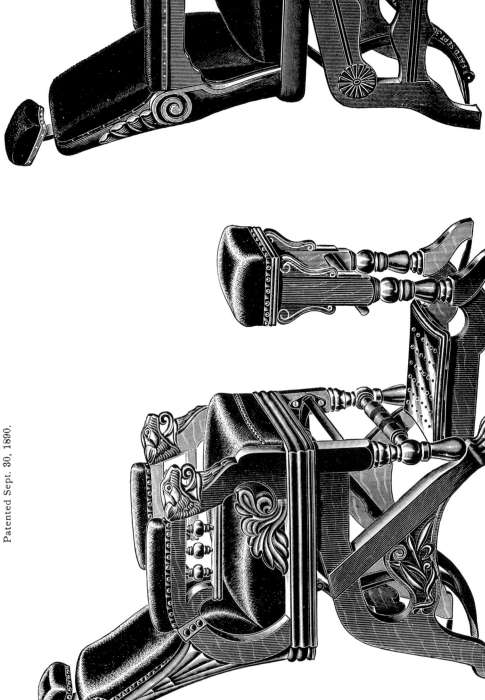

PRICE:

Made of OAK (antique finish), or of WALNUT.

Covered with best Mohair Plush, Crimson, Maroon, Green or Old Gold..................$45.00

KOCHS' BARBERS' CHAIR, No. 36.

WITH LIFTING TREADLE.

Patented Sept. 30, 1890.

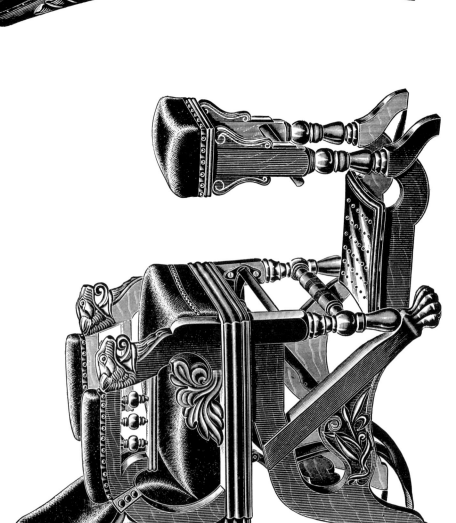

PRICE:

Made of OAK (antique finish) only.

Covered with best Mohair Plush, Crimson, Green or Old Gold..................$50.00

CHAIRS ARE FITTED WITH THE LIFTING TREADLE MACHINERY DESCRIBED

"Music did ... soothe the savage soul" in this Burlington, Colorado shop. The "Coke Dandruff Cure" was not meant to be taken internally. "We close Sundays" was a rare sign in a 1906 Tonsorial Parlor. These folks must have been regular church-goers. —Author's Collection

BOOT-BLACKING STAND, No. 427.

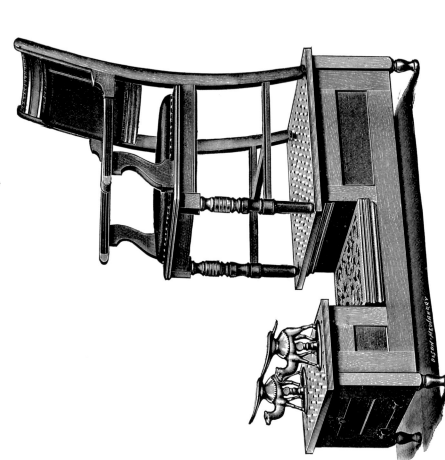

Made of OAK (antique finish) only. Top of stand covered with sheet brass. Nickel-plated camel foot-rests.

PRICES:

Complete, with seat and back upholstered with Leather or with best Mohair Plush, Crimson, Green or Old Gold............................$28.00

Complete, with Cane seat and back............................22.00

BOOT-BLACKING CHAIR, No. 421.

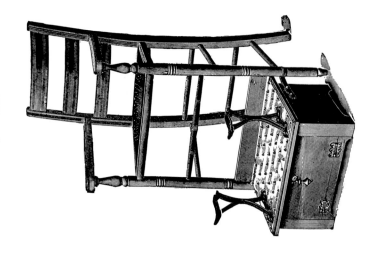

Made of Hard Wood, WALNUT or ANTIQUE OAK finish.

Price............................$7.00

BOOT-BLACKING CHAIR, No. 426.

Made of OAK (antique finish), or of WALNUT.

Price............................$10.00

Binghamton, N.Y. shop of 1890 featured ceiling-mounted advertising signs. Back counter cigar clerk is a lady. Bootblack wears a tie. Seven barbers, seven chairs, a high class shop. Dog on floor, next to spitoon, sleeps through it all. —Michael Griffin

TOOL BRACKET, No. 79.

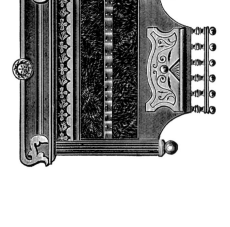

Made of OAK (antique finish), or of WALNUT.

Price..$3.00

TICKET BOARD, No. 80.

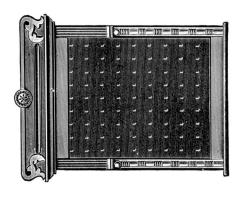

Made of OAK (antique finish), or of WALNUT, 81 hooks.

Price..$3.00

HALL RACK, No. 154.

OAK (antique finish), or of WALNUT, and furnished with German plate, 16x28.

Price..$20.00

INDEX HAND.

Made of wood, handsomely painted.

12 inch, price..75c.

ROTARY HAIR BRUSH BRACKET.

Price, each...$1.00

CASH DRAWER, WITH ALARM.

Combining security with convenience. Provided with five strong bolts. Combination susceptible of thirty-two changes. The strongest and best alarm till manufactured.

Price..$3.00

146

Are these fellows all gussied up for a 4th of July parade, or are they members of a Barbershop Quartet?

—*Author's Collection.*

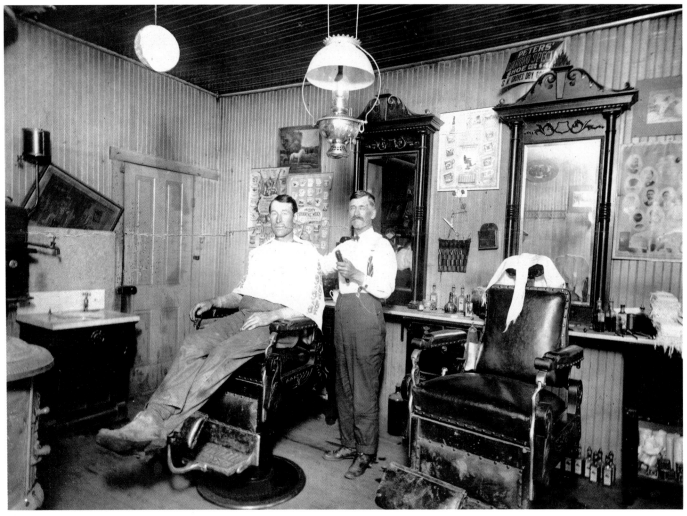

Sheridan, Wyoming, circa 1905. These well-worn chairs testify to a cowboy clientele. Wall decor includes three "Private Shaving Mug" posters and a "Choose your own hairstyle" chart. —Author's Collection

Cigars are showcased next to the mirror in this gas-lighted barber shop of the 1890s. —Author's Collection

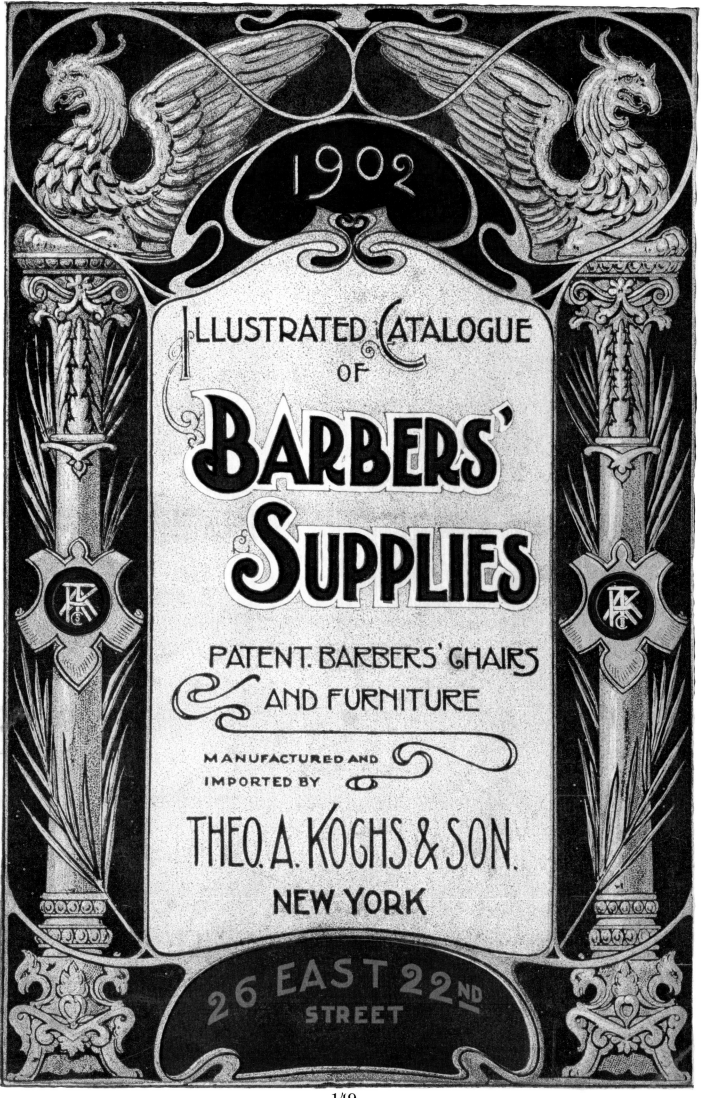

1902

ILLUSTRATED CATALOGUE
OF
BARBERS'
SUPPLIES

PATENT BARBERS' CHAIRS
AND FURNITURE

MANUFACTURED AND
IMPORTED BY

THEO. A. KOCHS & SON.
NEW YORK

26 EAST 22ND
STREET

MIRROR CASE, No. 195.

Made of carefully selected mahogany, highly finished. It is simply impossible to do justice to this piece of furniture in an illustration, or to describe it so that its elegance will be thoroughly appreciated. In every respect this mirror case is strictly high grade, and it is the best that it is possible to produce. The carving is most elaborate, the figures supporting the cornice being most artistic in conception and hand carved by experienced men. The work upon the top ornaments, workstands and other parts shown in our illustration as being carved is conscientiously done, and the mirror case throughout is a perfect specimen of the carver's and cabinet-maker's art.

Large size beveled French plates, 50x50, are used, and the workstands rest upon brass finished legs. The shelf is of marble, and dark colored marble is used upon the base, protecting the woodwork when the floor is cleaned. The lower compartment of each workstand is ventilated, is furnished with the Labor-Saving Door Opener, and, in fact, this mirror case is as perfect in every detail as it is possible to make it.

Height, 9 feet 7 inches. Length of mirror case arranged for three chairs (as shown above), 15 feet 7 inches.

PRICES:

Arranged for two chairs.........................$358.00
Arranged for three chairs......................... 525.00
Arranged for four chairs......................... 692.00
Arranged for five chairs......................... 859.00
Arranged for six chairs.........................1,026.00

END VIEW

MIRROR CASE, No. 736.

MIRROR CASE, No. 195.

MIRROR CASE, No. 199.

KOCHS' GOLD MEDAL
HYDRAULIC BARBERS' CHAIR, No. 97.

RAISING AND LOWERING.   REVOLVING AND RECLINING.

PATENTED DEC. 11, 1891; JAN. 11, 1898; FEB. 8, 1898.

Made of choicest Mahogany, richly carved and finely finished. Covered with the very best Mohair Plush or Leather of any color desired, and perfect in every detail. The metal feet are of solid brass.

PRICE, ... $125.00

COMBINATION FIXTURE, No. 208.

Made of oak, antique finish. The washstand is furnished with Italian marble 14-inch patent overflow basin and double Fuller basin cock for hot and cold water. German plate, 22x30, beveled. Height of fixture, 8 ft. 3 in.; width, 5 ft.

Price..$55.00

We carry this fixture in stock in antique finish only, but can furnish it in golden finish on short notice if desired. The colored illustrations of chairs on pages 5-24 of this catalogue show the difference in color of these finishes.

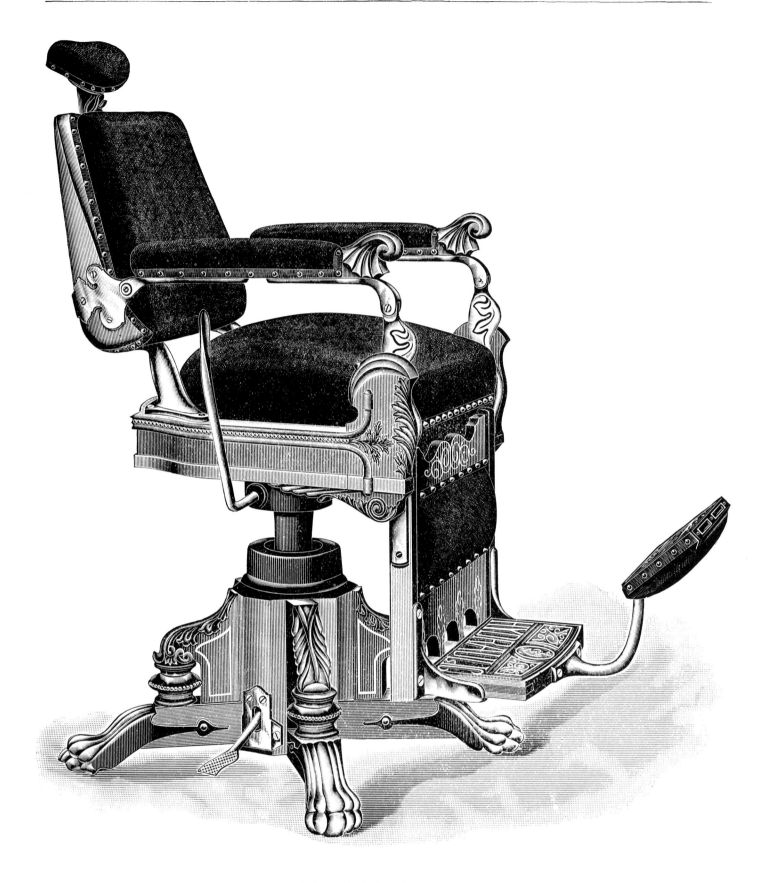

KOCHS' GOLD MEDAL
HYDRAULIC BARBERS' CHAIR, No. 93.

RAISING AND LOWERING.   REVOLVING AND RECLINING.

PATENTED DEC. 8, 1891; JAN. 11, 1898, AND FEB. 8, 1898.

Made of Oak, antique finish. Upholstered with Mohair Plush, crimson, green or old
gold, or with Maroon Leather. Solid brass feet are used upon this chair.

PRICE, ... $60.00

TOILET GOODS CASE, No. 678.

Made of oak, antique finish. A neat case for displaying perfumery and toilet goods for sale. Glass door, fitted with good lock. Height, 4 ft.; width, 2 ft. 6 in.

Price $7.00

COMBINATION CASE, No. 679. FOR MUGS AND TOILET GOODS.

Made of quarter-sawed oak, golden finish. The shelves for displaying perfumery and toilet goods are covered with glass doors, fitted with good locks. Height, 4 ft. 10 in.; width, 5 ft. 6 in.

Price $18.50

MUG CASES.

Made of oak, antique finish.

PRICES :

No. 451.   21 holes, 3 ft. 6 in. wide;
2 ft. 9 in. high.................$3.95

No. 452.   28 holes, 3 ft. 6 in. wide;
3 ft. 3 in. high.................$4.60

No. 453.   35 holes, 3 ft. 6 in. wide;
3 ft. 9 in. high.................$5.50

No. 454.   48 holes, 3 ft. 11 in. wide;
4 ft. 4 in. high.................$7.15

No. 455.   56 holes, 3 ft. 11 in. wide;
5 ft. high....................$8.25

MUG CASES.

Made of oak, golden finish.

PRICES :

No. 621.   21 holes, 3 ft. 6 in. wide;
2 ft. 11 in. high..............$4.60

No. 622.   28 holes, 3 ft. 6 in. wide;
3 ft. 5 in. high................$5.25

No. 623.   35 holes, 3 ft. 6 in. wide;
3 ft. 11 in. high..............$6.15

No. 624.   48 holes, 3 ft. 11 in. wide;
4 ft. 6 in. high................$7.90

No. 625.   56 holes, 3 ft. 11 in. wide;
5 ft. 2 in. high...............$9.00

ONE-BOWL
STATIONARY WASHSTAND, No. 106.

Made of oak, antique finish, with ventilated door. Fitted with Italian marble slab, 19x24 in.; 6-in. back; 14-in. patent overflow basin, with rubber plug, nickel-plated chain-stay, compression basin cock and shampoo sprinkler, with hose.

Price.................................$17.75

ONE-BOWL
STATIONARY WASHSTAND, No. 105.

Made of oak, antique finish, with ventilated door. Fitted with Italian marble slab, 19x24 in., with 6-inch back. Patent overflow basin, 14 in., with rubber plug and nickel-plated compression cock, chain-stay, chain and shampoo sprinkler, with rubber hose.

Price.................................$15.00

ONE-BOWL
CENTER WASHSTAND, No. 201.

Made of oak, antique finish. This washstand is fitted with Italian marble slab, 14-inch patent overflow basin and nickel-plated Fuller basin cock, chain-stay and chain; rubber plug and hose with nickel-plated shampoo sprinkler.

Price....................................$22.00

We carry this in stock in antique finish, but can furnish it in golden finish on short notice if desired. The colored illustrations of chairs (pages 5 to 24) show the difference in color of these finishes.

TWO-BOWL
CENTER WASHSTAND, No. 222.

Made of oak, antique finish, with Italian marble top. This washstand is made principally of wood, nicely carved and ornamented, and is preferred by many to washstands made entirely of marble. Furnished with nickel-plated waste and supply pipes, Improved Fuller Shampoo and Basin Cock, and 14-inch patent overflow bowls; nickel-plated feet.

Price.............. $48.00

PORTABLE WASHSTAND, No. 176.

Made of oak, antique finish. Fitted with Italian
marble slab, 19x24, 1¼ inches thick and countersunk, with 6-inch back. Door fitted with latticed
panel for ventilation. Patent overflow basin,
rubber plug, nickel-plated chain-stay and chain,
self-closing basin cock and shampoo sprinkler
and hose. Each washstand complete with water
tank made of zinc and pipe connecting to basin
cock.

Price $24.00

PORTABLE WASHSTAND, No. 177.

Made of oak, antique finish, beveled French
mirror plate, size 16x30 inches. Italian marble
slab, 19x24, with 6-inch back. Patent overflow
basin, rubber plug, nickel-plated chain-stay and
chain. Self-closing basin cock and shampoo
sprinkler, with hose. Door fitted with latticed
panel for ventilation. The water tank is made
of galvanized iron, japanned and nicely decorated.

Price $32.00

159

BRACKET, No. 531.

Made of oak, antique finish.   Lock on drawer.
Size of top, 12x26 inches.

Price...............................$2.75

BRACKET, No. 532.

Made of oak, antique finish.   Locks on drawers.
Size of top, 12x26 inches.

Price...............................$3.50

WORKSTAND, No. 206.

Made of oak, antique finish, wood top. Height,
3 feet.   Size of top, 13x24 inches.

Price...............................$6.00

WORKSTAND, No. 207.

Made of oak, antique finish.   Lower compartment ventilated and made with perforated metal
bottom. Height, 3 feet.   Size of top, 13x24
inches.

Price, wood top..................$ 7.50
Price, marble top................ 10.00

SHOW CASE, No. 506.

Made of oak, antique finish, 17 inches high, 28 inches wide and 3 feet long at base. This showcase fits counter No. 52.

Price $10.00

CASH DRAWER, No. 714.

Fitted with alarm and a combination susceptible of 32 changes.

Price $1.35

COUNTER, No. 52.

Made of oak, antique finish. Fitted with alarm cash drawer. Length, 3 feet; width, 28 inches. Showcase No. 506 fits this counter.

Price $18.00

CASHIER'S STAND, No. 48.

Made of oak, antique finish. Finished on all four sides. Fitted with alarm cash drawer and with door below. Size of top, 24 inches square.

Price $16.00

SHOW CASE, No. 507.

Made of oak, antique finish; 4 feet long, 2 feet 4 inches wide, 42 inches high.

Price $22.00

HAT AND COAT RACK,
No. 394.

Made of oak. Beveled German plates, 24x30, 6x12 and 6x6. Height, 8 ft. 1 in; width, 3 ft. 9 in.

We carry this in stock in antique finish, but can furnish it in golden finish on short notice, if desired.

Our illustrations of chairs (pages 5 to 24) show the difference in color of these finishes.
Price $25.00

No. 395. This hat and coat rack is made to stand in the middle of the room. The post is made of wood, oak finish, and the feet and hooks are bronzed iron. Height 6 ft. 6 in.
Price $5.50

No. 396. Hat and coat rack, with rack for umbrellas. The post is made of wood, oak finish, and the feet, hooks and rack are bronzed iron. Height, 6 ft. 8 in.
Price $6.00

CHILD'S CHAIR, No. 18.
Made of oak.

Cane seat and back, without foot-rest......,$5.00
Plush seat and cane back, without foot-rest. 6.00
Adjustable foot-rest, extra 1.00

CHILD'S CHAIR, No. 17.
Made of hardwood (oak finish).

Cane seat $3.25
Plush seat................................. 4.25

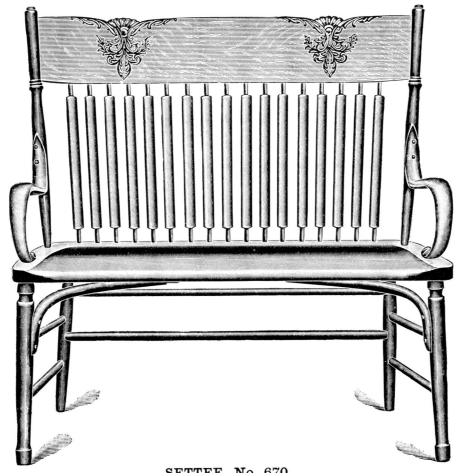

SETTEE, No. 670.
Made of oak, except seat, which is of elm, golden finish, 42 inches long.
Price, each $5.50

CLOCK, No. 704.

Made of oak. 12-inch dial. Height, 32 inches.

8-day, time $6.00
8-day, half-hour strike.... 7.00
8-day, time, calendar..... 6.50
8-day, half-hour strike, calendar 7.50

CLOCK, No. 702.

Made of oak, 8-day, time.
Price $7.50

CLOCK, No. 705.

Made of oak, 12-inch dial. Height, 24 inches.

8-day, time $5.50
8-day, strike 6.50

**GASOLINE
PENDANT LAMP, No. 683.**

Made of polished brass.

Price, complete, each..... $3.00

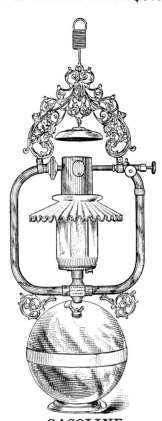

**GASOLINE
INDOOR ARC LAMP, No. 685.**

Made entirely of brass, oxidized copper finish. 600 candle-power. Burns 15 to 16 hours with one **filling and one pumping.** Length, 33 inches.

Price, complete with pump, mantle, chimney, shade, etc. $12.00

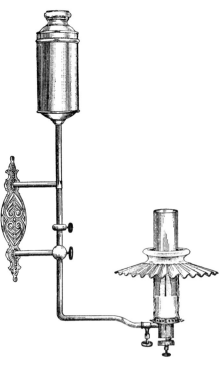

**GASOLINE
BRACKET LAMP, No. 684.**

Nickel-plated. Furnished with extra collar and set screw, so as to swing or remain stationary at any elevation.

Price, complete, each.....$5.00

COAT HOOKS.

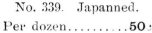

No. 339. Japanned.
Per dozen.........50c

No. 337. Oxidized copper finish.
Each $1.25

No. 338. Oxidized copper finish.
Each $1.00

No. 326. Japanned.
Per dozen 70c
No. 341. Nickel plated.
Per dozen.......$1.15

COAT RACKS.

Made of oak, antique finish.   Japanned hooks.

No. 465. With six hooks $1.15
No. 466. With nine hooks................................. 1.50

Made of oak, antique finish.   Nickel-plated hooks.

No. 397. With six hooks $1.50
No. 398. With nine hooks................................. 2.00

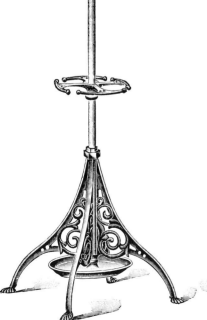

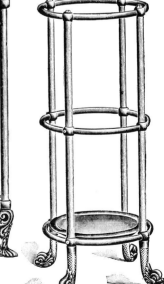

**HAT AND COAT RACK,
No. 393.**
Made of metal, oxidized copper finish. Height 5 ft. 6 in.
Price $5.50

**UMBRELLA STAND,
No. 384.**
A substantial metal stand, oxidized copper finish. Height 26 in., length 24 in., width 9 in.
Price.............................$5.50

**UMBRELLA STAND,
No. 385.**
Made of metal, oxidized copper finish. Height 24 in., diameter 10 in.
Price $3.75

LILAC WITCH HAZEL.
In 8-ounce bottles.
Per doz.................$2.40

**SOLIDIFIED
BRILLIANTINE JELLY.**
This is a highly perfumed dressing for the beard and mustache.
Per doz.................$2.00
Each.................... .20

LAVENDER WITCH HAZEL.
In 8-ounce bottles.
Per doz.................$2.40

JOCKEY CLUB COLOGNE.
In 2-ounce bottles.
Per doz.................$1.50

TOOTH POWDER.
A delightful powder for cleansing the teeth and hardening the gums.
Per doz.................$1.00

TRIPLE EXTRACT.
Jockey Club, White Rose **or** Jickey. Packed three bottles **in** a neat box.
Per doz.................$3.00
Per bottle............... .25

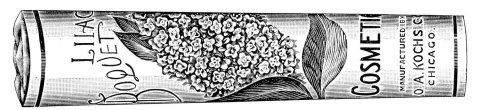

Kochs' Lilac Bouquet Cosmetic, exquisitely perfumed, pink color, per dozen 75c

Kochs' Special Cosmetic, well perfumed, yellow color, per dozen 40c

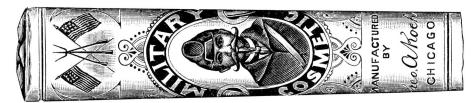

Kochs' Military Cosmetic, rose color, per dozen 50c

Kochs' No. 120 Cosmetic, white or black, per dozen..60c

KOCHS' MUSTACHE WAX, No. 996.

Large size, per dozen $1.00

KOCHS' MUSTACHE WAX, No. 997.
Small size, per dozen........................75c

HUNGARIAN MUSTACHE WAX, No. 998.
Per dozen....................................40c

Smith's Turkish Cosmetic, per dozen..............$1.20

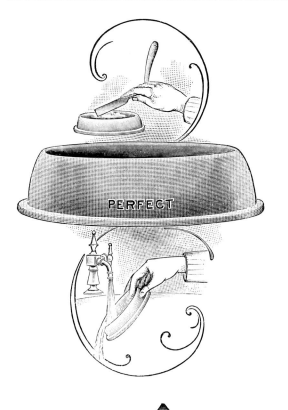

THE PERFECT RAZOR CLEANER.

Made of rubber of the proper shape and softness to thoroughly clean the lather from the razor. The razor cleaner is laid upon the breast of the customer, so that it is just as convenient as the regulation shaving paper, but as it is quickly cleaned by simply holding it under running water, its advantages are at once apparent. If you will use these razor cleaners in your shop, you dispense entirely with soiled shaving paper and the unsanitary condition that it creates. These razor cleaners are in universal use in Europe.

Each....................................25c

RUBBER MASSAGE BULB.

An indispensable article in all up-to-date barber shops where face massage has been introduced. Full directions for use with every bulb.

Each................................35c

SHAVING MUG, No. 737.
Nickel plated.

Each.......................................85c

THE ANTISEPTIC RAZOR STERILIZER.

A simple and effective method of sterilizing razors. The urn is filled with sterilizing liquid, into which the blade of the razor is dipped after shaving. This thoroughly sterilizes it and prevents any possible contagion when the razor is used upon the next customer. This sterilizing fluid is inexpensive, for the total cost of enough to operate a four-chair shop a whole month should not exceed five cents. The following is the

Formula for Sterilizing Liquid.

Dissolve ½ ounce boracic acid in one gallon of boiling water.

The urn should be refilled once a week. It is provided with a hinged cover and it is made of white metal, nickel plated, so that there is no danger of rust or of the formation of verdigris. Imitations are on the market made of brass, but these should be avoided.

Price of the sterilizer......................$1.50

Fibrone Checks.

Practically indestructible.

Per hundred $1.15

These checks are made in four colors, and with the following numbers: 10, 15, 20, 25, 30, 35, 40, 45, 50 and 60. The checks can, therefore, be used in complete sets for one, two, three or four chair shops, using a different color for each chair.

Cardboard Checks.

Best quality and finish.

Per hundred 30c

Brass checks, stamped with name and "Good for one shave" in plain sunken letters.

When ordering, be careful to write name distinctly. Extra charge will be made for any additional lettering wanted.

Per hundred $1.50

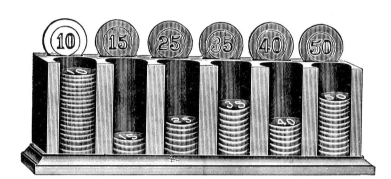

No. 906. Check Rack.

For Fibrone Checks.

Made of wood, ebony finish. A convenient and useful article, arranged to hold six different denominations of checks.

Each 75c

No. 841. Mustache Curler.

Each 10c

No. 839. Mustache Curler.

Ebony finished handles.

Each 20c

No. 853. Mustache Curler.

Each 5c

No. 859. Hair Curler.

Each 15c

No. 846. Hair and Mustache Crimpers.

Per package 10c

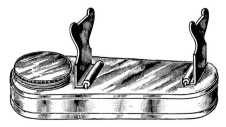

No. 884. Alcohol Lamp for heating curling irons.

Each 25c

No. 885. Alcohol Lamp, for heating curling irons.

Each 15c

CUSPIDOR, No. 888.
Made of heavy brass, highly nickel plated, self-righting.
Each...................................$1.00

CUSPIDOR, No. 889.
Metal, nickel plated, self-righting.
Each......................................25c

CUSPIDOR, No. 880.
Iron, enameled, self-righting.
Each.......................................50c

WOOD FIBER SPITTOONS.
The cleanest and most durable spittoon ever made. Far better than rubber.
13½ inches in diameter, each................75c
9½ inches in diameter, each.................50c

CUSPIDOR, No. 886.
Glazed earthenware, green color. Each................35c

JARDINIERE, No. 898.
Made of glazed earthenware, blended colors. For umbrellas or wet towels.
Each....................$3.50

CUSPIDOR, No. 890.
Urn shape, made of heavy brass, self-righting. Height, 12 inches. Price, each......$2.75

JARDINIERE, No. 897.
Glazed earthenware, green color, for umbrellas or wet towels.
Each....................$3.00

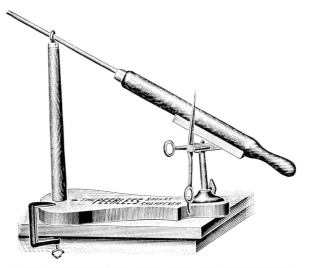

THE PEERLESS SHEARS SHARPENER.

A very convenient and handy arrangement for sharpening shears. It is adjustable to suit any size shears, and quickly and easily hones upon the shears a fine cutting edge. Full directions for use accompany every one.

Each $1.45

HOT WATER URN, No. 844.

Highly nickel plated. Capacity 3 gallons.
Price, each..............$7.00

BUNSON BURNER, No. 437.

For natural or artificial gas. Used under hot water urns or copper boilers.
Each........................25c

WILLOW WASTE BASKETS.

No. 306. 11 in. diam., each.40c
No. 307. 13 in. diam., each.55c

WILLOW WASTE BASKET, No. 318.

13½ inches diameter.

Each........................70c

COPPER BOILERS.

Capacity, 7 quarts.
No. 12. Round, polished.$2.75
No. 23. Round, nickel-plated 3.50
No. 34. Crescent shape, polished 2.75
No. 48. Crescent shape, nickel-plated 3.50

GASOLINE VAPOR LAMP, No. 436.

The most economical heater in the market; for use under hot water urns or copper boilers.
Each........................75c

EYE PROTECTOR, No. 316.

Made of green celluloid and isinglass. Worn by the customer while the beard is being trimmed.
Each 20c

EYE PROTECTOR, No. 315.

To be worn by the customer, effectually protecting the eyes while the beard or mustache is being trimmed. Made of fine wire screen, bound with leather.
Each 20c

FEATHERWEIGHT EYE SHADE, No. 313.

Made of green celluloid.
Each.....................................25c

EYE SHADE, No. 314.

Each 10c

STEEL TWEEZERS.

No. 870. Each 25c

No. 874. Each 15c

No. 871. Each 25c

No. 872. Each 10c

NAIL CLIPPER, No. 868.

Best quality. Thoroughly hardened.
Each.......................$0.20
Per dozen.................. 2.00

SAFETY CLAMPS FOR HAIR CLOTHS.

A very convenient and useful article, by means of which hair cloths can be readily fastened together.
Each $0.10
Per dozen.................................... 1.00

THE IMPERIAL MUSTACHE CURLER.

A perfect device for quickly curling the mustache. These pincers are made of aluminum and are fitted with firm springs.

Per pair 25c

BARBERS' COATS.

No. 267.

Made of white drill. Pockets, collar and sleeves trimmed with black striped duck. Black buttons.

Price..............$1.00

**VEST WITH SLEEVES,
No. 275.**

Made of best quality white duck. A very comfortable and neat garment, especially during the summer months.

Price................$1.25

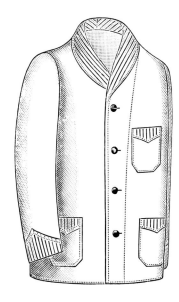

No. 268.

Made of white drill. Pockets, collar and sleeves trimmed with black striped duck. Black buttons.

Price..............$1.00

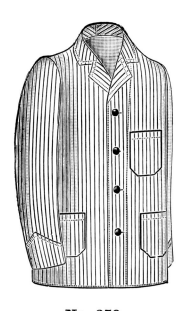

No. 278.

Made of white duck with black stripes. Black buttons.

Price..............$1.25

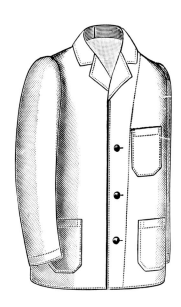

No. 264.

Made of white drill. The standard plain white coat. Black buttons. Price...........$0.75
No. 256. Same coat, but with standing collar. Price....$0.75

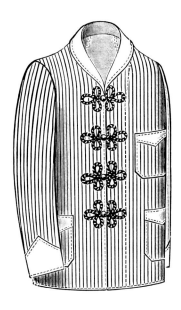

No. 265.

Made of white duck with black stripes. Fastened with braided loops.

Price...............$1.50

When ordering coats, always give us the breast measure, measuring under arms with the coat off.

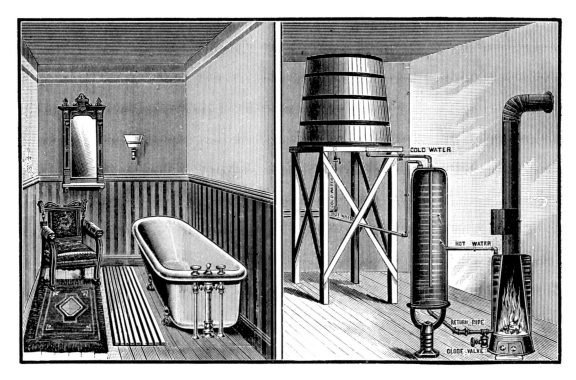

BATH OUTFITS.

COMPRESSED AIR OUTFITS.

Compressed air is now being used in modern barber shops to spray bay rum, witch hazel or perfumes, and dry the face after shaving. It is also used to blow away the loose hair after hair cutting and to dry the hair after a shampoo. The air is compressed and stored in an air tank by an air compressor which is run by the city water pressure. The compressor is noiseless and automatic, working when air is being used and stopping when its use is discontinued. Where there are no water works a double-action lever hand pump is used instead of the air compressor.

Prices, including Automatic Air Compressor.

Two-chair outfit.... $48.00   Three-chair outfit.... $52.00   Four-chair outfit.... $56.00
Five-chair outfit.... $84.35   Six-chair outfit..... $88.35

WILLIAMS' SHAVING SOAPS

Cleanse and **Stimulate** the action of the PORES.

Used in thousands of families *exclusively* for BATH and TOILET —antiseptic and *very healing*.

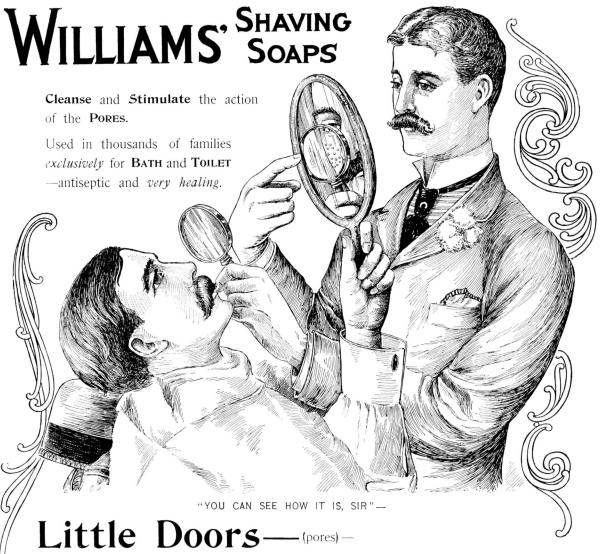

"YOU CAN SEE HOW IT IS, SIR"—

Little Doors —— (pores) —

myriads of them—unseen *but always open*—lead directly through the Skin—to the very life-blood of every human being.
Hence the *imperative necessity* that you guard these doors.
Let no impure particle enter—to mingle with the life-giving current.—Cleanse the passage itself—with pure and health-giving agents.
Herein lies largely—the secret of Fresh—Clear Skins.

Nothing comes nearer the skin than your SHAVING SOAP—You apply it with the brush—and, as it were, *force it* into those willing little doorways. Is your Shaving Soap PURE? Are you using the famous—

"WILLIAMS'" Shaving Soaps?

It is well to remember that for a good deal over HALF A CENTURY—these soaps have been made by the *same firm* —in the *same place*—and with the same scrupulous regard for every detail in manufacture.
It is worth something to know—that in the thousands of Tons of these Soaps—which have been sent all over the world—NOT ONE OUNCE of impure fats or other objectionable—dangerous matter—was ever contained.

CAUTION.—Cold, windy weather is upon us. Chapped faces invite cutaneous diseases. Be very firm with your barber. See that he uses none of the cheap, vile, impure Substitutes for Williams' Soaps. Insist that he use **WILLIAMS'**—and *only* **WILLIAMS'.** It heals the face—and keeps it soft and smooth. You pay a fair price for a Shave—you are entitled to all of the *comfort* and *protection* that the use of standard toilet preparations insures.

WILLIAMS' SOAPS—*in three principal forms*—are sold by all *Dealers.*

"Genuine Yankee" Soap, 10c.   Williams' Shaving Stick, 25c.   Williams' Barbers' Soap, 40c.

Oldest and most famous cake of shaving soap in the world. Millions using it.

Strong, metal-lined case. For Tourists' and Travelers' use. Don't fail to ask for WILLIAMS'—and take *no other.*

This is the kind your barber should use. It is also most excellent for Toilet use. Tons of it sold yearly to *families.* 6 cakes in a package—40c.

NOTE.—If your dealer does not have these soaps—we mail them—to any address—postpaid on receipt of price.—All three kinds sent for 75c. in stamps.
London Office and Warehouse: 64 GREAT RUSSELL ST., W. C.   Address **THE J. B. WILLIAMS CO., Glastonbury, Ct., U. S. A.**

BARBER SHOP QUARTETS

It's 1903 and "Sweet Adeline" is the season's song hit. Pen and ink sketch by Wm. Mark Young.

Barbershop quartets are famous for their unique blend of a capella harmony. Their origin is steeped in mythology; but modern "barbershoppers" owe a debt of gratitude to lawyer Owen C. Cash and businessman Rubert Hall, who in 1938 led a group of two dozen gentlemen in an old-time songfest atop the roof of a hotel in Tulsa, Oklahoma. Thus began "The Society for the Preservation and Encouragement of Barbershop Quartet Singing in America," now headquartered in Kenosha, WI.

The pleasing combination of barbershop chords is a purely American innovation dating from the 1880's. The melody is sung by the second tenor and the other three parts harmonize around it. (In most other styles of singing the melody is carried by the highest voice.) It is a real challenge to sing a separate first tenor part, above the melody, while a bass or baritone is belting out his own part right in your ear.

Mention is made in literature as far back as the 17th century of musical instruments in barber shops. However, the term "barbershop quartet" seems to have been coined in the fourth decade of the 20th century.

There is little doubt that the popularity of music halls and vaudeville shows in the 1880's and 1890's set the stage for a vibrant marriage of gospel and saloon-style singing that eventually became known as barbershop harmony. But the only pre-1940 reference I have found to "barbershop harmony" is a piece of sheet music, circa 1900, for a minstrel show featuring a "Chorus of 100 Male Voices," all in blackface.

Male quartets were the rage of the period and their popularity extended well into the 1900s. The Sears & Roebuck catalog of 1908 promoted "Vocal Quartets with Male Voices" as being "the most popular talking machine records on today's market." However, no mention is made of any title bearing the word "barbershop."

The absence of this term was, to me, very perplexing. In all of my research among letters, books, photos, and advertising of the pre-1939 period, the only time I found any reference to "barbershop" harmony was in that minstrel show piece. I wondered, *did anyone really sing inside the shaving place?* All that rhythm could have been very dangerous!

Above is a reproduction of a 19th-century painting of the famous singing barber "Figaro," from Rossini's opera *The Barber of Seville*, first produced in Rome in 1816. Figaro symbolized a carefree Don Juan, a razor-wielding Casanova of sorts. Some scholars claim that Figaro actually existed in the person of royal barber to Louis XVI, of France, and was a respected member of the king's court. —*Bettman Archive*

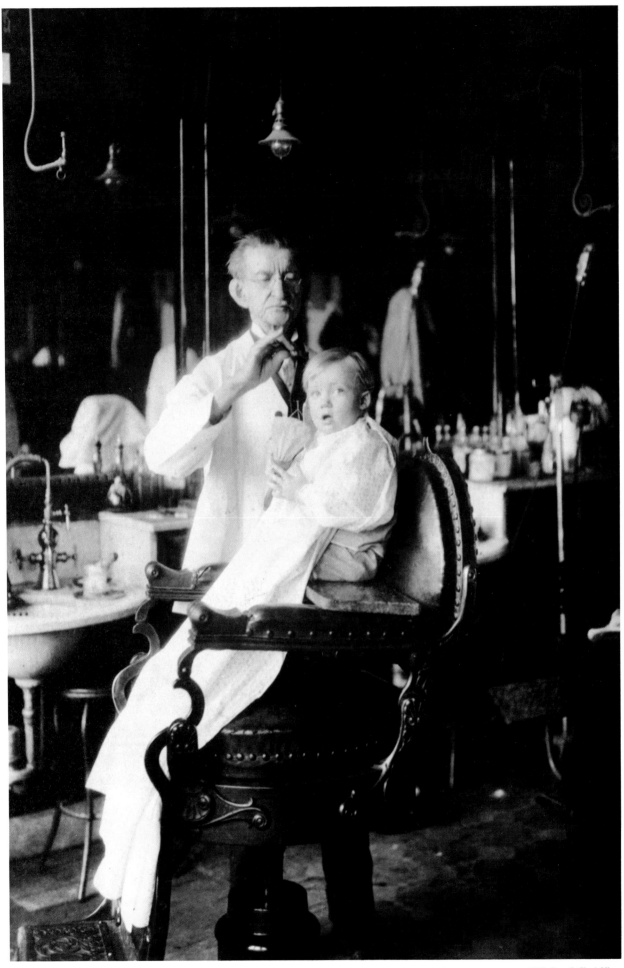

"First Haircut" circa 1910.　　　　　　　　　　*Michael Griffin*

MY LIFE AS A BARBER

by William Gambino

You might say that I was born into the trade. My Dad was an orthopedic shoemaker; however, my three uncles were all barbers who owned their own shops, and six of my cousins also became tonsorial artists. I begrudged the long hours, but I stuck with the profession for fifty eventful years.

It all began in 1905, when I was six months old. My parents decided to move from Brooklyn, New York to Flushing (Queens), New York, which was about an hour's trolley car ride out into the countryside. My dad opened up a shoe repair shop next door to my Uncle Tony's barber shop in Flushing.

At the age of twelve, I began casting about for various ways of earning some pocket money. After school hours, I found odd jobs to do in my father's shoe repair shop, but the grass looked greener over the fence at Uncle Tony's shaving place.

There, I could work all day Saturday and up to six hours on Sunday, and also pick up a few tips during the week when the shop was open from 9 a.m. to 11:00 p.m.

I swept the floor, lathered faces, applied lotions, combed hair and kept hot towels coming at a rate of up to three per shave. Razor honing was also my responsibility.

Regular customers came in about three times a week for a shave followed by a comb-and-brush treatment with hair tonic. Once a month, we would also shave the back of their necks, up to the hairline. These personal grooming services were performed (in 1917) for two dollars a month plus a ten-cent tip for the "boy." I earned up to three dollars a month in tips and another two dollars from sweeping, mopping and mug-washing.

I also curled moustaches. In those days, long moustache ends were grown and then waxed and curled with a warmed-up slate pencil. One Sunday, in walked Don Giovani; it was his wedding day and the occasion called for a special job. My assignment was to curl his moustache as the devil would have done it. Meanwhile, my eleven-year-old girlfriend, Millie, wanted to borrow my bike and I refused. She was very upset about this and as I was curling Don Giovani's moustache, Millie opened the screen door and kicked me. I pulled away, to push her, and as the devil would have it, the whole end of Don Giovani's moustache came off.

All hell broke loose. I got slapped, Millie ran away on my bike, and my dad rushed in to see what happened. After much discussion, the hair over the other side of Giovani's lip was cut to match. Upon looking in the mirror, Don Giovani smiled and said he thought it looked better. I received a ten-cent tip and got fired.

At the age of sixteen, after two years of high school, my dad and uncles figured it was time for me to attend a barber college and learn the trade properly. The college was located in the Bowery in New York City. Tools of the trade were purchased from the school for twenty-five dollars, another twenty-five bucks went for the first two months' tuition.

On my first day at school, the teacher questioned me

Flushing, New York, 1917. Bill Gambino, the boy barber, sits on his bicycle (center). His father, a shoe repairman, stands in doorway. Millie, his eleven-year-old pal, appears at right. Uncle Tony is inside the barber shop playing his mandolin.

about my experience. I was ushered to the end of the huge shop to a section that was curtained off around a single barber chair. I set up my equipment on a small table which held a mirror to see the customer.

The first victim brought in was a Bowery hobo, dirty, smelly and ragged. I set the chair back for a shave and washed his face. Then I lathered him up as the instructor looked on. The instructor told me to shave the hobo and then abruptly walked away.

I froze when I started to shave him, my hand was shaking like a leaf. The poor guy turned his head, gave me a fearful look, and aked me if I had ever shaved anyone before. Like a stupid kid, I said, "No, you are number one." He jumped off the chair, pulled the cloth from around his neck and ran out of the shop, lather flying in the wind.

Needless to say, I was chewed out plenty, and with the next customer the instructor stood by my chair. After tackling a shave, pulling and dragging and bringing forth many cuts, I finally got the knack. The following week, I was advanced to the paying customer's section. There I got to know the other students better.

One smart aleck, whose dad owned a shop, thought he knew a bit more than the rest of the class. One day as we watched him cut hair, he encountered some stray sprouts on top of the ears. Being a show-off, he made an artful swipe, missed, and nipped off the top of the customer's ear. Blood all over the place, lots of yelling and a grand mess! The student was sent home and the customer was rushed to a hospital.

One day, after school, some of our older classmates took a group of us to a burlesque house a few blocks away, I think it was called "The National Burlesque Theatre." It was located on the roof of a building. A half an hour into the spicy event, all hell broke loose. New York's finest broke into the room and arrested the whole audience! My dad gave me and my friends a very serious lecture. "A girlie show was no place for a 16-year-old."

In a few months I graduated and set out to look for a job. I tried many shops, but they were not interested in a wet-behind-the-ears kid with precious little experience. Finally, I stumbled onto a basement shop in the Bowery that needed a helper.

An 1808 Barbershop as depicted in an 1882 lithograph.

On my very first day I watched the boss shave a customer and gently place a hot towel over his face. Suddenly, he looked out the window and motioned for me to go to the back of the shop. Then he grabbed my hand and jerked me out the back door into the alley.

Bang, bang ... shots rang out! We rushed back into the shop to find our customer dead, the towel still covering his face; it was a gang hit! I grabbed my tools and left for good.

Following that episode, a family pow-wow was held, and my uncles agreed to shift me from one shop to another, within the family, until I had enough experience to find a permanent job.

I hated working for my uncles and cousins. All they would let me do was wash faces, handle hot towels, lather heads and comb hair. My fingers grew raw from rubbing wiry beards.

Eventually, I found a full time job in Greenpoint, near Brooklyn. My Uncle Barney had a shop close by, and it was his responsibility to keep his eye on this 18-year-old barber.

My new boss was named Jimmie. His was a two-chair shop with living quarters in the back. Jimmie's wife worked downtown and he would leave me in charge while he spent time with a lady friend. After three months of illicit pleasure the missus came home early one day and Jimmie's alibi was closed forever.

Back in Flushing, I found work in a small barber shop located above a drug store. It was a cheap-rent place with dark, narrow, low-ceilinged rooms. Most of our customers were immigrant Italian construction workers. Everybody there smoked Italian "De Nobili" cigars. My clothes stank of tobacco, my mouth tasted of smoke, and I was sick at my stomach much of the time.

One day the owner decided to put in a telephone and start a taxi service with two Model T Fords. The drivers lounged in our waiting-chairs between calls. During slow periods, the conversation usually centered on girls. (I put up with that awful tobacco smoke, just to learn more about girls.)

Shortly thereafter my chance came. One of the drivers said he would fix me up with a married woman for two dollars. A few days later it was all arranged. I was told to dress up in my best outfit because "Marge was very fussy." The address they gave me was a block down the street and two flights up.

My nineteen-year-old knees were shaking when I reached the top of the stairs. I adjusted my tie and knocked on the door. Suddenly there was cursing, yelling and screaming. I heard two shots and a thud on the floor. I ran down the stairs and headlong into the arms of the law.

Just when I thought my number was up, the policeman burst out laughing. The shots were firecrackers. The whole thing was a gag!

As time went by, I heard of an opening in Speedy Demola's barber shop. This shop was located on the outskirts of Flushing; it was a three-chair establishment. Speedy had a son who was 19 and his dad wanted him to learn barbering so that one day the shop would be his. It was the first establishment in which I had seen an electric clipper used; the year was 1924.

The clipper was attached to a rotating cable strung across the shop and hooked up to an electric motor. The clipper heads would vibrate at great speed and were quite noisy when in use. They had to be well oiled and have fast motion so that no hair would be pulled. This was especially true with youngsters who came in with several months of growth, their hair all matty and dirty.

Speedy's son Louie hated barbering. His love was automobile repair, which he would work at during the quiet hours. Louie owned a Model T Ford with no body and no windshield, just a motor and frame for which he paid $10. He didn't have enough money to repair the car and so I bought it for $15. We bolted a wooden crate to the frame to sit on and attached an umbrella in case it rained. I painted the whole thing red, including the umbrella. We drove this "car" on a vacant log next door until we missed a curve and smashed it up on a huge boulder.

As I gained more experience I started looking for work in New York City. At the age of twenty, I found a job in a hotel barber shop. Tips were good, but it so happened that many *nice guys*—gays—frequented this shop. While shaving these gentlemen, one would often feel their hands moving to one's private parts. Pulling away when I was thus selected, I would place a cold razor on the culprit's throat and whisper how that I hated the sight of blood. The hand was quickly removed!

A fellow apprentice, named Dominick, would be called upon to do room-service from time to time; this involved shaving customers in their rooms. Dom was a short, cherub-faced fellow with a soft pink complexion. One day Dom went on a call that would normally take about 20 minutes. Over an hour passed and no barber. The house detective and I went to the room. We found poor Dom tied up over a chair, his pants pulled down. He cried that he had been raped by three men. He said he was grabbed by them as soon a he entered the room and they all had their jollies at his expense. From then on I refused any room-service calls and shortly thereafter I quit the hotel barber shop.

My next job was in Long Island City. The boss there was an old German gentleman called Butch. He had hoped to hire a German barber, but I was the only qualified person who applied for the position. The shop was located in the Borough Hall area, and all the commissioners had their offices and staff there. The mayor of New York at that time was Jimmy Walker.

My very first customer was a chef from the restaurant in the basement. "New barber, huh?" said the chef. "He'd better be good, because I'm very particular." And as he sat in the chair he described in detail the exact effect he wanted—not too short, not too long, a nice curve at the neck, and the sideburns just so. "Yes, sir," I said ... and went to work.

At the end of the operation I held up the mirror, the usual formality. The chef's face became the picture of horror. He gasped ... the words wouldn't come. At last he managed to express himself. "Ruined! I'm ruined!"—and he clasped the sides of his head tragically. Butch came over. "Cut it all off!" the chef suddenly commanded. "Do you mean that?" I, who had lavished unusual care on the coiffure, asked. "Yes, yes; you've

This three-chair barber shop is typical of the establishments I worked in as a youth. —*William Gambino*

spoiled it! Cut it all off!''

"Hear that?'' I said to the boss. "He says he wants it all off.'' The boss said "Do what the gentleman wants.''

So again I went to work, and before long the chef had a perfect Sing-Sing haircut. Once more I raised the mirror. The customer beamed delightedly. "Ha!'' he exclaimed, "that's fine, fine! Look, Mr. Barber—that's the way I wanted it in the first place!''

In the rear of the lobby was a luncheonette and next to it was our partitioned-off barber shop. All of the office gang were continually marching in and out of the luncheonette. It was a lively place to work. Two years later, my kindly old boss "Butch,'' who was in his late seventies, suffered a heart attack and died. The shop and the lunch counter both closed shortly afterwards. The year was 1926, the end of an era was approaching.

That same year I turned twenty-one years of age and decided to work my way to the West Coast. My parents called it madness!

I hitch-hiked to Niagara Falls, took a few Kodak snapshots and went on to Erie, New York. I took an overnight boat ride across Lake Erie to Cleveland, Ohio.

My first job in Cleveland was at "Chick's Barber Shop,'' a four-chair establishment with two manicurists and a bootblack. Chick found me a one-bedroom apartment in the Hollywood section of Cleveland.

Sunday was my day off. I cleaned up my room and left the door open. Many young ladies went by with friendly hellos. I was puzzled by the fact that there were so many women around. After speaking to the manager, he told me they were prostitutes and to "Be careful.''

About a week later around midnight there was a terrible commotion, noisy shouts, etc. My door was broken down; the police had raided the joint. I was arrested (and released within one hour with an apology.)

I moved out of the area to another apartment. During my stay at Chick's, his girlfriend shot him; then one of his manicurists became pregnant and tried to blame me. I had nothing to do with her condition so I quickly moved on.

My next stop was St. Louis. The evening I arrived I was held up at gun point and my money taken before I found a place to sleep. I had about 75 cents in change left and bought two hamburgers that tasted like bread and fat.

After walking around for a long time I finally found a flophouse for 25¢ a night. I was led upstairs to a room that had been partitioned off into tiny cubicles. The lock was a padlock and I was cautioned to keep it fastened.

If you wanted to wash, you had to go down to the end of the hall to a bathroom which supplied paper towels but no soap. There was water in my room, but it was not drinkable. Time to go to sleep.

I heard some people talking so I peeked over the partition and saw a huge room full of cots; they were the 10¢ sleeping quarters. I was used to a good home life and this all made me wonder why I ever left to go on such an adventure.

During the night I started to scratch. On went the light. I was covered with bed bugs. I cleaned myself thoroughly and placed the bed sheets on the floor to sleep. What a night. That was enough of St. Louis.

I hitchiked west across Missouri to Kansas City where I got a job in a small barbershop. The owner told me it was only a two-month position. He was a fight promoter and was going on the road with his boxer.

Finding a private room in a boarding house, for $10 a week with two meals a day, was a stroke of luck. Edith, the cheerful blonde lady who ran the boarding house, came into my room the first night, got into bed with me, and asked if I would like to make her happy once in a while. For two months, I was a very happy 22-year-old!

In November, my parents started to demand that I come home for Christmas and because my aunt and uncle were coming through Kansas they would pick me up for the trip back.

I will never forget that journey. My aunt and uncle and myself in the front seat, a dog and baggage and several pieces of furniture in the back. The trip took 8 days. For all of those 8 days it rained. We each took turns driving.

We made a stop in Ames, Iowa. The temperature had dropped to 10 below zero and our overnight stay was in a small cabin with one bucket of coal. I went to bed with my clothes on and almost froze to death. The bucket of coal did not last through the night. We all wanted to get home as fast as possible.

As we drove through Pennsylvania, it was dark. We reached the outskirts of Scranton and could look down on the city below from the top of our road. Then we spotted a side road which we decided to try because we thought it might be a shortcut. There were no street lights, it was raining, the car lights went on and off and the brakes did not hold due to the constant rain. We were part way down the road when our car lights went out again and the brakes failed completely. We felt sure this was the end!

Suddenly the lights came on for a few seconds, time enough for us to see that we were almost to the edge of a cliff. I grabbed the wheel and managed to get us back on the road. We crashed through a fence and into the back-yard of someone's home. We were thrown out; the dog, baggage and contents were strewn all over the place. There was little damage to the car, but I was knocked unconscious and during that period I saw myself dead in a coffin, surrounded by parents and family, all dressed in black. Plenty of flowers and crying people. The rain ended and we limped home to hot food and warm beds.

Back home in Flushing I took many short term jobs. I was 25 years old before I finally found a decent position. Depression days were upon us, the year was 1930. My salary was $17 a week for 12 hours a day, plus a half day on Sunday.

I enjoyed working in Vincent's barber shop. Haircuts were 35¢ and shaves cost 15¢. In addition to their regular trade, this shop had a "choice" clientele. For the select group there were deluxe 50¢ haircuts and 25¢ shaves in an exclusive section at the back of the shop. Vincent also owned a beauty parlor which gave me the opportunity to learn hairdressing. We gave permanent waves, did hair curling, bobbing, setting, bleaching and tinting.

Next door was a florist who had a son named Jack, a year older than I. We got along great. Just around the corner was the Flushing Hospital and many nurses came in for hair care services. We also had calls to shave hospital patients. One very nice orderly from the hospital used to frequent our barber shop. He came in twice a week for a shave. At first I could not understand why the lather turned pink on his cheeks. Then I realized that Burt used rouge. Each time Burt came in, my friend Jack, the florist, would tease him. One day Jack was going to a special show and was wearing a suit that looked like a Mexican horse blanket. Burt fell in love with that multi-colored suit.

Burt was due for a two-week vacation from the hospital and planned to visit his parents who lived in Buffalo. Arrangements were made to lend Burt the suit. It was a perfect fit. Several months went by. No Burt, no suit. Jack inquired about Burt at the hospital and found them also concerned, as they had not heard from him either. Jack got Burt's address and wrote to his parents. The parents wrote back, saying that Burt had passed away and had been buried in a "borrowed suit."

Over the four-year period I worked in Vincent's shop, I was required many times to provide personal grooming services at the hospital. I had to shave patients with pneumonia while wearing a mask and a hospital gown. Some patients were so immobile that I had to cut their hair while they were lying in bed—one half side at a time.

Barbers are in constant peril from drunks, children, and mentally ill people who make sudden unexpected movements (or throw up on you). Then there are those foolish souls who won't stop talking during a shave.

Diseases of the scalp and head lice are also dangers we faced. You must be constantly disinfecting yourself and your tools so that none of these problems are passed from barber to barber, or from customer to customer.

Once my boss Vincent planned a two-week vacation. It was all set. A middle-aged barber named Ralph was hired to fill in. At the end of the day we both went home by trolley car, which was a half a block away from the barber shop. On the way home, when we passed the hospital, Ralph would cross himself. "You can die in there," he always remarked.

One day during Vincent's vacation, a call came in to shave a patient. I was busy and finally convinced Ralph to go. He tried to find the room, in vain, and wound up taking the freight elevator. As Ralph got on the elevator, there were two dead bodies on guerneys, all covered with sheets. Two orderlies were leaning on one of the stiffs. Ralph asked them what was on the stretcher and when told he rushed back to the barber shop, crossing himself, and mumbling "No more, no more!"

A priest happened to walk in the shop later that day and when told of the incident, he threw holy water on Ralph and told him the devil had left him. Ralph was smiling all the rest of the day.

Unbeknownst to Vincent, Ralph had sleeping sickness (narcolepsy), which meant he could fall asleep at any time, any place—sitting, standing or working. Vincent had developed a bad cold and decided to keep Ralph on a few more days. One day, I had to go to lunch and I told Ralph to be careful and not to go to sleep. When not busy he frequently would lower the chair back, lay in it, and go to sleep.

During that lunch period, he did lower the chair and fall asleep. The shoemaker from next door came in and saw Ralph snoozing. He went back to his store and got a jar of black shoe polish. He deftly painted Ralph's face to resemble a minstrel singer and sneaked out. In the meantime, someone else entered the shop, saw a sleeping Negro, and helped himself to the contents of the cash register, about $30. When I returned from lunch, I found Ralph fast asleep next to the empty cash register. There was a lot of explaining to do. Vince kept him on a few more weeks until all the money missing from the cash register was worked off.

My biggest problem at Vincent's was the beauty parlor next door. There was a middle-aged woman who had a crush on me; she was very fat, with a face only a mother could love. She wore several big diamond rings on her fingers and was obviously worth a couple of million dollars. Many times when I was behind the closed curtain with her, trying to work on her hair, she would grab me and kiss me. I put up with this because she was a big tipper. One day she propositioned me. She told me she would set me up in an aprtment, give me money and a car and all I had to was make love to her once a week. She left smiling, and told me she would be waiting for my answer. She never got one.

At the age of 26, I met the girl I married and a new life began. Now that I had the responsibility of a wife, more money was required. I wound up buying a one-man shop in Flushing. My older sister lived close by and we rented an apartment near her.

The barber shop was on a side street in a quiet neighborhood. Rent was $15 a month. This was in the middle of the depression and President Roosevelt was promising a chicken in every pot.

Vincent had paid me $17 a week plus tips, a total of $100 a month. Shortly after opening my own business, I was earning $50 a week, twice the money, which was a welcome change. Slowly, as time passed, more and more new customers frequented my little shop and most of the old customers stayed with me. My success with children's haircuts was a big factor in the growth of our business.

Barbering is a profession which takes from five to seven years to master. One must learn to be patient, each customer has his own idea of the type of haircut he desires. It has become a very personal business. Children require an especially careful approach, more so if they have been frightened by other barbers.

The psychology of barbering is acquired by experience. In a multiple-chair shop one can observe how certain customers favor certain barbers. They like the handling, the gentleness, or perhaps the advice a barber gives them on personal problems. Jealousy is a big factor in this business; one barber hates to be passed up in favor of another.

One-man shops have no such problems, but the shop must be clean and sanitary and the barber must be meticulous in the care of his instruments.

In the early days, before the hand clipper was invented, a haircut was accomplished by a comb, scissors and a razor. Then the hand clipper came into being in the 1880's and was a wonderful time-saver. In the early 1900's the motor clipper evolved. It consisted of a small motor hanging from the ceiling with a cable rotating at one end, which reached a noisy clipper six or eight feet away.

Then came the individual, motorized hand clipper. I recall the first one, manufactured by Oster; it was quite noisy. Later, a smaller one was introduced by Andes. This was very quiet and did not require the changing of cutter heads. A lever on the side of the clipper moved the blade to different settings for variations of closeness.

Scissors manufactured in Germany and Switzerland were the preferred instruments. The blades went from a five-inch to a seven-inch size. The larger size was mainly used for the heavier hair growth of children and ladies.

Barbers made extra money by giving a shampoo, a singe or a massage. When the customer got "the works"—a haircut, shave, shampoo and massage—the whole thing took about an hour. This put the barber under pressure if many customers were waiting, and was discouraged on busy weekends.

The practice was, "No children or ladies on Saturday." Usually, ladies' haircuts were available only if it was a combined barber and beauty shop, which was partitioned off.

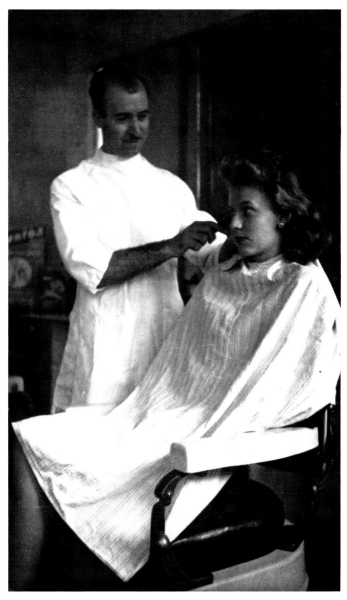

William Gambino works on a pretty customer in his Flushing, N.Y. Barber Shop in 1954.

Many styles came in and out of fashion. If a famous movie star had a certain type of haircut, all the ladies wanted the same thing. Each head of hair was different and it took many visits to refine the different styles each client wanted. A customer would come in and tell me to "cut it like the last time." Without a photographic memory, a barber is in trouble!

In a one-man shop, the barber soon learns how each customer wants things done. He also becomes almost a father confessor. Customers start relating personal problems. Teenagers would sound off about the way their parents treated them and by listening to each one, even if no advice could be given, the barber becomes a psychologist.

He knows the inner feelings of many, and tells them to none. My elderly customers talked constantly of their wives, lost by death. I heard the terrible difficulties of men out of jobs, with no hope for the future. Barbers are also called upon to make loans and to accept I.O.U.'s for haircuts.

Children were my greatest joy; but they were tough to handle because a first haircut always brings fear. I kept a jar full of lollipops on hand to give the kids after the hair cutting was over. At first, I would give them a lollipop during the haircut, but that proved to be disastrous. Falling hair would stick to the sucker or it would bang a jerking head, etc. Candy was served only after haircuts from then on.

One day a new customer came in with a little boy named Jerry. He was placed on a small seat that fit across the arms of the barber chair. I did not know that Jerry had a weak back and could not sit without being held.

In one second, I saw him falling foward. I moved fast and caught him when he was just inches from hitting the floor. I scolded his parent for not telling me about Jerry's back. After that, I tied Jerry to the chair.

There was a large showcase in which I kept little toys for five cents to amuse the children. One day a four-year-old named Alex was brought in for a haircut. There was no way his mother could get him to sit in the chair to get a haircut, and he needed one badly. A few days later, a group of children came in for toys. Little Alex tagged along, staying in the shop and talking. He rode in on his tricycle, and it suddenly dawned on me that maybe I could give him a haircut-on-wheels. I placed the sheet around him while he sat on his bike and he stayed still. He was told a free lollipop was his after the cut. He went home to surprise his family (who left town the next day).

The barber often cuts a poor child's hair free of charge, or takes a chance on ever being paid for making some job-hunter presentable. The number of defaults in the latter category is surprisingly small.

In 1941, World War II started and many of my customers were drafted. A lot of local businesses had to shut their doors because of drafted owners. One day, a customer, Jim, came in with his son. Little Jim Jr. sat in the chair. His father thought he should have a military haircut. Well, the hair clipper I used scared the daylights out of him and the little fellow would only consent to a haircut if no clipper was used, just the shears.

On the next haircutting trip, his visiting cousin, the same age, came along for a haircut, too. I sat both boys together and covered each with a different cloth. Jimmy's cousin wanted the clipper to be used because I let him flip the switch to start the clipper. Young Jimmy watched. He got up enough courage to want to start the clipper. I let him hold the machine "real tight" (if dropped, it would break the blade). He lost his fear of the clipper and from then on there was no problem giving him his military haircut.

As time went on, the continual loss of customers due to the war forced me out of business. The shop was sold and converted into a beauty parlor. Luckily, I found out about a friend who was about to be drafted by the military, and ran his shop until he returned.

At the age of 45, my hair started falling out. One barber told me it was "Because you have given too many haircuts to young children." Another said that maybe my hat was too small and it was cutting off the circulation to my scalp. Anyway, my dad had a full head of hair and I wasn't very happy about my premature loss.

One day, a real-estate broker friend of mine told me he knew of a lady who could solve my "problem" and perhaps make me wealthy at the same time. The story follows, as printed in the *Queens County Times*.

After selling about 200 jars of my baldness cure, for a total of $490, I appeared on a New York City T.V. show for an interview. A big mistake! Several weeks later, an agent from the Food and Drug Administration knocked on my door. His first question was had I paid the New York State sales tax? "Of course, we pay it on all the products we sell here," I answered.

Then the agent took a sample of "Maidenhair," for testing, and told me not to advertise or sell any more of the product until I had received federal approval. Needless to say, the government laboratory never got back to me, and my dreams of riches faded away. Now I know what Mrs. "A." meant when she cryptically told me "You'll find out."

— **William Gambino**

June 28, 1950

Queens County Times

Baldness Conquered? Bill Vows He and 35 Others Have New Hair

by C.W.N.

Lotions to grow hair on bald heads have come and gone, and invariably they have failed. The search for the successful formula has been on a par with the quest of perpetual motion.

And yet Bill the Barber lowered his head for me today and I swear I saw hairs on what used to be the lone prairee!

I do hope I'm not self-deceived; I sincerely don't want to mislead Queens County Times readers. But as nearly as I can recall, without having had the foresight to take a census two months ago, the hirsute population of Bill's bean has really increased in the interim.

He himself says it has, and he ought to know. I'm inclined to believe Bill because I've known him personally (William Gambino is the formal name) and have patronized his shop these ten years or more.

Bill not only let me examine his darkening dome, but also exhibited before-and-after photos of other baldies who appear to have experienced the same happy phenomenon.

To be sure, you saw nowhere any rich mat of wavy locks; the picture was more like that of a promising garden in early spring; yet the tender shoots were clearly visible. Bill believes it takes a year to get the full crop.

But let him tell it:

Bill's Story

About eight months ago a customer and friend of mine who is a real-estate broker came into my barber shop quite excited. "I have just the thing for you!" said he.

"I just sold a house to a woman who has a scalp cream made of tropical herbs.

"That scalp cream grows hair!"

Being a barber and baldheaded myself, I scoffed. He pleaded. I remained skeptical. I had tried all that was humanly possible, so why take any stock in this guy's wild yarn?

Polish Your Sconce With *Delilah* HAIR ENCOURAGER Finds You Bald Or Makes You So.

But every time he came in for his haircut this Mr. X, let us call him, insisted, demanded and commanded that I go see the woman who possessed the wonderful formula.

Ha-ha! I yessed him along to a fare-theewell.

One day he came in with a determined look on his puss. Hard as nails. Do or die. He had made an appointment with the woman and I'd better honor it or else, by the seven sniffing dogs!

It so happened that at the moment I had in the chair a Mr. Y, who had been bald 30 years. As soon as Mr. Y caught the drift, both of them were on my neck.

So I gave in and went to see the lady, but I still thought her idea fantastic.

She gave me several jars to experiment with. Mr. Y being willing to act as the guinea pig, I sloshed it on his dome.

Imagine my amazement when, within 25 days, hair started to grow!

So I tried it on myself—and now I too have hair growing.

I tried it on 35 other customers. It worked on them all. God bless that woman!

Everybody else laughed at me. My family doctor said I had "a high-standard imagination."

I asked Mrs. A. why she didn't commercialize her great product, and why she wasn't by now one of the world's outstanding successes. Her reply was a cryptic "You'll find out."

I asked her for the distributorship. She granted it.

Feeling all set, I prepared ads for the magazines and jobbers.

Now I started "finding out." All my ads, down to the tiniest, were refused.

But—seeing is believing, said I to myself; I won't give up!

Discovery of the Formula

In a subsequent talk with Mrs. A I asked how she came upon such a great formula. The answer was a story.

"About 200 years ago," she said, "a great-great-uncle of mine was a missionary priest who traveled extensively and had lived among the Hindus, Persians, Chinese, Mexican Indians, and many other peoples.

"He noticed that when a native lost a patch of hair, the medicine man would gather herbs, mix a paste, and apply it. Several months later hair would fill the bald patch.

"Amazed, he recorded his findings. The medicine men not only cured baldness but many other ills.

"But the formula book my relative compiled was laid aside and forgotten for two centuries."

Then, Mrs. A related, she herself fell ill and lost her hair. The family gathered and decided to try great-great-uncle's formula.

It worked. Then they tried it on Mrs. A's nephews, with the same happy results.

But as for commercializing it—the family has been trying to do that for 10 years.

"It's easier to grow hair on a bald head," says Mrs. A, "than it is to get anybody to believe it can be done."

And here Bill the Barber takes up the story:

"And so have I failed to commercialize the stuff—so far, that is. Yet I have seen it, in my own shop and with my own eyes, benefit my own customers, even myself! It actually eliminates dandruff, relieves scalp itch, checks falling hair.

"I still say seeing is believing. I'm not licked yet."

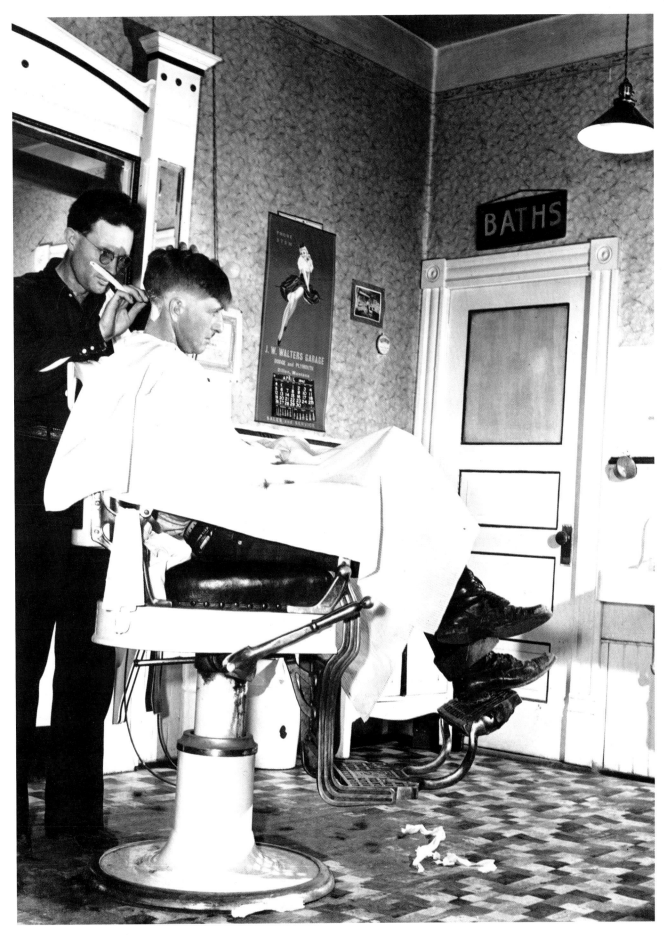

"Bare Bones" Barber Shop in Wisdom, Mont., April, 1942. One mug, one razor, one bathtub and one very serious operator. —*Library of Congress*

W.M. Mallory takes a break in front of his Main Street "Harlem Barber Shop" in Oxford, North Carolina, Nov. 1939. (Below) "Hair Straightening $1.00" and "No Profane Language" appear on signs in this Washington, D.C., Black-owned barber shop, July, 1942. —Library of Congress.

"You gotta get Wildroot Cream Oil, Charlie . . . It keeps your hair in trim . . . You see, it's non-alcoholic, Charlie . . . It's made of soothing lanolin." Mr. Vaccarelli opened this barbershop in Manayunk, Penn. shortly after his arrival from Italy. —Karen D'Alessandro. (Below) A rural shop of the 1920's. —Author's Collection

Lesson   Subject   Two

HONING AND STROPPING

HONING AND STROPPING

Honing

Things to Remember

If a barber lacks skill in honing he hides behind the camouflage of temperamentality.

The mechanical skill of honing razors is acquired only by practical experience, but there are certain rules governing this work that you must always observe.

First, the razor must always be kept perfectly flat on the hone. Second, it must be drawn forward with edge first on a diagonal stroke. Third, the edge must never touch the hone in a backward stroke when putting it in position for the second movement. Fourth, every part of the edge must touch the hone with equal pressure and the same amount of draw across the stone at all parts.

You could obtain the same results by laying your razor diagonally across the hone and drawing it straight forward across the edge, but this makes the process of honing more difficult. It is best to lay the razor on the hone with the back of the blade straight with the end of the hone, holding the razor in a position that enables you to turn it in the hand without turning the hand.

This movement will require considerable practice but it can be acquired and it is one of the things by which the old barber gauges your skill as a workman.

Things to Remember

One will learn by the draw when the razor is taking an edge. There will seem to be a suction to the hone.

Testing an edge on the flesh after honing, is very deceptive. One cannot determine an over-honed edge.

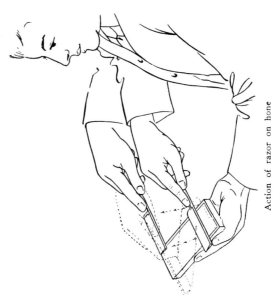

Starting position of razor on hone

Honing is not a knack; it is a science and must be learned, not acquired.

Action of razor on hone

A Lesson from "The Barbers' Manual," by A.B. Moler. Revised edition, 1927.

Things to Remember

It is well to practice on an old razor or on a slow cutting hone that you do not damage a perfectly good instrument and continue to practice this until it becomes perfectly easy and natural.

After the mechanical skill has been acquired, the testing of the edge to determine its fitness is next in importance.

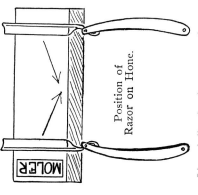

Position of Razor on Hone.

Line of direction for razor on hone

You determine the edge by testing it on the nail. Usually the barber moistens his thumb nail, and by drawing the edge over the nail lightly, it will tell you the condition. If a razor has a thick blunt edge, it will ride over the nail without making any impression as would any blunt instrument, but if it is honed thin, it will cut in and draw as you move it over the surface. If it has a rather gritty grating feeling, it will indicate that the razor is too rough and this may be when it is not quite honed to an edge or when it has been over-honed to the

A smooth even draw just heavy enough to feel the cut gives the best edge.

An uneven edge cannot be kept sharp. Hone evenly from heel to point.

Things to Remember

degree where the edge breaks and crumbles giving it that disagreeable gritty feeling.

It is necessary to test the edge frequently as you hone, in order to detect its condition, and as you find it is taking an edge, hone

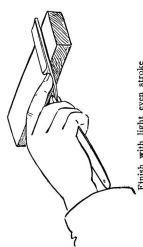

Finish with light even stroke

Testing edge after honing

very cautiously for an over-honed edge is as bad or worse than one not sufficiently honed. There is little danger of over-honing when a water hone is used. This is why it is recommended from the beginning, but as the water hone is a little too slow for the workman who wants to make time, the Swaty hone here has its place in the kit.

A nick in the edge of the razor causes it to jump as it is drawn over the nail.

An overhoned edge feels rough, like a file. It can be smoothed by drawing over a match or like surface, a few times, then rehoned.

This Lesson is reproduced directly from the 1927 edition of "The Barbers' Manual," by A.B. Moler. Mr. Moler founded a chain of barber colleges in 1893, and published the first edition of this textbook in 1898.

Neither the razor nor strop should be colder than the temperature of the room when stropping.

Stropping

A razor unless freshly honed should always be stropped on the canvas strop first just enough to draw out the edge and finish on the leather. There is a friction in stropping on the canvas that heats the metal, thereby expanding it and bringing it out to a keener edge so enough stropping should be given on the canvas to heat the blade, from one-half to one dozen strokes.

The strops should be held tight and a sufficient pressure given the razor on the strop to feel the draw and the razor must be held perfectly flat on the strop. It can be drawn perfectly straight, but there will be no harm if drawn diagonally on the sur-

Freshly honed razors need only the leather strop. A freshly honed razor is one just off the hone.

Stropping position

The more shaves you give, without honing, the more stropping will be needed. First with canvas, second with leather.

face and it should be turned on its back for each stroke without lifting it from the strop.

There is quite a knack turning the razor in the hand without turning the hand itself. It should be so held that it can be easily rolled in the hand, making the process of stropping much easier and more graceful.

After the proper number of strokes on the canvas, turn the strop over, bringing the leather side up, and strop on this the same as on the canvas, generally about the same number of strokes.

If a razor is freshly honed it should not be put on the canvas strop but should be

Too much stropping or too heavy is as bad as not enough, and too lightly.

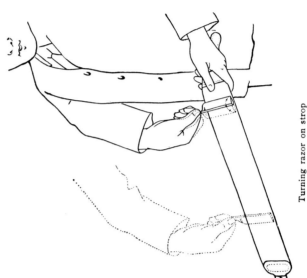

Turning razor on strop

Things to Remember

Exercises

PRECEDING our lesson in shaving, we give a number of exercises that are essential in enabling one to take the proper positions in handling razor and to put the hands in proper condition for shaving.

These exercises can be practiced to advantage preceding the actual work at the chair but in your endeavor to put this into effect, if for home practice, be sure that you have followed instructions carefully.

You must note that a razor is never carried straight forward toward the edge; it must always be held so that the cutting edge will strike the object to be cut at an angle or like sawing, for it is the teeth or roughness in the edge (too fine to be detected with the naked eye) that does the work like the teeth in a saw, therefore every stroke with a razor blade must be a sliding stroke. Too much emphasis cannot be given to this particular point, for if not practiced properly, your exercises would be of no avail.

The several positions that one must acquire in getting at all parts of the face, are four in number called Free Hand, Back Hand, Double Back Hand and Reverse Hand. The object in using the left hand while working with the right is to imitate the actual shaving movements. The left hand is always used to draw the skin tight under razor and the exercises must be with the left hand.

A Lesson from "The Barbers' Manual," by A.B. Moler. Revised edition, 1927.

Things to Remember

A razor is carried over the face, not dragged or pushed.

Cutting strokes like cutting remarks, penetrate if not handled skillfully.

---

stropped immediately on the leather and usually a little more stropping at first than will be required after the edge has been smoothed.

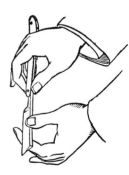

Testing edge after stropping

You test the edge of your razor after stropping by drawing it over the flesh or ball of your finger. Draw the razor carefully over the surface or you may draw your finger over the edge, to detect its condition.

If in perfect shape, it will have a smooth, keen cut that will not permit you to draw very far without cutting through, but if it is rough it will have a rather disagreeable feeling, although it may cut into the flesh just as quickly as the keen edge.

This, however, would not give a satisfactory shave where the smooth, keen edge is necessary to do the work properly. If you were to look at the blade through a microscope you would find it has teeth like a saw and the honing and stropping is given to obtain just the proper set or size to the teeth.

Things to Remember

A stropped razor gives its answer to the flesh, not the nail.

The razor should be stropped just before the shave; no other time. This is on account of the heat given to the razor by the friction of stropping. The heat expands the metal, giving a better edge.

Now cover the customer with a chair cloth by swinging it over the customer, not by standing back of the customer and swinging it over the head. There are conditions, such as extremely hot weather, when the chair cloth is not spread over the customer, but this is the unusual, not the usual procedure.

Now take your face towel from the stack on your workstand right by your elbow, unfold it and place it diagonally over the customer's chest and with the first finger of the right hand lifting the neck band at the collar button and tuck the edge of the towel in at the neck band with a sliding motion with the first finger of the left hand.

Now cross the other end of your towel over, turn the customer's face toward you and tuck in the other side, changing hands.

See that the linen is smoothly and neatly spread for the manner of handling linen often decides in the boss's mind whether or not you will hold your first job. Now pick up your cup and brush and if you are working with an individual washstand in front of your customer, do the rinsing of the mug in a manner that will show your customer, if he may be looking, that you are giving him sanitary service. This should be done quickly and noislessly and only a little mixing after the water has been emptied from your cup, just a sufficient amount to fill your brush with a lather about the consistency of thick cream. If the lather in the brush is too moist, it will run down the customer's neck; if too

---

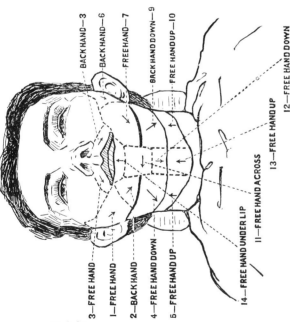

3—FREE HAND
1—FREE HAND
2—BACKHAND
4—FREE HAND DOWN
5—FREE HAND UP

BACK HAND—3
BACKHAND—6
FREE HAND—7
BACK HAND DOWN—9
FREE HAND UP—10

14—FREE HAND UNDER LIP
11—FREE HAND ACROSS
13—FREE HAND UP
12—FREE HAND DOWN

Diagram of Face for Shave.

As your customer takes your chair, raise the headrest several notches and try to turn the chair in a manner that will make it easy for him to be seated, and as you swing the chair in position, also recline it at the proper angle, making it comfortable for the customer, still easy for you to operate.

Avoid letting the chair down to its extreme limit and pumping it up to height to suit you for the customer is never comfortable laying perfectly flat. The head should be higher than the feet. The chair will be partially reclined always.

A Lesson from "The Barbers' Manual" by A.B. Moler. Revised edition, 1927.

Lathering. Left hand turning head

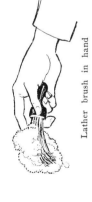

Lather brush in hand

Too many fingers in the froth spoils the broth.

To rattle your brush in the mug keeps your customer awake. If he wants to sleep, let him.

stiff, it will dry quickly on the face and you will not get the benefits that the lather is intended to give to the operation.

You apply the lather with the handle of the brush in the palm of the right hand, allowing the ends of your fingers to work down into the bristles to keep them from spreading too much and to enable you to handle the brush more easily. It must be used with a rotary movement, which not only works the lather into the roots of the hair, but enables the brush to make more lather in itself as you go over the face in a rotary movement.

Apply the lather to all parts of the beard that is to be shaved using care around the mouth at the nostrils and at the ears. After the face has a good coat of lather, take the brush between the thumb and finger of the left hand, holding the hand at the headrest, not at the customer's forehead, in a manner that will enable you to turn the head from right to left without raising it from the headrest, and with the right hand rub the lather well with a rotary movement so that the soap will be worked well into the roots of the beard.

After a little rubbing, generally from two to three minutes, you re-place your lather brush in the cup, pick up a turkish

There is a difference between a steamed towel and a soaked one. Steam your towels.

Cut and scald and you will have more time for the ball-game tomorrow.

or steam towel. Fold it once lengthwise, hold it under the hot water until thoroughly saturated, wring it out reasonably dry, having it as hot as the hands will bear it comfortably, and spread it over the face by holding it at the two ends, bringing it from the lower part of the neck over the entire face, including the forehead and eyes.

Applying hot towel

Allow the towel to remain on the face to steam while you strop the razor, then remove the lather and be careful not to rub against the grain of the beard. Re-lather the beard and proceed with the shave.

195

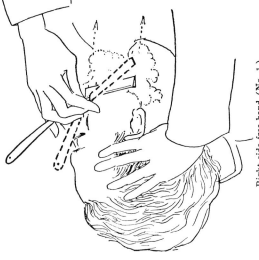

This illustration shows the improper position of the razor. The dotted lines show the proper position. This precautionary illustration should assist you to the right position.

As much depends upon keeping the skin tight under the razor as does the condition of your razor, for comfortable shaving.

Right side free hand (No. 1.)

Movements

The razor is to be held in the right hand with the handle between the little and third finger and in such a manner that it will enable you to draw the razor forward with a diagonal cutting stroke. The razor must not be drawn straight while shaving, it must have a sliding, cutting stroke.

After stropping the razor start at the right side of the face at the hair line, shaving down with a free hand stroke to the jaw bone, holding the surface that you are going over smooth and tight with the left hand. As you continue to shave continue to bring the left hand close to the surface that you are shaving that you may draw the skin tight, and continue with the same kind of a stroke until the right side of the face has been shaved to the corner of the mouth. This is movement No. 1.

Another precaution regarding the back hand stroke may help. Keep the elbow up and carry the razor; do not push it.

Position for back hand

Allow me to caution you at this point regarding the use of lather paper. The regulation size for lather paper is 4x6 inches. Always wipe your razor off in the center and *not* around the outer edge as you are apt to do.

At this point you use the back hand stroke, which is reversing the razor in the hand, and so held that it will enable you to give a sliding stroke with the point of the razor in advance and shave to the point of the chin.

Also be careful that you shave the corner of the mouth with the back hand movement. This is movement No. 2.

The proper placing of a customer in a chair that he may be comfortable is as important as the actual shave. Avoid dropping the headrest too low or reclining the chair too much.

Do not attempt to shave with an old-fashioned razor unless a medical doctor is in attendance.

In shaving the upper lip, avoid pinching the nose with the left hand; just touch it lightly.

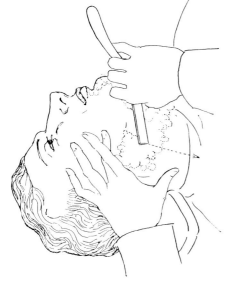

Free hand down (No. 4.)

You now start at the point of the chin, holding the skin tight between the thumb and second finger of the left hand and shave down on the side of the neck as far as the grain of the hair will allow, being cautious always not to touch a hair against the grain. Continue to shave over this surface as far back as the ear. This is movement No. 4.

You will now step back of your customer for movement No. 5, a free hand stroke shaving the lower part of the neck up with the grain, stretching the skin on the neck between the thumb and fingers of the left hand, shaving on the surface that is so stretched.

If the finger of the left hand is placed lightly against the side of the nose and the thumb at the corner of the mouth, the skin on the upper lip can be stretched, making the shave much easier.

The left side of the upper lip is frequently shaved with the free hand stroke from the corner of the mouth toward the nose, but it is not advisable in case of a heavy growth.

Back hand (No. 2.)

When you have completed this section of the face, which is from the corner of the mouth to the point of the chin as far down as the jaw bone, you will again use the free hand movement over the right side of the upper lip.

With the left hand you will touch the nose lightly to enable you to place the razor on the upper lip, shaving first the portion under the nose. Finish the right side of the lip with the free hand movement. This is movement No. 3.

There is some question, by barbers, regarding the best manner of shaving the upper lip. Some prefer to shave against the grain, shaving from the corner of the mouth to the nose on either side, but experience has taught us the beginner can better master this stroke by using the free hand on the right side and the back hand on the left.

The direction the hair points coming out of the skin is called "with the grain." The opposite is called "against the grain." Shave with the grain all that it is possible.

197

Things to Remember

There is a knack in keeping the fingers of the left hand dry to better stretch the skin; and a knack in stretching the skin when the fingers are moist. Never use alum.

Left side down back hand (No. 9.)

Now with the back hand shave the opposite side of the upper lip, movement No. 8, then continue shaving the opposite side of the neck, starting at the point of the chin, shaving down as far as the grain will allow. This is the back hand stroke No. 9. Now step back of your customer, with the free hand stroke, shave the lower part of the opposite side of the neck up, No. 10.

The careful barber watches carefully the grain of the beard on the neck, and shaves with it.

Left side up free hand (No.10.)

Keep your straight razor collection under lock and key.

Things to Remember

In shaving the left side of the face, a great deal depends upon the position in which the customer's head is placed. It should be turned to the right but done without cramping the neck.

Keep the shave clean without scattering bits of lather over the shaved portion of the face. It looks mussy and interferes with your drawing the skin tight under the razor.

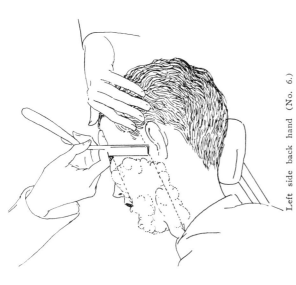

Left side back hand (No. 6.)

Now turn the face toward you with the left hand placed at the back of the head at the headrest. You turn the head while slightly lifting it and the customer will let it roll either direction you choose to place it, again strop your razor and re-lather—if the lather has become dry—and learn to use your razor and lather brush in the same hand. Take your position directly back of the chair and with the back hand stroke start at the hair line on the other side of the face, shaving down as far as the lower part of the ear. This is movement No. 6. Now use the free hand and shave the side of the face to the point of the chin as far down as the jaw bone. Also be careful that you shave the corner of the mouth with this free hand movement. This is movement No. 7.

Treat a straight razor as you would a loaded pistol.

198

Things to Remember

The natural inclination seems to require the razor handle between the second and third fingers but it should be held between the third and fourth.

There is a nicety in handling the shaving paper as well as the linen. It easily musses. Learn to keep it neat, and your sleeves out of the lather spread on it.

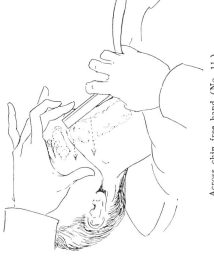

Across chin free hand (No. 11.)

Now turn the face up, always using the left hand for this purpose. Shave across the chin toward you with the free hand movement No. 11, and hold the skin tight under the razor by stretching it between the thumb and forefinger of the left hand.

Your first stroke is with the point of the razor, beginning at the upper part of the chin; your next stroke is with the center of your razor just a little lower on the chin, and the third stroke is with the heel of the razor still farther down. I wish to caution you here to be sure and use every part of your razor in shaving the chin.

Now shave down with the free hand stroke No. 12 as far as the grain of the hair will allow, then step back of your customer and shave lower part of the neck up, free hand No. 13. Now you have left only the under lip to be shaved and you keep your position back of the customer, shaving up

Things to Remember

Number fourteen is a peculiar sliding and dipping stroke. It can only be acquired by practice.

with the free hand and stretch the skin down by placing the finger of the left hand around the chin holding the skin tight. This is movement No. 14.

Under lip free hand (No. 14.)

You now apply the hot towel as before and allow it to remain on the face while you strop your razor. Now hold your razor as for the free hand stroke except that you are sliding the razor further into the hand and with the ends of the fingers of the same hand, hold the water bottle and give a dash of water into the palm of the left hand, moistening it so it will slide over the surface of the face readily while going the second time over.

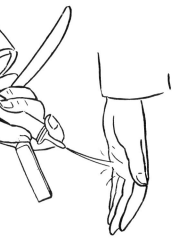

Water bottle and razor

If the floor is not to be scrubbed, confine the spray of water to moistening the hands, not the floor. Moisten only sufficiently to wet the palm. The customer may not be ready for his Saturday night bath.

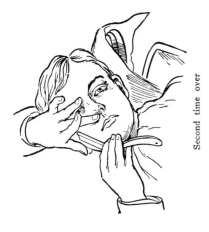

Second time over

Remove the towel and start the second time by shaving rather crosswise of the grain, not entirely with it, as you did the first time nor entirely against it as most barbers do.

The first stroke can be on the right side of the face from toward the eye to the ear, continuing down the side of the face to the jaw bone. You now continue down the side of the neck with the grain and up on the lower part of the neck as you did the first time over. Turn the face toward you and shave the opposite side giving the first stroke on the side of the face from the ear toward the eye, always being careful not to scrape or use undue pressure. Just a firm steady stroke for it can be too light as well as too heavy.

You will be able to use the free hand stroke over nearly the entire surface the second time over and there is no rigid or set rule about doing this part of the work. If your first time over has been carefully

The difficulty here is to keep the finger and thumb from slipping on the moist surface of the skin. There is a knack to it. If there weren't, barbering would be easy.

Ascertain whether your stroke is too light or too heavy by trying on a true friend who will tell you the truth, then let him try on you, and you will learn a lot.

performed, there should be little shaving necessary the second time. It is intended only to catch the rough spots.

Now lay your razor down, pick up the steam towel used before, saturate it again with hot water and place it over the face as hot as the customer can comfortably stand it. Sometimes a cream or menthol preparation is applied to the face before the hot towel that steams it into the pores of the skin, but this may be according to the method of the shop or your customer's desires.

You may now remove the steam towel, and this is the time to talk Facial treatments, but as it is not part of this lesson we will omit it. Now apply your face lotion, going through several of the facial movements, after which you remove from the breast the towel tucked in around the neck, straighten it, lay over the face and dry first by rubbing it over the face, always taking note of the spots that may be left moist, the corners of the eyes, around the nostrils, the lower parts of the ears, etc.

Always thoroughly dry the face before proceeding with any other part of the work, as it is uncomfortable for the customer if the face is only partially dry. Just a little fanning with the towel held at each end is sufficient and in many instances no fanning at all is the customer's wish.

You now apply talcum powder by sifting a very little into the towel folded in the hand.

The art of turning the head on the headrest is an important one. In this, the customer detects the barber's disposition or state of mind. An easy, careful movement is necessary.

If a razor is put on the face too lightly, it denotes lack of confidence. If too heavily, it denotes carelessness. Have confidence without carelessness.

Never lay a razor down open; close it carefully with the finger and thumb at each side of the shank to keep the edge from striking the handle.

Dry the customer's face well. You know how it feels to wash your face and let the wind dry it. Wipe dry, before fanning.

Tonic or even water can be so poorly applied to the scalp that it loses its effect. It must be carefully distributed through the hair and well rubbed in to be effective.

The reward for good hair combing is like the reward for painting a good picture. The pleasure of looking at it. Artistic temperament recognizes this.

HANDLING TOWEL

This movement in actual work at the chair is used not only for drying every part of the face but for washing it as well, and the properly trained barber never picks up a towel for this use that he does not handle it in this manner. There is a nicety in handling linen that commands business, and it should be practiced until all movements become easy and graceful. It can be practiced with a handkerchief or any cloth of convenient size.

I wish to caution you about applying powder, do not pat a customer's face but go over the face in a downward stroke, and after having been applied, wipe off all you can with the dry towel or with the hands. If the face has been left moist, the powder will show in white spots. This is one reason why careful drying is essential.

Now raise your chair with the customer to an upright position in the chair, ascertain what other work may be desired, and

EXERCISE NO. 8

Hold the right hand directly in front of you with palm up, using the left hand to spread the center of the towel over the open palm. Now with the left hand, grasp firmly all of the lower folds of the towel and turn the fingers of the left hand toward the left, bringing them down underneath the left hand, raising the left hand as you turn, bringing the folds at the back of the right hand and at the same time turning the right hand over with back up.

The folds of the towel are now held in the left hand at the back of the right hand.

The towel is easily shifted in the hand as it takes up the moisture from the face by simply sliding it from the center of the towel slightly toward one or the other edges.

This enables you to hold the towel smoothly over the palm of the hand, thereby giving use of the entire palm of the hand with its naturally soothing effect.

if no tonics or scalp treatments are to be given, consult your customer as to whether he desires the hair to be combed wet or dry. If wet, apply the moisture from the water bottle, a sufficient amount of water to be used to moisten all of the hair, not a part of it, for it must all be moistened if any. Apply it with the bottle held in the right hand and with the left hand rub the moisture through the hair using a rotary movement.

Lesson   Four

Subject   Things to Remember

HAIRCUTTING

Things to Remember

In this lesson here we omit the instruction given in another lesson on the barber's position at the chair. You will get that at another time, so we will proceed by seating our customer, spreading the hair cloth from the front, and by placing the protecting towel around the neck before bringing the hair cloth in contact with the customer.

To allow a haircloth to come in direct contact with the customer's neck is not sanitary unless a clean one is used, for each customer. State laws require protectors.

the hair cloth prevents the cut hair from working down the neck.

If a cotton strip or a prepared paper protector is used the hair cloth is pinned over it in the same manner and the edges folded down as is the towel.

Now sift a little talcum powder from your neck duster around the neck to prevent the cut hair from sticking. Now use your brush and comb to straighten the hair and put it in its proper position to be cut.

After having given the proper study, and frequently it requires your stepping back from the chair a distance to better observe the lines, you are ready for the actual work.

Generally the clipper is used on the lower part of the neck with all haircuts, but not elsewhere for the long trims.

Start at the lower growth of the hair on the left side and clip up to the point at which you want to leave off, then gradually bring the blades out from the hair as you continue to cut, thereby making a gradual taper at the clipping line.

After completing with the clipper you now use your shears and comb. The shear should be so held in the right hand with the points nearly toward you, as illustrated, and the comb held in the left hand parallel with the blade of the shear, which enables you to cut rather at one side instead of directly in front, and it enables you to get at the work more easily.

If you were cutting directly in front of yourself, there are many places in the trim

Many barbers maintain the part need not be combed from the hair before cutting, but the writer's experience and advise is to the contrary.

With the prevailing styles, little clipper work is required. Hand made haircuts take the lead at present.

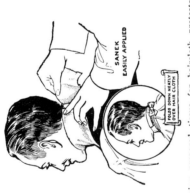

Using prepared tissue for haircloth protector

Protection strips are less expensive than laundry work, and used with less effort than a towel.

If a towel is used for this purpose, it should be the face towel, and one side, the long way of the towel, tucked carefully under the neck band from the back toward the front on each side, then the balance of the towel raise and fold around the neck from the back and held in place under the chin with the left hand. Now bring the hair cloth up to the towel and with both hands hold it close to the towel. Pin at the back of the neck and fold the part of the towel that protrudes above the hair cloth down over the hair cloth, making a neat protection that in addition to protecting

A Lesson from "The Barbers' Manual," by A.B. Moler. Revised edition, 1927.

202

Handling the shear and comb properly seems to be an awkward position, but the barber must learn not to cut directly in front of himself, or he will grow round shouldered in the service.

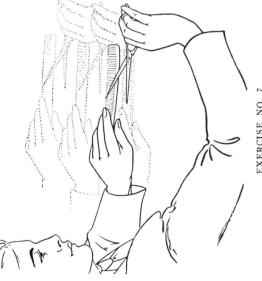

EXERCISE NO. 7

Hold shear in the right hand with the third finger in the ferrule and the little finger resting on the short lip that is made for it.

The first and second fingers are to be bent over the handle of the shears in such a manner that it will hold it firmly in the hand. The ferrule should never be allowed to pass beyond the second joint of the finger. The thumb in the other ferrule never allowed to pass the first joint.

that would require you to stoop very low to get the proper vision and to handle the instruments. Acquire this habit first of all, as it will save you much time in becoming a professional hair-cutter.

Start your shear and comb work on the right side at the lower edge just in front of the ear, cutting only a little at a time, and as you continue to cut up, gradually run out of the hair by turning the teeth out each cut, generally leaving off about the hat-band line. The comb must be so held that it can be easily turned in the hand to comb up while cutting and down through the hair to straighten it.

A shear and comb artist has the same opportunity to display skill as does the sculptor or painter; therefore acquire skill and become famous.

If while cutting up through the hair it tangles or folds under, bring the blade of the shear underneath the comb to hold the hair straight and comb up through the hair so that it will fall straight over the blade of the shear, then bring the comb underneath the shear again in place for the next cut.

I wish to caution you here in the manner of using your shears. Always use the full length of the blade by starting at the end of the comb, with the heel of the shear, and close them quickly, which will give a smooth cut.

Continue around, changing the position of the shears and comb back of the ear from a parallel line to about a 45 degree angle back of the ear.

As you cut back of the ear, you are to change the angle of the shears and comb as you did on the other side back of the ear, to avoid cutting a bare spot as you would if you were to hold the shears and comb horizontally.

This is necessary on account of the change in direction of the growth of the hair back of the ear. Use the same care as you work over the ear and around in front of it, that you did on the other side, and keep the length of the hair on both sides as nearly the same as possible.

There will be a pronounced ridge at the point where you left off with the shears and comb. This will be reduced by cutting over the fingers. It is known as the finger work.

The hair line has more to do with the expression of a hair-cut than any other one thing. Draw graceful lines.

The gradual taper from the short hair to the lower edge to the longer hair at the crown is the most shapely. Avoid abrupt edges.

Styles are elastic. They admit of many variations in length, outlines, and tapers. It is the artistic haircutter who builds them to fit.

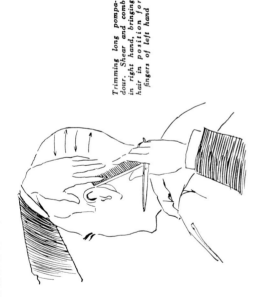

Trimming long pompadour. Shear and comb in right hand, bringing hair in position for fingers of left hand

The pompadour is trimmed by taking your position at the side of your customer, start your work back of the ear at the ridge and work from you, combing the hair up through the fingers, trimming it lightly, and work around to the other side of the head back of the other ear.

Shear in right hand. Comb transferred to left. Fingers holding hair for cut, point of shears out, to increase length of hair going up

Good judgment in laying out styles is as important as the actual cutting.

The more times over the same surface, not only spoils the original design in mind but adds that many more nicks.

Trimming ends of long pompadour combed forward, working from right to left. Only slight trim required

Now start at the point where you have just left off and come back just the opposite direction from the way you have cut, cutting over the fingers in the same manner, working back and forth in this way cutting a little at a time until you have reduced the ridge, and if the entire top and front is to be shortened, continue to work in this manner back and forward until you have gone over the entire surface, finishing with the longer hair at the forehead.

If the long hair on top is not to be cut, you can use what is known as the reducing cut on the side of the head by combing all of the hair over to one side, picking up the ends with the comb the same as cutting over the comb, trimming the ends lightly. Comb the hair back in place and if the ridge still shows, repeat until the hair will lay smooth at the sides as it is combed back. Treat both sides alike.

When you have completed the cutting, use your neck duster quite briskly in brush-

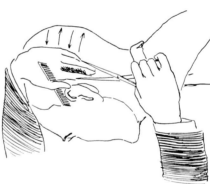
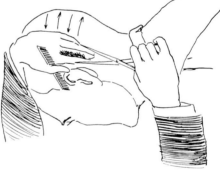

To get proportion is more important than smoothing the surface.

Careless emptying of a hair-cloth disturbs waiting patrons and appearance of the shop.

In most foreign countries barbers do not shave the neck. Why isn't this good practice? Only the primitive Chinaman shaved the scalp. Who wants to be primitive?

ing the cut ends of the hair from the head and especially around the neck.

Empty the hair from the hair cloth by picking it up from the lower end, bringing it up to the upper edge, pick it carefully off the customer in order that the hair does not drop onto the garments, turn from your customer, drop the top edge of your hair cloth, holding to the lower end, and shake well to remove all of the cut hair. Now spread it again as before, bringing the hair cloth close up to the neck band, but do not bring it in contact with the customer's neck, and use the towel that you have had in use around the neck to tuck in over the hair cloth at the back of the neck. This is to protect the customer's garments while combing and shaving the neck.

Now use fresh lather around the hair line over the ears and down the back of the neck. Whether or not the neck is to be shaved clear around, it is best to lather the neck to avoid showing a high water mark on the sides where you have put the lather. Rub the sides a little to prepare them for the shave.

Strop your razor a little before shaving the neck. It will not need as much stropping as would be required for the face shave, for the hair on the neck is easier shaved.

Now shave the neck, starting in front on the right side, make the outline true and even and work carefully around the ear to the point where the shear has indicated the line, at the same time combing the hair to-

Careless combing is unforgivable; it is even more important than cutting.

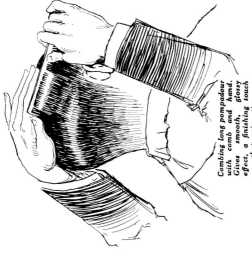

Combing long pompadour with comb and hand. Gives smooth, glossy effect, a finishing touch that gains tips

Will it be an artistic finish or yours, with this customer?

ward the line. The free hand stroke will be used for the righ hand side, but the back hand stroke will be used on the left side in front, and the double back hand, back of the ear.

This is the only place a double back hand stroke is used with the razor.

For the long pompadour we comb straight back, and you may do this by standing directly back of your customer, first using the brush and comb alternately.

After you have straightened the hair on the top and sides, untangling it all, laying it in its proper place, lay your hairbrush down and with the comb follow through the hair from the front to the back with the hand instead of the brush. This will give a smooth and more finished appearance and is pleasing to your customer.

Cutting to overcome defects is a part of the barber's work. A trained eye detects defects at a glance.

Side view, short pompadour shaved straight. Clippers slightly used on sides and lower neck. Avoid a ridge by cutting over comb with teeth turned out

MEDIUM POMPADOUR

This style is very popular, as is also the longer pompadour, and differs only as follows:

Use the clipper just at the very lower edge entirely around, and gradually taper with the shears and the comb from the clipper line, finishing the haircut as described for the long pompadour.

The combing of the long pompadour, in fact, the combing of any haircut—where a sufficient amount of hair has been left to permit of nice combing—is as important as the actual cutting, and this will prove your worth as a tactfully skillful barber.

A haircut, to be most becoming, like a suit of clothes, must be built to order.

Because a certain style is becoming in one instance, do not use it in all. Learn to deviate. Increase your stock in trade by variety.

Full round effect in back, like college cut, with long pompadour front and short burnsides.

If the shape of the head seems to be rather long and narrow, it will be your attempt to broaden the appearance by leaving a sufficient amount of hair on the sides of the head to fill out and overcome the narrowness, at the same time combing the top of the hair rather flat, which helps broaden the appearance of the features.

If a head seems to be rather flat in the back and wide, a sufficient amount of hair should be left at the back of the head to fill out and give the head a longer appearance. If the head seems to be rather flat and wide on top, you must try to leave enough hair on top so that it may be loosely combed back from the forehead or roached up in a manner that will overcome the flatness, and if a head seems to be round like a ball an attempt should be made to so draw your lines that it will give it a longer effect.

Many barbers would be good haircutters if they did not so often run out of hair.

206

Things to Remember

The time was when the barber who could cut the best pompadour was most in demand, but there is not much demand these days.

More time is necessary to trim a perfect short pompadour than any other style.

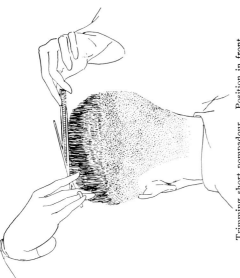

Trimming short pompadour.   Position in front

Things to Remember

The porcupine effect of a short pompadour probably quilled it.

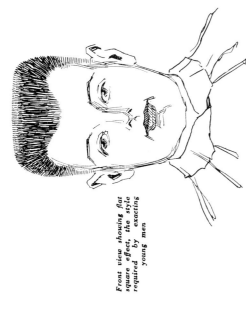

Front view showing flat square effect, the style required by exacting young men

In cutting a short pompadour, if you have trouble in keeping the hair on end, you must use hair dressing, or even a stick of mustache wax, applied by running the wax back and forth through the hair over the comb. The wax holds the hair in place while you make your form. You take your position for this work on the left side of the chair and turn your customer's head slightly toward you and start your work at the forehead in the center, getting the length you desire, and cut straight back over the comb until you reach the crown, gradually running shorter as you comb back. You will notice you are combing and cutting from you in making your form through the center.

The pompadour should have a flat appearance across the top unless the head is unusually broad, so you must be careful about trimming the sides too close. Trim a little from the cut you have made, first on one side and then on the other to get the proper shape, and after you have it formed as illustrated, continue to cut lightly over the top to give it a softer and more velvety appearance.

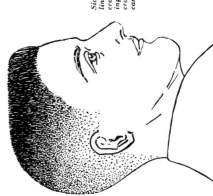

Side view shows straight line effect from front to crown, gradualaly tapering to shorter hair at crown. Clipper line carefully trimmed away.

An exact eye measurement is required for perfect pompadour work.

A Lesson from "The Barbers' Manual" by A.B. Moler. Revised edition, 1927.

Lesson   Five

Subject
HAIRCUTTING

Things to Remember

Cutting over the fingers enables the barber to get his measurements. Going over the surface must be done systematically, not promiscuously.

Trims

Trims vary in length according to the customer's wishes and that they may be better classified, we will call them long, medium and short trims, each cut by the same general rules or principles, the only difference being the length of the cut.

You will start the work at the lower edge, using the clipper just on the back of the neck if your customer prefers, or entirely around the lower part of the haircut, starting just in front of the ear on the right side, working around the lower growth of the hair to the opposite side, observing the instructions regarding the clipper that is given in the preceding article on clippers. Always be careful about using the clippers too high. The tendency is to do too much clipper work.

You will now start with the shears and comb cutting from the edge you left with the clippers, up through the hair, cutting close to the clipper line or scalp at first and gradually running out of the hair from two to three inches above the clipper line.

The fault with most barbers in cutting a trim is in taking too much off.

All haircuts must be proportioned. The trim, most exacting of all cuts in this regard.

Cutting side over finger. Comb and shear in same hand. Comb just releasing hair shown in fingers

This is called the shear and comb work. When you have trimmed away the entire head you are ready for the part of the work called cutting over the fingers.

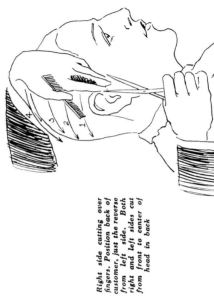

Right side cutting over fingers. Position back of customer, just the reverse from left side. Both right and left sides cut from front to center of head in back

Baldness, scalp scars and defects may interfere with the general rule of haircutting. Good judgment must be displayed in these cases.

A Lesson from "The Barbers' Manual," by A.B. Moler. Revised edition, 1927.

Allowances must be made for age, profession, countenance, etc. Study conditions.

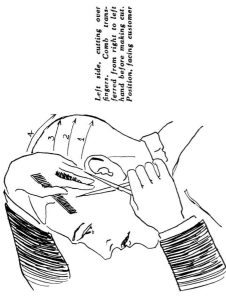

Left side, cutting over fingers. Comb transferred from right to left hand before making cut. Position, facing customer

A carefully made outline is like striping a painted job. It gives the expression.

Make your start at the ridge you have left with the shears and comb, starting on the right side, working around the direction as illustrated for cut No. 1. You will work from front back to the center of the head in the back, then step around your chair and cut the opposite side just the same, working back with the second No. 1, just as you did the first one, then take No. 2, which is a cut just a little higher. Cut first one side and then the other, then follow by No. 3 and No. 4.

This covers the entire surface, but you must remember each cut, No. 1, 2, 3 and 4, is left a little longer than the one below it so that the longest hair will be on the top of the head.

There are variations from this rule according to the length of the hair, the size of the head, etc., but generally this is a very good rule to be guided by in all long or medium trims. Always avoid cutting it short directly over the crown.

In cutting over the fingers, they may be bent. The shape of the head and a slight curve given to each cut, with the shear blades to make a smoother job or a nicer fit.

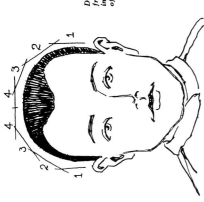

Diagram of the cuts from one to four, showing position or direction of fingers for each cut.

The diagram above is intended to make the work more plain, but a good deal of practice will be necessary to enable you to acquire the positions for the several cuts.

As there is no diagram of exercises for this cut, about all that you can do for your benefit before actually doing the work will be to get your hands and wrists limbered and in condition to take the position easily.

Your position at the chair cutting the left side will be rather at the side in front of your customer, working from the front back, where your position for cutting the right side will be back of your customer, cutting from the front back or toward you, each time going to the center of the head in the back.

When you have reached the top of the head for No. 4, your fingers will be horizontal, one side of the top of the head, No. 4, should match with the other side, No. 4, and it is well to make an extra cut or a proof of your work by combing straight back over the top in the center of the head to see that both sides are cut evenly.

A barber cannot judge all of his work at close range. He should step back frequently to get a better view of the work.

Things to Remember

Many barbers disagree with the instructions given here for front outline, but there will be no mistake if this rule is followed.

Front outline. Heel of shear at temple, point near eyebrow. Left side illustrated

After completing the cut, you may make your front outline by combing all of the hair over on one side and trimming it just lightly at the edge, then comb it all over to the other side of the head and trim it lightly as shown in the illustrations.

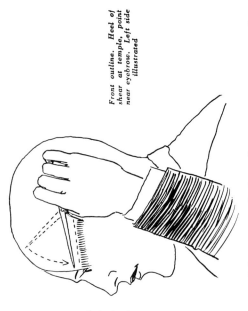

Front outlines. Varied in height according to length of hair. Right side illustrated

A final touch may be given to the haircut with the shears and comb after combing the hair, but very little should be necessary.

Things to Remember

If each front outline is trimmed while the hair is parted, and one side higher than the other, difficulty will arise the next time the hair is parted. Long, ragged edges will comb over the short ends.

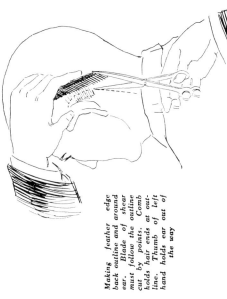

When work is properly done, front hair combs to a "V"

When it is combed down straight over the forehead, if the work is properly done, it will form a perfect "V." You may now trim the outlines back and over the ear as illustrated, making an even distinctive edge that gives the nicer finish to your haircut.

Unless the feather edge outline is combed toward the edge, there will be an irregular outline when the work is completed, that is difficult to overcome and is unsightly.

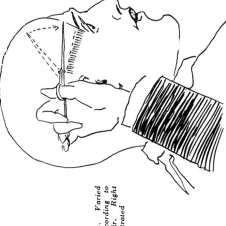

Making feather edge back outline and around ear. Blade of shear must follow the outline cut by points. Comb holds hair ends at outline. Thumb of left hand holds ear out of the way

Lesson Six

Subject
HAIRCUTTING

Things to Remember

The difficult part is erasing the clipper line. This re- quires careful shear and comb work.

Half Crown

You have learned to handle your clipper in the exercises and preparatory training, so we will start by learning just how high we are to use the clipper for the half crown.

The clippers should be run about as high as the hatband line clear around the head,

A shorter taper is necessary where clippers have been used around the lower edge of the haircut.

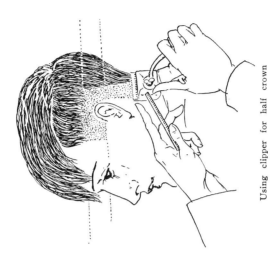

Using clipper for half crown

Salesmanship is a much abused word. True salesman- ship works best, if you are sold on what you are trying to sell.

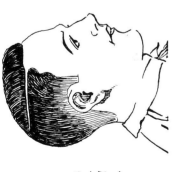

Side view, short trim shaved neck, short burn- sides, side part combed up

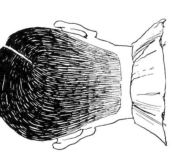

Back view, short trim with shaved neck. Styles now point to very little neck shaving

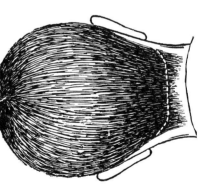

Back view, medium trim. Neck may be shaved at dotted line, if required. Center part combed down and back

Customers do not want to be annoyed but are susceptible to suggestions. Have you a "good number" to offer?

A Lesson from "The Barbers' Manual," by A.B. Moler. Revised edition, 1927.

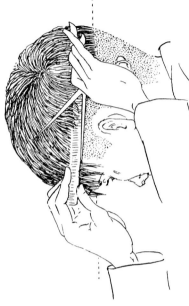

Shears and comb for half crown

The mind's eye is the barber's blue print, and like all blue prints is expensive to alter after the plans are laid.

Until the fingers become accustomed to the shear ferrule there will be a desire to use rubber shear pads, but the experienced barber has learned they are only a handicap.

A wig effect must be guarded against in all half and full crown cuts. It is overcome by a carefully trimmed clipper line.

although frequently the line is left a little lower for the style we will call the long half crown.

You will note that a long half crown differs only slightly from a short trim, but we so name them that you will be able to better classify styles.

If a medium or a short half crown is to be cut, you would, of course, cut the hair on the top and sides proportionately longer or shorter.

Clip clear around, being cautious to run the clipper out of the hair at the lower edge to taper it gradually. This saves work with the shears and comb.

After having completed the clipper work start with the shears and comb at the temple on the right side, cutting away the abrupt edge and tapering it with the short hair left by the clippers into the longer hair at the edge of the line.

In doing the shear work, you will note the shears and comb must be handled in a manner that will enable you to work more at one side of the work rather than directly in front of it. This avoids stooping to an awkward position in parts of the work that will be difficult to get at if you were cutting directly in front of yourself.

The cutting out of this clipper line is the most difficult part of this haircut, for if the pronounced ridge shows where the clipper left off, the haircut has the apearance of a wig placed on the head, and this you must overcome by carefully trimming away the lines. This is accomplished by using the fine end of your comb at the clip-

per line, running up and out of the hair as you cut. If the hair tangles underneath the comb, or folds under, place the blade of your shear underneath your comb, straightening the tangled ends before making the cut.

Always be careful to turn the teeth of the comb outward, as this will allow the hair to fall into the teeth of your comb, and pull your comb out of the hair sufficiently

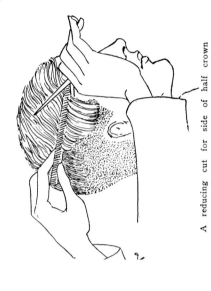

A reducing cut for side of half crown

This illustration would indicate a quantity of hair being removed at one cut. Note the error and remove but a little each cut.

A Lesson from "The Barbers' Manual" by A.B. Moler. Revised edition, 1927.

Things to Remember

Things to Remember

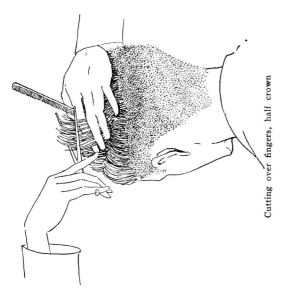

Cutting over fingers, half crown

This cut would indicate the finger work is being done before the clipper line is cut away. Note the error and trim the clipper line first.

A careful study of style is essential in all haircutting, and there is to be the same careful gauging of length in crowns and half crowns as there is in trims.

to enable you to work with your shears close to your comb.

Work around, keeping the taper the same in the back and on both sides. When completed, start cutting over the fingers, starting just a little above the temple on the right side and work back to the crown. Always avoid cutting it short directly over the crown.

You will note we illustrate and describe this finger work for the longer trims, as cuts No. 1, 2, 3 and 4, but with the half crown we will eliminate No. 1, taking No. 2 at the side of the head just where you have left off with the shears and comb starting at the temple on the right side in front and work back to the center of the head in the back. This requires about six to eight cuts.

You now step around to the other side of your chair, starting at the temple in front cutting No. 2 back to the center of the head, just opposite on the No. 2 on the other side that we have just finished.

Now No. 3 which is just a little higher, working from the front back to the crown, usually from five to six cuts.

Next, No. 3 on the opposite side, being careful to get both sides the same length.

Now you use No. 4, which is directly on the top of the head on one side, cutting back from the forehead to the crown, each cut a little shorter than the last one, about four to five cuts in all. Now No. 4 on the other side is made on top, cut in the same manner about the same number of cuts, that both sides will be alike.

You have now gone over the entire surface and are ready to make your front outline. You will do this by combing all of the hair over to one side and make your outline about the height of the clipper line on the side and about parallel with it, although this will vary according to the length of hair your customer desires for the half crown.

Now step around to the opposite side and comb all of the hair over on the opposite side, leaving no part, and trim the front outline on the other side in the same manner and the same length.

After this is done, if the hair is combed down over the forehead, it will be a perfect "V" shape.

No set rule will make an artistic haircut. It is only a foundation upon which to build. The finish is a matter of good taste.

Seasons of the year govern styles. A full or half crown is a summer haircut.

The reason a half crown cut is difficult is that there is so little chance to display real taste.

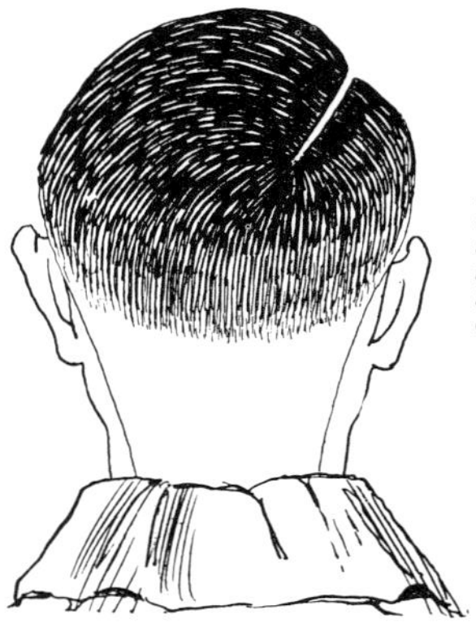

Back view of low, full crown or short trim, a compromise between the two. Illustration shows too pronounced clipper outline, result of 00 clipper work

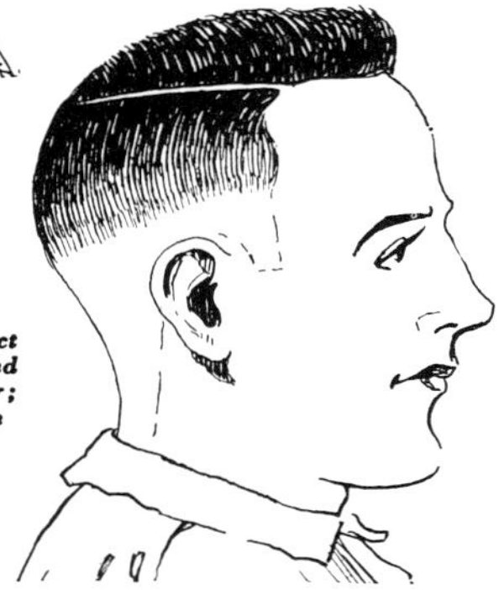

Side view shows effect of same exaggerated style, too abrupt taper; very dressy otherwise

If the hair on the crown of the head is inclined to stand up when cut for a half crown, the use of hair dressing may be necessary to make it lay smooth.

face. Start on the right side, using the free hand stroke, generally making your outline straight back from the point of the eye, running into a graceful curve over the ear, just at the hairline, or the outline may be lower on the side in front of the ear, according to your customer's wishes. Shave straight down the back at the hair line, being careful that your line is drawn so that it will be the most becoming to the customer. There are variations here that only practice and study will enable you to accomplish.

A Lesson from "The Barbers' Manual" by A.B. Moler. Revised edition, 1927.

Have you ever sat in a barber shop and been sprayed by the sprinkle of cut hair from the haircloth? If you have, you won't do it to others.

If a customer desires the freedom of his arms above the chaircloth, so adjust it that he may feel free and at ease.

You will now use your neck duster with a little powder sifted into it, if it is not a fountain neck duster, carefully brushing the cut ends of the hair from around the protecting towel, brushing the hair quite vigorously to remove all of the cut ends, and lightly brushing over the face to remove the ends that may have lodged there, and which are always disagreeable.

Now remove the haircloth by brushing and lifting one side at a time, then remove the protecting towel, carefully dusting the cut ends of the hair as it is removed. Now pick up the lower end of the haircloth, bring it up to the upper edge and carefully lift it off your customer, being careful not to drop the cut hair on the customer's garments.

You will now cover your customer again with the haircloth by spreading it from the front, being careful not to let the haircloth come in direct contact with your customer, and cover it from the back with the towel you have used as a protector, tucking in the edge of the towel, as you did previously. This protects the garments while shaving the neck and combing the hair.

We will now shave the neck and you will use fresh lather to apply to the sides, over the ears, and down the sides, and you will lather clear around even though the neck is not going to be shaved across the back. We apply the lather in this way as it constitutes better barbering.

For shaving the neck you will strop your razor but slightly as the growth of hair is not as heavy on the neck as on the

214

There are as many ways of combing the same head of hair as there are ways of cutting each. Learn the most becoming styles and comb becomingly.

Side view finished half crown. Hair roached up

Back view finished half crown

You will note, you may comb the hair on this side down perfectly flat and smooth, or may roach it up in front to show the different effects.

Now step around to the opposite side, brush and comb the hair smooth, and now comb the hair down perfectly smooth and observe the effect. Then again comb it up to get just the right artistic touch to the work.

This completes the half crown, and I want you to note, it is only a few degrees removed from a close trim.

Have you ever had a barber comb your hair to feel as well as you comb it yourself? If you can do this for your customer, he will come a long way to patronize you.

You have seen barbers wipe the lather from their razor blades onto their hands; a repulsive operation. Don't get that habit.

Now step to the other side of your customer and, with the back hand stroke, make your outline on the opposite side just the same height and as near the same shape as you did the other, making a graceful curve over the ear at the hairline, but we change to the double back hand stroke, to shave back of the ear. This is the only place the double back hand stroke is used.

Now wash the lather from the neck with a hot towel, and dry with a dry towel. The same care must be given in drying the neck as in drying the face after shaving.

To comb the hair, moisten as you would for a tonic, thoroughly moistening and thoroughly rubbing the moisture through the hair. Replace the water bottle on the stand. Now step back of your customer and give a few light massage movements to thoroughly distribute the moisture.

Now take your position back of the chair with your comb in the right hand and brush in the left, take your comb and throw the hair forward over the forehead, and then take your position on the side that your customer parts his hair and make the part with your comb and be careful to make the part straight in itself and straight with the head, then take your comb and simply throw the hair on the opposite side, out of the way, until you are ready to step around the chair to comb in position. As you walk around the chair you follow your comb with your brush. And, also, avoid your brush coming in contact with the ear as this is very annoying to your customer.

Sometimes a part is straight in itself, but not straight with the head; and sometimes it is straight with the head but crooked in itself. It must be straight in itself and with the head.

Full Crown

We will now change this style to the full crown cut.

By again using the clipper, this time to the temple, leaving your outline from one to two inches higher than for the half crown. This brings the line about to the crown in the back of the head, and leaves this portion horse-shoe shape on top of the head. You will use the same care and skill in running the clippers out of the hair at the line, that you have been cautioned about using for other cuts.

You can make your work much easier if you use your clipper, starting at the temple with one side of the clipper blade up, working back and around to the crown. This so tapers the line that it makes your shear and comb-work much easier.

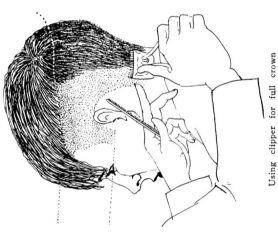

Using clipper for full crown

Frequently there is a curl on the back of the neck and the clipper must be turned in different directions to cut it properly. This is also true in cutting well up on the sides of the head where the grain of the hair changes.

You are now ready to cut over the comb with your shears, and the shear and comb work must be carefully done at the edge where the clipper has left off. Take your position at the side of your customer and start on the right side of the temple, cutting back to the crown.

You will note this is quite similar to the cutting of the half crown at the edge, but as the grain of the hair changes toward the crown, you must change the angle of your shears and comb accordingly, to cut against the grain. Trimming the outline is the biggest part of this haircut. As you note, there is little shear work to be done. The full crown is the easiest hair-cut that we have and requires the least work. It, however, is not adaptable to men

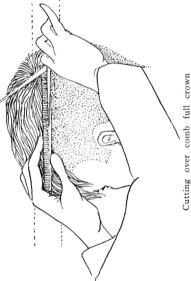

Cutting over comb full crown

Things to Remember

of all ages. It is generally preferred for little boys or for laboring men who do not care to have the abundance of hair on their head to keep clean.

After both sides have been trimmed, comb the hair up between the fingers, working from the front back, cutting over the fingers instead of the comb.

You will note, with the other cuts we use cuts No. 1, 2, 3 and 4, but with the full crown cut, we will need only No. 3 and No. 4, or perhaps if it is a short crown cut, you will need only No. 4, starting from the front to the angle and position of No. 3, cutting back to the crown over the fingers, each cut a little shorter than the last, usually four to five cuts.

Now trim the opposite side in the same manner over the fingers from the front back, giving about the same number of cuts. Now you have No. 4 on one side of the head from three to four cuts and No. 4 again on the other side of the top of the head about the same number of cuts.

We have now completed the shear and comb work over the fingers and you will comb the hair all over to one side of the head as we did before, making the front outline about the height of the clipper line and at the same angle. This makes the outline just a little higher than for the half crown.

Now step around to the other side and cut your outline the same as the other side, the same height and the same angle, then comb the hair down over the forehead and

It is better to leave a pronounced clipper line than to cut nicks trying to get it out. Strike the happy medium by trimming smoothly and not overdo.

A full crown may be roached or combed flat. Judge the style from the countenance.

Things to Remember

if the work has been properly done it will form a perfect "V" with the longest hair in the center of the forehead.

We will now dust the hair and linen again, remove our haircloth, comb the hair to give you the effect. Moisten the hair as before, thoroughly rubbing the moisture through the hair and scalp, giving a light scalp massage, and brush and comb again. This time, you may comb all of the hair over to one side, making no parts, and this may be roached up in front or it may be combed flat. Study effects when combing hair and try to turn out the best looking job you can.

Now we will show another effect, this time making a part near the center or at the center, if your customer prefers, roaching both sides up, slightly back. The combing is the most fascinating part of barber business, and you must acquire a taste for this if you expect to enjoy your work.

A double ought clipper may be used at the lower part of the neck, but should not go higher.

As much pains should be taken in combing the short trims as the long. Frequently they are more difficult to make look well.

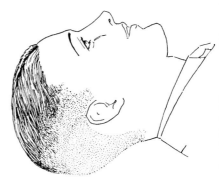

Side view finished full crown. Hair roached back

A Lesson from "The Barbers' Manual" by A.B. Moler. Revised edition, 1927.

There are many differences in ladies' and men's haircutting, but if one has become a good men's haircutter, it will not be difficult to acquire ladies' work.

LADIES' AND CHILDREN'S HAIRCUTS

THE proper cutting and arranging of bobbed hair has become one of the most important and profitable part of the barber profession, and we are extending a great effort toward the attainment of the best results in ladies' haircutting.

You will find that ladies are the most critical customers, and are expert judges on this class of service.

First, and the most important part, is to ascertain just what style hair cut your customer prefers, and after deciding on the style you should picture in your own mind just how that hair cut ought to look after you have completed the work.

Outline for the first cut

Never make lower outlines the exact height you desire them; allow for retrim.

In all ladies' haircuts, ascertain whether or not the hair is to be worn straight or curled. If curled, allow for the shrinkage.

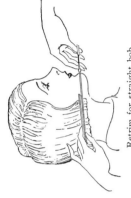

Retrim for straight bob

If you are trimming a long head of hair that is being bobbed for the first time, you will find out just how your customer desires the work. If it is to be a straight bob, see that the hair is properly parted and combed smoothly and evenly straight down all around before making the trim.

If the hair is to be curled later, you must allow for shrinkage, but if not your outline should be one-half inch lower than you intend to have it when you have completed for you will be obliged to trim around a number of times to even it after your first

Thinned outline with shear points

This illustration shows trimming with the points of the shears from the outer edge. This is only desirable for ragged edges, not for thinning.

Things to Remember

If the lower hair line at the back of the neck grows irregularly, it may be scalloped with a pronounced edge, like drapery, but this is one of the extremes.

Pointed outline

This thins the heavy hair away, leaving it fairly smooth, better than it can be done by working over the fingers as you do for the men's haircut.

You start about one-half inch back of the ear on the right side and thin around to within one-half inch of the ear on the left side. After having completed this thinning process, you may use your clipper on the back of the neck to the proper height either to an outline you may have designated, which may be a "V" shape or straight around or any other design your customer prefers, and from the clipper line trim the

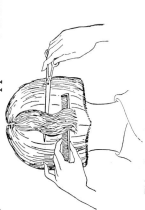

In lifting a strand of long hair as illustrated, it may be thrown out of the way and the shorter hair underneath, trimmed with the shears and comb.

Thin edge produced by outside cut

THE BARBERS' MANUAL

Things to Remember

If the lower hair line at the back of the neck grows irregularly, it may be scalloped with a pronounced edge, like drapery, but this is one of the extremes.

Pointed outline

This thins the heavy hair away, leaving it fairly smooth, better than it can be done by working over the fingers as you do for the men's haircut.

You start about one-half inch back of the ear on the right side and thin around to within one-half inch of the ear on the left side. After having completed this thinning process, you may use your clipper on the back of the neck to the proper height either to an outline you may have designated, which may be a "V" shape or straight around or any other design your customer prefers, and from the clipper line trim the

In lifting a strand of long hair as illustrated, it may be thrown out of the way and the shorter hair underneath, trimmed with the shears and comb.

Thin edge produced by outside cut

Bangs are dangerous. It is easy to make and unmake good effects.

To specialize in ladies' hair-cutting, one should also specialize in ladies' hair-dressing.

Heart shaped bang

fair knowledge of the work you will be able to cut any style if you will first consult your customer and ascertain the exact style that she wishes.

If bangs are worn, they may be trimmed in any manner your customer desires. You can part from the forehead about an inch back from the hair line, the amount you want to cut into bangs, and trim it the shape or style your customer desires. Sometimes the bangs are trimmed in what we know as the heart shape or they may be trimmed diagonally across the forehead or straight across or "V" shape, rounding or any other style your customer may desire.

If this were a child's haircut, I would bring the outline nearly to the top of the ear and use the clippers to that point. Children's haircutting does not vary greatly from the women's straight bob, except in the height of the outline.

A Lesson from "The Barbers' Manual," by A.B. Moler. Revised edition, 1927.

If hair is to be combed straight back flat like a man's pompadour, it can be cut the same except that it should be longer on the sides and in combing back, partly cover the ears.

An artistic ladies' haircutter must be an artistic hair-comber. Water waving, finger waving and like waves are necessary for proper effect.

balance of the back of the head by cutting over the comb about as high as you would for a long trim.

Now blend the sides just back of the ears by using the English trim slightly which will smooth the abrupt edge from the long hair covering the ears to the short hair back of them. If a heavy, blunt line is left on the sides, thin just the lower edges by using the English cut, but do not allow the shears to slide up the strand of hair more than an inch or two from the ends. This process is to thin away the underneath part of the blunt edge which will allow the outer edge to turn in, giving a better style to the cut.

Be careful that you have the hair combed out well around the ears as quite frequently the hair will fold around back of the ear and if it is not combed out when cutting it will show ragged ends later. And if you will part the hair around the ear, you will not only be getting these long ends but you can gauge your work better, as the lobe of the ear is your gauge in cutting the proper length.

If your customer wears a dip on the side, be careful that you leave this hair that lies in front of the ear longer, as the dip will take up the length and blend in with the rest of the cut.

There are various styles of ladies' hair cuts, and I would advise that you study the charts carefully and become familiar with the various styles. However, after you have become a haircutter and have a

BIBLIOGRAPHY

Associated Master Barbers. *Standardized Textbook of Barbering.* Chicago, IL: A.M.B.A., 1939.

Bridgeford, Frank C. *The Bridgeford Barber Instructor & Toilet Manual.* Kansas City, MO: 1904.

De Zemler, Charles. *Once Over Lightly, The Story of Man and His Hair.* New York: Stratford Press, 1939.

Diderot, Denis. *A Diderot Pictorial Encyclopedia of Trades and Industry.* Paris, 1751: Reprint by Dover Publications, Mineola, NY, 1959.

Doyle, Robert A. *Straight Razor Collecting, An Illustrated History and Price Guide.* Paducah, KY: Collector Books, 1980.

Fitch, F. W. *Square Deal Magazine* (Editorial). Des Moines, IA: F. W. Fitch Co., 1925.

Frankfurth, William. *Hardware Catalog.* Milwaukee, WI: 1886.

Glass-Works Auction Catalog. East Greenville, PA: 1991, 1992.

Griffin, Michael J., Editor. *Barber Shop Collectibles Newsletter.* White Plains, NY: National Shaving Mug Collectors Assoc., 1980–1993.

Hambleton, Ronald. *The Branding of America, from Westinghouse to Gillette.* Camden, ME: Yankee Books, 1987.

Hazen, Edward. *Panorama of Professions and Trades.* Philadelphia: Uria Hunt, 1837.

Holiner, Richard. *Collecting Barber Bottles: Pictorial Price Guide with History.* Paducah, KY: Collector Books, 1986.

Koch, F. A. & Co. *Illustrated Catalog of Cutlery for Barbers.* New York: 1927.

Kochs, Theo A. & Son. *Illustrated Catalog of Barbers' Supplies, Chairs and Furniture.* New York: 1894, 1902 and 1926 editions.

Koken, Ernest E. *Illustrated Catalog of Barber's Supplies.* St. Louis, MO: 1905.

Krumholz, Phillip L. *A History of Shaving and Razors.* P.O. Box 4050, Bartonville, IL. Ad Libs Publishing Co., 1987.

Krumholz, Phillip L. *The Complete Gillette Colllectors' Handbook.* P.O. Box 4050, Bartonville, IL: 1992.

Lasselle, W. H. & Co. *Illustrated Catalog of Jewelry & Silverplate.* Berlin, MA: 1902.

Mansfield, Howard. *The Razor King.* Invention & Technology Magazine: Spring 1992.

Marshall Field & Co. *Illustrated Department Store Catalog.* Chicago, IL: 1890.

Moler, A. B. *The Barbers' Manual.* Chicago, IL: A. B. Moler, 1911 through 1927 editions.

Nard, Anthony J. *Barbershop Auction Catalog.* Milan, PA: 1991.

National Shaving Mug Collectors' Association. *Membership Information:* Penny Nader, 320 S. Glenwood Street, Allentown, PA 18104.

Paidar, Emil J. & Company. *Illustrated Catalog of Barber Shop & Beauty Parlor Equipment.* Chicago, IL: 1921.

Powell, Robert Blake. *Antique Shaving Mugs of the United States.* P.O. Box 833, Hurst, TX: 1972.

Powell, Robert Blake. *Occupational & Fraternal Shaving Mugs of the United States.* P.O. Box 833, Hurst, TX: 1978.

Proctor, Richard Wright. *The Barber's Shop.* Manchester, England: Thomas Dinham & Co., 1856.

Rehder, Denny. *The Shampoo King, F. W. Fitch and His Company.* Des Moines, IA: Waukon & Mississippi Press, 1981.

Reynolds, Reginald. *Beards, Their Social Standing, etc., Through the Ages.* New York: Harcourt Brace Jovanovich, 1976.

Rohrer, Joseph. *Artistic Marcel, Water, Permanent Waving and Hair Bobbing.* New York: Institute of Beauty Culture, 1924.

Sargent & Co. *Hardware Catalog.* New Haven, CT: 1884.

Sears, Roebuck and Co. *General Merchandise Catalogs.* Chicago, IL: 1903, 1908 and 1911.

Severn, Bill. *The Long and Short of It, Five Thousand Years of Fun and Fury Over Hair.* New York: David McKay Company, 1971.

Smith Brothers. *Illustrated Price List of Hair Dressers' Sundries, etc.* Boston: 1882.

Todd, John M. *Sixty-two Years in a Barber Shop.* Portland, ME: William W. Roberts Co., 1906.

Vom Cleff & Co. *Illustrated Catalog of French and German Hardware and Cutlery.* New York: 1906.

Waits, Robert K. *Safety Razor Reference Guide.* 594 Endicott Dr., Sunnyvale, CA: 1990.

Wohl, Sigmund. The Razor's Edge, Auction Catalog. P.O. Box 429, Bronxville, NY: 1992.

PRICE GUIDE TO

A word about prices. A veteran price-guide author, a barber-shop-museum owner, a shaving historian, and two "barberiana" auction houses were asked to provide ballpark value ranges for all of the tonsorial-related items illustrated in this book. Between them, these folks have bought and sold about 5,000 bottles, mugs, razors, poles, chairs, and backbars over the last couple of years. Their estimates varied widely, especially on the signs and furnishings. Anyway, we bravely recorded their appraisals and take no responsibility for any losses you might incur as a result of treating them too seriously.

To sell any antique for top dollar, you must have a near-perfect item and offer it to a motivated buyer (usually in a major metropolitan area). To "buy right," you must find a motivated seller (usually divorced or widowed), or attend a rural estate auction on a day when all the antique dealers in the county have gone fishing.

The important thing is to buy what you like, live with it for a couple of decades, and pass it on to the next generation (for a fat profit, if possible.)

—The Author

p-35 Barber Supply Catalog 1882, 16 pgs. $75-$100.

p-36 Atomizers, plain style $18-$25. Boilers, complete and fine $100-$200. Bench Bottles, clear $20-$45, colors $50-$80. Barber Bottle Caster set $150-$200. Bell Bottom $150-$250 set, fancy labels under glass bring more. Pretty Girl, labeled under glass $350-$600 ea. Etched Ruby Bottle $125-$200.

p-37 Shaving Brushes, fine: Crown $10-$18. Patent Wedge $10-$18. Rosewood $20-$30. Bone $25-$35. Fancy Handle, Nickel plated $18-$22. Ebony $10-$15. Enameled $8-$12. Hair Brushes, plain $5-$8 (not collectable except in fancy boudoir sets). Neck Brushes $20-$30.

p-38 Hand Clippers, early models with exposed leaf spring $20-$35. Concealed spring type (not shown) $10-$15. Lightning Machine clippers $200-$300. Horse clipper $5-$15. Electric clippers (not shown) ceiling mounted motor with cable, "Race" brand, complete $150-$200.

p-39 Labels, unused circa 1880–1940, average artwork $1-$4. Large, ornate artwork (not shown) $5-$20. Clipper parts $1 up.

p-40 Combs, bone $10-$15, ivory $30-$40, Tortoise shell $15-$18, hard rubber $1-$5.

p-41 Tool Bracket, carved walnut $400-$500. Patent cup $30-$60.

p-42 China Mug, medium, $15-$40. Large with advertising $35-75.

p-42 China Mug, medium, $15-$40. Large with advertising $35-75.

p-43 Requisite mug, plain $15-$40 (decorations could raise price). Numbered mugs (used to fill up empty spaces in barber shop racks, also used in shops attached to hotels, and on military bases) $40-$60 each, best price when in sets. Champion $30-$40. Toilet $20-$40. Popular $40-$60. Brushes $10-$15.

p-44 Powder or Sponge Bowls in art glass $50-$125 each, more money in sets with bottles, less in clear glass. Hamburg Razors, plain horn, fine cond. $15-$25. White bone $20-$30. Barber Shears $8-$15 (brand new scissors today cost $15-$60).

p-45 Razor Strop, plain leather, single $10-$20. Requisite Strop $8-$12. Shaving Soap, bars in orig. pkg. $5 up.

p-46 Mug Cases sell at collector-attended auctions for an average price of $20 per cubby hole. Those shown with attached top crests (which have often been removed by barbers who tired of dusting them) could bring $450-$1,000 each (maybe more in the big city).

Work Stands $300-$450. Looking-glass brackets $95-$150. Wash Stands $300-$600.

p-47 BARBER CHAIRS (in excellent condition). Nos. 2 & 3 $700-$1,000. Union metallic $1,500-$2,000 or more (few of these survived).

p-48 Barber Chairs such as these have been purchased in "as found" condition for as little as $250. Those shown might fetch $750-$1,500 in fine condition. Additional carving would add to value.

p-49 Barber Chairs (top row) $500-$700. No. 5 $700-$900. No. 9 $600-$800. Some decorators prefer these lightweight wooden chairs over the later iron-based hydraulic models which can buckle floors.

p-51 Koch's Columbia, No. 4 was the most highly carved model offered in their 1892 catalog $2,000 to $4,000 fully restored.

p-52 Koch's Columbia chair, machine carved, circa 1898 $1,000-$1,600.

p-53 Koch's Gold Medal oak barber chair with cast iron base painted to match wooden trim $1,000-$1,800. This transitional (1891-1909) style bridged the gap between wooden chairs and all-metal chairs. Highly carved deluxe examples sell for as much as $4,000 in restored condition.

p-55 Paidar brand chair from 1921 catalog. Worn condition $200-$350. Replated and reupholstered $400-$750. (Add 25% for N.Y. or L.A.)

p-56 & 57 Kochs' barber chairs from the 1920s sell in the same $200-$750 price range. Deluxe "Koken" porcelain enameled chairs from the same period have brought twice as much.

p-58 & 59 Child's chair with hobby horse head $1,200-$2,500. (Plain style, without head $700-$1,500.) Both styles were also made in Japan when Koken was bought out a few years ago. Pedal car style chairs $1,500-$2,000.

p-60 Kochs' folding chair No. 52 is very rare $250-$500.

p-61 Child's wire chair No. 77 $250-$500. No. 540 shoe shine stand $95-$175. No. 100 Child's Seat $50-$75. Oak shoe shine stand with 2 chairs $350-$600. No. 502 Twisted wire shoe shine chair $350-$600.

p-62 Sterilizers. No. 65 Red Cross, Nos. 30 & 31, Nos. 50 & 51 Vulcan and Nos. 10, 11 & 21 $500-$2,500 each, depending on condition. (Not shown are wall-hung nickle plated towel steamers $500-$1,200.) Very few of these large sterilizers escaped the scrap metal drives of World War II. They were replaced by commercial linen rental and laundry services.

p-63 Formalin lamp No. 1820 $35-$55. No. 14 Sterilizer $35-$60. (Not shown) Oak sterilizer with glass doors 10 in. x 12 in. $80-$125. White painted wooden sterilizer with glass sides 10 in. x 14 in. $50-$60. Sterilizer Jars $40-$80.

p-64 Barber Pole approx. 8-ft.-tall $600-$1,500. Fairly common in Midwest and on East Coast, but rarely seen in California. More elaborate turnings would increase value.

p-66 This 12-foot pole, circa 1880, would be a rare find. A museum piece!

p-67 Barber Poles from Koken's 1905 catalog. Nos. 3 & 4 $800-$1,000. Nos. 1 & 2 $1,400-$1,600. Nos. 7 & 8 $1,200-$2,000 (we've never seen one with a built-in lantern).

p-68 Barber Poles, circa 1900 $800-$1,500 each. Acorn top increases value, and old paint is very important to collectors.

p-71 Small barber poles in fine condition $300-$400. Index hand $100-$195. No. 15

"Baths" pole with gabled base and advertisement $1,800-$2,500 (maybe more).

p-72 Barber Pole with carved fleur-de-lis $1,500-$1,800.

p-73 No. 46B $200-$300. No. 636 $200-$300. Nos. 2 & 7 $800-$1,500. Nos. 607 & 608, 42-inch-tall $400.

p-74 Nos. 627 & 628 $300-$400. Nos. 3 & 4 $800-$1,200. Nos. 6 & 7 $1,200-$1,500.

p-75 Small pole $300-$400.

p-77 Non-revolving barber poles from 1910-1925. Nos. 56 & 58 $250-$450. No. 62 $600-$1,200. No. 57 $800-$1,200. No. 20 $500-$750. No. 59 $500-$1,200. No. 45 $500-$600.

p-78 Revolving cylinder poles with light. (Can be either keywind or electric motor driven.) Nos. 7, 9 & 10 $800-$2,500 ea., depending on age and condition. Highest prices are found at Antique Advertising and Coin-op Machine Shows in large cities.

p-80 Revolving wall-mounted poles (windup style is the most desirable). No. 18 $250-$500. No. 6 $450-$900. No. 2 $450-$900. No. 21 is the rarest at $600-$1,000.

p-81 Arm pole No. 537 $200-$350. No. 471 with backet $500-$800. No. 174 $400-$800. No. 43 $250-$400. No. 907 $300-$400. No. 49 with light $350-$450.

p-82 Art Glass globe $600-$800 (watch for re-productions).

Not shown: Koken leaded glass barber pole, flat-sided, hexagon-framed in bronze with white porcelain enameled cap. These wall-mounted, striped poles often hung in fancy hotel barbershops. Recent price range $2,000-$4,000. (Several years ago a couple of people with auction fever ran one up to $12,000.)

Opal glass globes $50-$70. Canteen style $55-$85. Index Hand, wooden $100-$195. Transfer decal-type window sign, unused $15-$25. Porcelain enameled sign No. 447 $25-$40 (watch for reproductions). No. 446 $75-$125. No. 448 $100-$175.

p-83 Electric Sign No. 126 $225-$350. Globes for poles $55-$85. Flashing sign with 9 interchangeable ads $800-$1,200.

Not shown: Handpainted Showcards, advertising 10¢ shaves, 25¢ haircuts, etc. Original old examples have sold at auction for $300-$800. Figural Trade Signs in tin or carved wood (oversize scissors, razors, etc.) 12 in. to 14 in. $75-$150. 36 in. and larger $300-$500. Early Tin Signs advertising Wild-root Hair Oil 12 in. x 36 in. $150-$300. Gem Razor, chromo lithograph on tin razor blade dispenser with mirror $500-$800. Automated Gem Razor sign of man shaving with moving arm, cardboard 22 in. x 29 in. $3,000. Auto-Strop tin litho, 9 in. x 9 in. $100. "Look Better/Feel Better" tin sign 48 in. $125. Lucky Tiger (damaged) die-cut cardboard sign 24 in. $100-$150. Florida Water, paper sign 14 in. x 18 in. $350.

p-86 Razor Strops, 1880-1886, fine condition $10-$20. J.R. Torrey Razors, black rubber handle $10-$20. White bone handle $20-$30.

p-89 English Razors, circa 1800. White bone with scrimshaw anchor $150-$200. Tortoise shell $140-$180. Ivory with metal inlay $150-$250. Horn with mother-of-pearl or ivory inlay $150-$200. Tortoise shell with inlay $180-$200. Plain horn with "Magnum Bonam" ("Large and Good") engraving $100-$170.

p-90 Straight Razors: Queen, with hard rubber handle, marked "Henry Sears & Sons, 1865," but actually mfg. circa 1880-1900 fine condition $30-$35. No. 40 Tortoise shell $25-$35. No. 492 black rubber $8-$15. Nos. 493 & 494 $10-$16. Nos. 670 & 700 $16-$22. p-91 Atomizers, clear $20-$50.

BARBERSHOP COLLECTIBLES

Note: All quotes for razors are for fine condition. Rust, nicks, and other blemishes can depreciate price by ⅔ or more. American-made straight razors are currently the most sought after by collectors. Sheffield-made (English) are second in demand, and Solingen (German) are third.

p-93 Perfecto Razors $20-$32. Lucifer $10-$20. Wizard, real tortoise shell $28-$38 Admiral, plastic handle $20-$30.

p-94 Vom Cleff & Co. No. 97 (has desirable "worked back" on top of blade) $45-$70. No. 101 $45-$55. No. 99 $75-$95. No. 180 $25-$35. Nos. 194 & 194½ $30-$40. No. 177 $45-$80.

p-95 Pocket Knives: Nos. 7816 & 290 $40-$60. Nos. 2534 & 2306 nude designs $60-$80. Razors: No. 191 Fancy $30-$40. No. 191 Plain $10-$20. No. 193 Ivory $35-$50. Nos. 212 & 212½ $30-$50.

p-96 Razors: No. R66 $35-$50. No. R68 $30-$45. No. R72 $35-$50. No. R74 $30-$40.

p-97 No. R58 $20-$30. No. R60 $20-$30. No. R62 $18-$30. No. R64 $30-$45.

p-98 Arc Magnetic $22-$30. High Art $30-$35. Acme $10-$20. Winner $20-$30. Autocrat $25-$32. Personalized (made to order) $15-$20 unless a famous name. Surprise $25-$30. Antiseptic $28-$35. Regal $25-$30. Hollow Ground $10-$20. Reliable $25-$35. Ern, set of (4) $80-$110.

p-99 German Bismark $10-$20. Tree Brand, Pearl $30-$40. Boker 6L18135 - 37 $10-$20. No. 6L18165 $10-$20. No. 6L18166 Magnetic $15-$22. No. 6L18192 Figaro $15-$25. No. 6L18199 Jos. Allen $10-$20. No. 6L18200 $20-$30. No. 6L18202 $25-$35. No. 6L18203 pearl handle $95-$135. No. 6L18255 pipe $10-$20. No. 6L18261 IXL $10-$20. No. 6L18257 $10-$20. No. 6L18265 imitation ivory $20-$30. Nos. 6L18258 & 66 pipe $10-$20. No. 6L18315 Wade & Butcher's $10-$20. No. 6L18321 $10-$20. No. 6L18334 Joh. Engstrom $12-$22. No. 6L18335 $12-$22. Adj. razor guard $20-$30.

p-100 Safety Razors (1910 and earlier). No. 6L18449 $40-$60. No. 6L18465 Star set $80-$120. No. 6L18467 set $80-$130 if wedge-type blade. No. 6L18469 set $100-$135 (wedge blade). No. 6L18475 Gillette set (single ring style) $20-$30 (double ring is scarcer) $150-$200. No. 6L18500 Aluminum box $15-$20. Shaving Brushes. No. 6L18544 $12-$18. No. 6L18548 $12-$16. Nos. 6L18551 & 52 $10-$15. No. 6L18554 $6-$10. No. 6L18559 $8-$12. No. 6L18572 $18-$25. No. 6L18574 $10-$15. China Mugs $15-$30 ea. No. 6L18578 Brush $18-$25. No. 6L18579 $4-$10. No. 6L18582 $10-$20. Shavade No. 6L18583 $6-$12. Aluminum Mugs $20-$30. Razor Strops Nos. 6L18653 thru 6L18660 $5-$12. Double belt style Nos. 6L18664 thru 6L18676 $20-$30. Single belt $18-$22.

p-101 Shaving Sets. No. 6L18372 $35-$45. No. 6718386 $90-$110. No. 6L18395 $40-$60. No. 6L18396 $60-$80. Mirror No. 6L18400 $15-$25. No. 6L18402 $50-$75. No. 6L18404 $25-$35. Outfit No. 6L1842, Ever Ready $30-$40. No. 6L18424 $75-$90. No. 6L18412 Superior $80-$100. No. 6L18414 $180-$250. No. 6L18437 Wilbert $60-$75. No. 6718442 set $120-$150. No. 6L18444 Combination $180-$250. No. 6718440 Strop $30-$35. No. 6L18473 Autostrop set $50-$75 for early model.

p-102 Magazine Ads and Covers, shaving-related (full page) 1890-1940 $8-$25 each.

p-112 Occupational Shaving Mugs (Koken Barber Supply Catalog, 1905) No. 533 Tailor

$500-$600. No. 534 Cobbler $600-$750. No. 535 Butcher $200-$300. No. 536 Baker, with good detail $400-$600. No. 537 Grocer $500-$600. No. 538 Dry Goods Store $500-$650.

p-113 No. 539 Stone Cutter $700-$800. No. 540 Brick Mason $450-$600. No. 541 Cabinet-maker $500-$600. No. 542 Plasterer $600-$700. No. 543 House Painter $600-$700. No. 544 Harness Maker $550-$650.

p-114 No. 545 Blacksmith $300-$500. No. 546 Two Blacksmiths $450-$550. No. 547 Boiler-maker $500-$700. No. 548 Machinist $400-$550. No. 549 Trainman $350-$450. No. 550 Train with 4 cars and added scenery $450-$550. (An even finer train might fetch $800.)

p-115 No. 551 Horse and Buggy (often mistaken for a doctor's mug), common at $250-$380. No. 552 Carriage Driver (early taxi) $500-$650. No. 553 Grocer (name and address on wagon ads to value $600-$800. No. 554 Stake wagon $550-$700. No. 555 Trainman's mug with Missouri Pacific Railroad emblem on caboose $300-$400. No. 556 Stationary Steam Engine $250-$400 (A factory engineer, foreman, or maintenance man might have chosen this fairly common design.)

p-116 No. 557 Electric Street Car. (If conductor is included in the picture) $500-$600. No. 558 Cowboy $600-$800. No. 559 Hunter $300-$400. No. 560 Fisherman $350-$450. No. 561 Bicycle Rider $750-$850. No. 562 Baseball Player $800-$1,000.

SHAVING MUGS (Not pictured): Telegraph Key $200-$250. Mortar and Pestle $250-$350. Barber shop with 3 barbers and 3 customers $800-$1,300. Barber shop with 1 customer, mug rack in background $600. Other mugs not shown, recent auction prices realized: Musical Instruments $250. Bartender $250-$550. United Mine Workers emblem $150. Stove Retailer $700. Two-wheel bicycle $500. Tinsmith's Tools $200-$400. Brewery Wagon $500. Moose Head, fraternal mug $200. Undertaker and Hearse $800. Fireman, horse-drawn pumper $450. Masonic Symbol $80. Touring car $600-$1,000. Farmer and plow $200-$500. Hammer, saw and plane $150. Grocer, counter scene with customer $300-$700. Another grocery store interior, marked "Koken" on bottom $1,300. Airplane, single-wing with wire struts $3,100 (a very rare occupation). Coal wagon $600. Farm wagon $360. Bar Room scene, good detail, 3 customers $660. Another Saloon with poor details and hairline crack $150. Fireman's Hat, Axe, Ladder, etc. $1,100. Shoe Salesman at work $1,400. Carpenter at bench $500. Brewer's logo of 2 lions and a beer keg $450. Battleship Maine, under full steam, flag flying $2,250. Shoe, hightop style with adv. motto $600. Gymnast on horizontal bar $2,500. Motorcyclist $1,300, $2,000 and $3,000. Horse head $60-$150. Bust of pretty woman, profile, in oval frame $275. Painter's bucket and brushes $400. Butchershop interior $250. Handcuffs $600. Oil field tower $500. Three oil rigs $1,000. Delivery truck $800. Furn, Eastlake set $520. Bank Teller $770. Cattleman in top hat, leading prize steer $400. Telegraph pole with insulators $465. Fireman standing next to a rig with 12 helmets on it $990. Coronet, musician's $220. Linemen, telephone poles, houses, etc. $1,050. Beer mug emblem $120. Trousers, vest and jacket, displayed hanging in mid air $575. Pocket watch, gold "Wal-

tham" $350. Miller's Flour Barrels $1,540 (with local documentation). Broom-maker $350. Chauffeur driving open automobile $1,430. Piano player (lots of detail) $1,320. Bakery van and horse with name and address $880. Lineman climbing telephone pole $1,800. Doctor, sitting with patient, taking pulse and looking at his watch (presale estimate was $3,000). Mug sold for $8,300. Dentist and patient $1,650. House painter on scaffold (crack in base) $360. Typesetter in Colonial costume $385. Horse and buggy with attendant $650. Draftsman's Tools $360. Sewing machine $450. Navy seaman waving flags $700. False, teeth, Dr. Peterson, Dentist $600. Pool Hall, billiards, 4 men, good details $1,924.

Note: most of the shaving mugs above were offered in very good to fine condition. No chips or cracks or faded images. Even their bright bands of burnished gold were relatively unworn or had been reapplied and refired. Common everyday trades bring the lowest prices. Offbeat occupations are what advanced collectors seek out. Shaving mugs with artwork depicting Peanut Vendors, Yacht Builders, or Race Car Drivers are worth their weight in gold.

p-120 Personalized (non-occupational) Shaving Mugs. These are standard designs from Kochs' 1894 and 1902 catalogs. No. 49 $100-$125. No. 54 $50-$75. No. 56 (Black wrap) $100. No. 65 (comic) $300-$400. No. 69 $50-$150. No. 70 $100-$150. No. 78 $25-$50. No. 79 $75-$150. No. 80 $250-$350. No. 81 $75-$100. No. 82 $150-$250. No. 87 $250-$350.

p-121 Personalized Shaving Mugs. No. 89 $250-$350. No. 91 $50-$75. No. 93 $75-$100. No. 94 (rare comic) $250-$350. No. 95 $75. No. 96 $100-$150. No. 97 $50. No. 98 $50-$75. No.99 $150. No. 101 $50-$100. No. 102 $50. No. 103 $35-$50.

p-122 No. 109 $35-$65. No. 114 $75-$150. No. 119 $50-$100. No. 123 $50-$100. No. 124 $50-$100. No. 125 $75-$125. No. 129 (Listed in orig. catalog as a comic design) $350-$450. It would be worth three times as much if it had really belonged to a minstrel performer. No. 130 (What is black and white and read all over?) $350-$450. No. 139 $50-$75. No. 154 $75-$100. No. 155 $100-$150. No. 156 $75-$125.

p-123 Shaving Mugs. No. 120 $50-$100. No. 121 (often mistaken for an undertaker's mug) $50-$100. No. 122 $75-$125. No. 126 $75-$125. No. 127 (scenic) $150. No. 128 (scenic) $150. No. 140 $150. No. 141 $75-$100. No. 147 $50-$75. No. 158 Fisherman $250-$350. No. 159 $450. No. 160 (would be worth more if it had really belonged to a jockey, otherwise $500-$600 for its decorative value).

p-126 Silver-plated mugs average $40-$75, depending upon the amount of original finish and applied decoration remain. Replated mugs and those with matching brushes run much more.

p-127 No. M156 Shaving Stick container $15-$22. (Not showen are solid sterling silver mug and brush sets $300-$400.)

p-128 Barber Bottles, auction prices. (upper left) $385 pair. (middle left) Amethyst with yellow enamel $522 pair. (bottom left) Deep teal blue Tonic and Shampoo set $440. (upper right) Enameled scene of trees on frosted clear glass, 8 in. tall $800 pair. (middle right) milk glass with hand-painted flowers $302 pair. (bottom right) Palmers Perfumes, bay rum with label under glass $500 each.

BARBER BOTTLES

(Not pictured) Auction prices of Barber Bottles: Trees enameled on frosted clear glass, green and yellow, 7⅞ in. tall, smooth base, rolled lip, 3 bulges in tapered conical shape $800 pair. Cranberry hobnail on opalescent white, 7 in. $100. Teal blue set of 10½ in. enameled floral Tonic and Shampoo bottles $440 pair. Hobnail satin glass in canary yellow 6⅜ in. $176 pair. Rib pattern, green with yellow and silver enamel, Persian decoration, 6¾ in. pontiled with sheared lips $165 pair. Mary Gregory decorations in white on olive green. Child playing $522 pair. Mary Gregory decorated 8 in. bright green bottle with rolled lip $286. Milk glass hair tonic bottle, lettering on sky blue background $220. Milk glass Bay Rum bottle 9 in. tall with enameled flowers $200. Fiery opalescent milk glass with handpainted swallows in flight, Bay Rum $275. Banded vertical venetian glass, light bulb-shape, pontiled bottom $220. Old mill scene, Bay Rum in white letters on deep amethyst 7¾ in. pontiled bottle with rolled lip $357. Venetian glass with red, green and blue vertical bands on clear 8⅞ in. bottle $330. Hobnail clear glass with flashing, 6¾ in. tall $330. Cobalt blue, ribbed pattern with tiny orange and yellow flowers, 7 in. $50-$100 yellow amber, coin-spot pattern 7 in. $71. Milk glass Witch Hazel, floral decor $150-$230. Molded lizard climbing the neck of a Lubin, Paris bottle $495.

p-132 Flint glass water bottle, clear $50-$75. Opaque white Sea Foam bottle $80-$100. Opaque white Bay Rum $75-$100. Powder Stands in canary, blue, or amber glass run $15-$25 ea. Pomade Bowls, $20-$25 in colors $15-$20 clear. Metal Powder Box $10-$15. Pressed glass Powder Jar with cover $20-$30 (cut crystal runs much more).

p-133 Hair Tonic, unopened bottles of Florida Water, Bay Rum, etc. $15-$35, depending on form and label artwork. This price range also covers most other hair-care product bottles made before 1941.

p-134 Barber Bottles. Venetian glass $100-$150. Sparkling pattern, pressed glass, clear $50-$75. Blue or amber $75-$115. Marbled bottle in rose, blue or amber $100-$150. Ruby red $135-$175. Venetian glass bowl $35-$50. Clear flint glass, patterned $20-$30. Marbled glass bowl in colors $30-$45.

p-135 (See page 133 prices, these are in same range.)

p-136 Rotary Brush $40-$50. Gold Lapel Pins, barber emblem $125-$350 (these are rarely found). Travel Case with accessories $200-$300. Razor Pockets $12-$30.

p-138 Electrotypes: copper or lead, advertising cuts, printing mats, etc. $10-$35 ea. Business cards, blotters, and postcards made from these type-high cuts are actively traded at $5-$15 ea.

p-140 Three-Bowl Washstand, a rare find $1,200-$2,400. Two-Bowl style with marble top $1,000-$1,800.

p-141 Barber Chairs, circa 1890 $300-$1,500, depending on condition and extent of carving).

p-142 These were top-of-the-line models. Fully restored could bring $2,000. (Swivel-style carved recliners are worth more.)

p-143 Photographs of Barber Shops are highly collectible. Original 8x10 $25-$100 each. Smaller photos, postcard-size through 5x7 $10-$50. Reprints on modern Kodak stock are widely available at antique paper shows for $5 each. Stereo view cards from the turn-of-the-century sell for $8-$15.

p-144 Boot-Black Stands. No. 421 & 426 $400-$800 ea. No. 427 with camel foot rests $600-$1,200.

p-146 Carved Index Hand $100-$195. Rotary Brush Bracket $20-$45. Cash Drawer $125-$200 (still being made). Hall Rack $250-$350 in the Midwest, $450-$650 in California. Tool Bracket No. 79 $200-$400. Ticket Board No. 80 $125-$300.

p-149 Trade Catalog, dated 1902, has color section, 198 pages 8x10 in. $350-$500. 1915 to 1927 catalogs $50-$125.

p-150 Back Bars (Mirror Cases). Only a few examples have survived with all of their gingerbread intact. They were troublesome dust-catchers. When "sanitary barbershops" became the rage in the early 1900s, many shop owners removed the elaborately carved top crests from their backbars and used the area for merchandise display. A few barber shop owners even painted their golden oak fixtures with several coats of germ-free white enamel to match their newly purchased porcelain enameled chairs.

Pricing these backbars, sight unseen, is next to impossible. All the rules of antique furniture appraisal would apply. Is the hardware original? Are the mirrors beveled? Is the wood veneered or solid? Has the piece been professionally refinished? Rule-of-thumb prices are $500-$2,500 for single-chair back bars, $800-$4,500 for two-chair back bars, $1,000-$8,000 for three-chair set-ups. The later, plainer, 1920-1940 barber shop interiors sell for second-hand furniture prices. At a recent barberiana auction, an art deco back bar with marble-framed mirrors and two porcelain enameled barber chairs sold for a mere $800, including work station cabinets.

p-152 No. 97 Barber Chair $600-$1,800. This was one of Kochs' most expensive chairs in 1902.

p-153 No. 208 Mug Rack and Wash Stand combination $1,500-$3,000.

p-154 No. 93 Barber Chair $600-$1,200.

p-155 Toilet Goods Display Case No. 678 $200-$300. No. 679 Combination Mug Rack and Display Case $850-$1,200.

p-156 Mug Racks average $20 per cubbyhole at auction, and higher at antique shops and shows. 48-hole with top crest $750-$1,000. The earliest shaving mug racks had solid partitions between the cubbyholes. Most of those illustrated here have bars only on the front to separate compartments. These were easier to dust.

p-157 Washstands, marble top $250-$500 ea. for single-bowl style with rectangular base.

p-158 Deluxe washstand No. 201, highly carved $350-$750. No. 222 two-bowl washstand $500-$1,000 with plumbing.

p-159 Nos. 176 & 177 are very rare. Portable washstands worth $1,500 and up (we've never seen one).

p-160 Nos. 531 - 532 Wall Brackets $100-$195. Nos. 206 & 207 Workstands $200-$400.

p-161 No. 506 Countertop Showcase $250-$400. No. 714 Cash Drawer $150-$250. No. 52 Counter $200-$350. No. 48 Cashier's Stand $150-$250. No. 507 Show Case for cigars, hair tonic, razors, etc. $400-$800.

p-162 Nos. 395 & 396 Upright Hat Racks $100-$150. No. 394 Hall Stand hat and coat racks are $250-$400 in the Midwest. Antique shops in big cities ask $500-$1,000 for refinished examples.

p-163 Nos. 17 & 18 Child's Chairs $300-$500 each. No. 670 Settee $300-$500 in golden oak.

p-164 Barber Shop Clocks, made exclusively for the trade, had a reversed face and movement so that they would read correctly when reflected in a backbar mirror. (Not shown) A reverse face Waterbury Octagon case with 8 in. drop $500-$700. The conventional clocks shown on this page sell for $250-$350 each.

Gasoline Lamps (which are seen more often in barber shop photographs than the kerosene-type oil lamps) bring $85-$225 each.

p-165 Nos. 327 & 339 Coat Hooks $8-$15. Nos. 337 & 338 $20-$30. Nos. 465, 466, 397 & 398 hooks on wooden plaque $30-$50. No. 393 Hat & Coat Rack $125-$175. Nos. 384 & 385 Umbrella Stands $75-$95.

p-166 Bottles, mass-produced, empty $10-$15. Full with bright labels $15-$35.

p-167 Cosmetic containers, paper tubes $6-$15 (the military trademark would bring more). Talcum Powder tin containers (not shown) $25-$50 with elaborate lithographs on metal.

p-168 Perfect Cleaner, rubber bowl $6-$12. Face Massage Bulb $5-$10. No. 737 Metal Shaving Mug $10-$20. Nickel plated Antiseptic Urn $40-$50.

p-169 Fibre Checks $1-$2. Brass Checks "Good for Shave" $10-$15 each. No. 906 Check Rack $15-$25. Nos. 39, 841, 853 moustache irons $8-$15. No. 859 Hair curling irons $6-$12. No. 846 Crimper $3-$4. Nos. 884 & 885 Curling Iron Heaters $10-$16.

p-170 Cuspidors/Spittoons. No. 888 weighted brass $55-$85. No. 889 nickel plated $35-$60. No. 880 Enameled Iron cuspidor $65-$100. Rare colors in enamelware, such as mottled chocolate-and-white granite (not shown) are worth up to $350. Wood Fibre Spittoon $40-$60. No. 886 Glazed green earthenware $80-$100. No. 890 tall brass, weighted $75-$150. Beware of reproductions with raised nameplates or embossing. (Not shown) Japanned tinware spittoons in colors, sometimes affixed to a protective tin mat $60-$100. Two-piece white porcelain cuspidors $25-$35. Nos. 897 & 898 Towel Jars (Jardinieres) $80-$150 in unsigned earthenware. Ceramic umbrella stands by famous pottery houses can bring prices in the thousands. (Consult a general antiques price guide.)

p-171 Scissor Sharpener. A rare Peerless jig $200-$300. No. 844 Hot Water Urn $50-$200. No. 306 Willow Waste Basket $30-$40. No. 318 Woven-style $20-$30. No. 12 Copper Boiler $100-$150. No. 436 Vapor Lamp $20-30.

p-172 Eye Protectors. No. 316 $5-$10. No. 315 $3-$5. Nos. 313 & 314 eyeshade $3-$5. Tweezers $1. No. 868 Nail Clipper $2-$5. Hair cloth clips $1. Moustache Curler $8-$12 pair.

p-173 Barber's Uniforms: 1890-1910 $35-$125 ea. (Not shown) Striped hair cloth sheet that covered customers $75.

—THE END—